ADULTHOOD

IS A ~~MYTH~~ GIFT!

Other books by Sarah Andersen

Adulthood Is a Myth
Big Mushy Happy Lump
Herding Cats
Oddball
Fangs
Cryptid Club

ADULTHOOD

IS A ~~MYTH~~

GIFT!

A celebration of "Sarah's Scribbles"

SARAH ANDERSEN

Andrews McMeel
PUBLISHING®

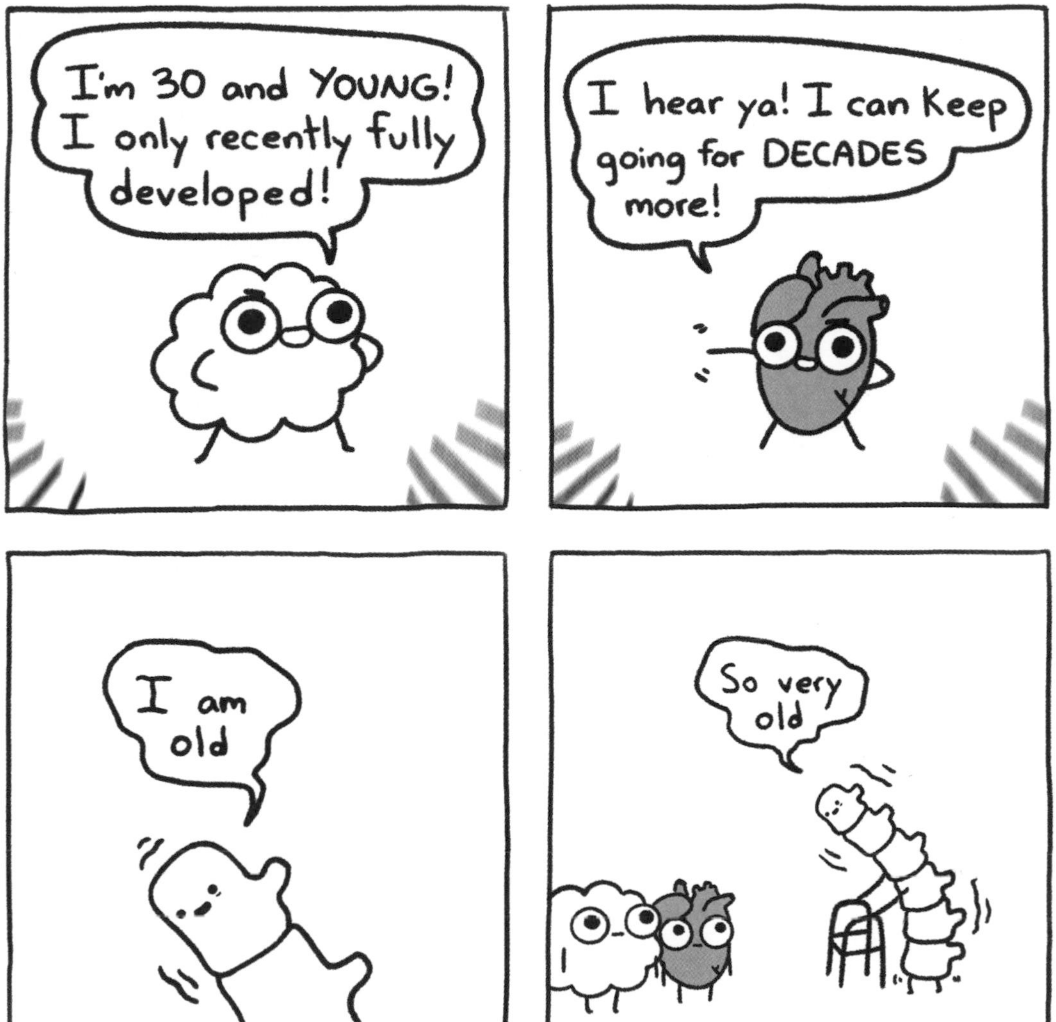
I'm 30 and YOUNG! I only recently fully developed!
I hear ya! I can keep going for DECADES more!
I am old
So very old

YOUNG ME

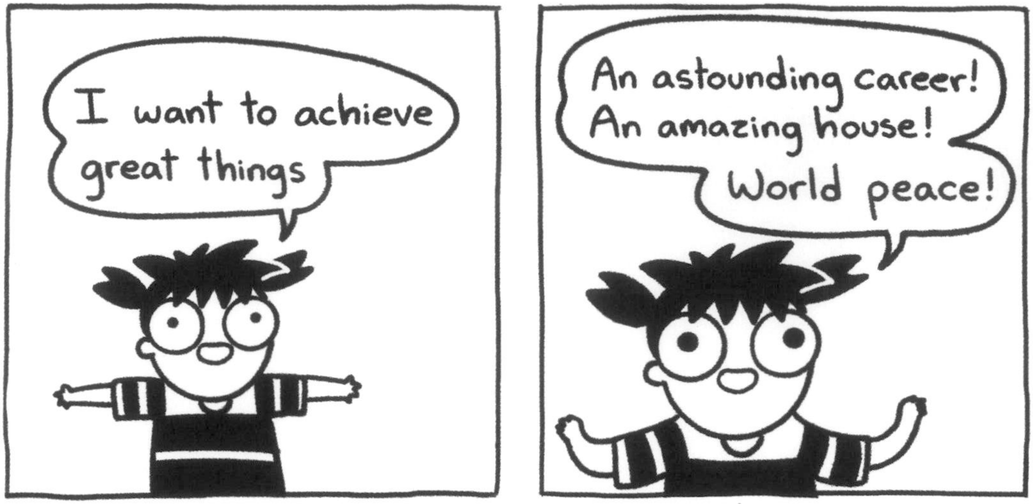
I want to achieve great things
An astounding career!
An amazing house!
World peace!

ADULT ME

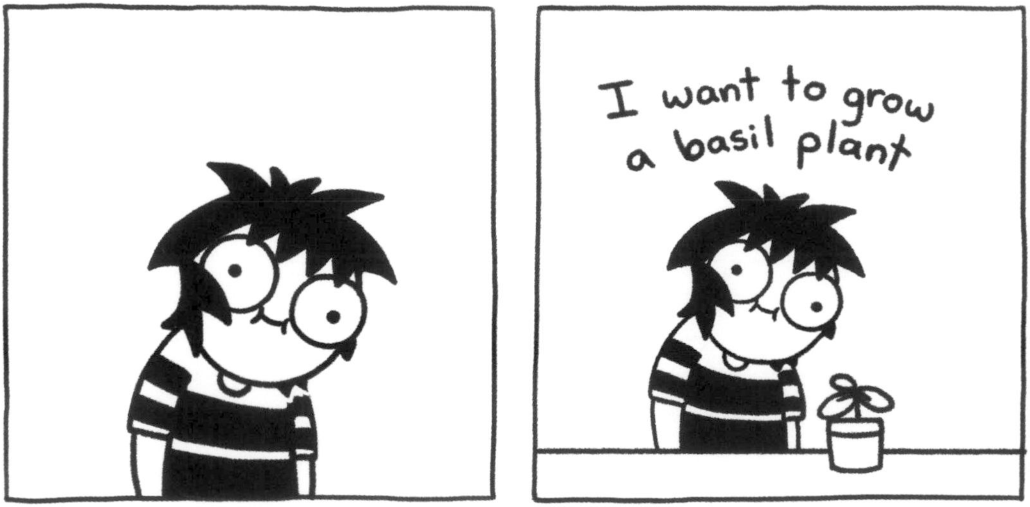
I want to grow a basil plant

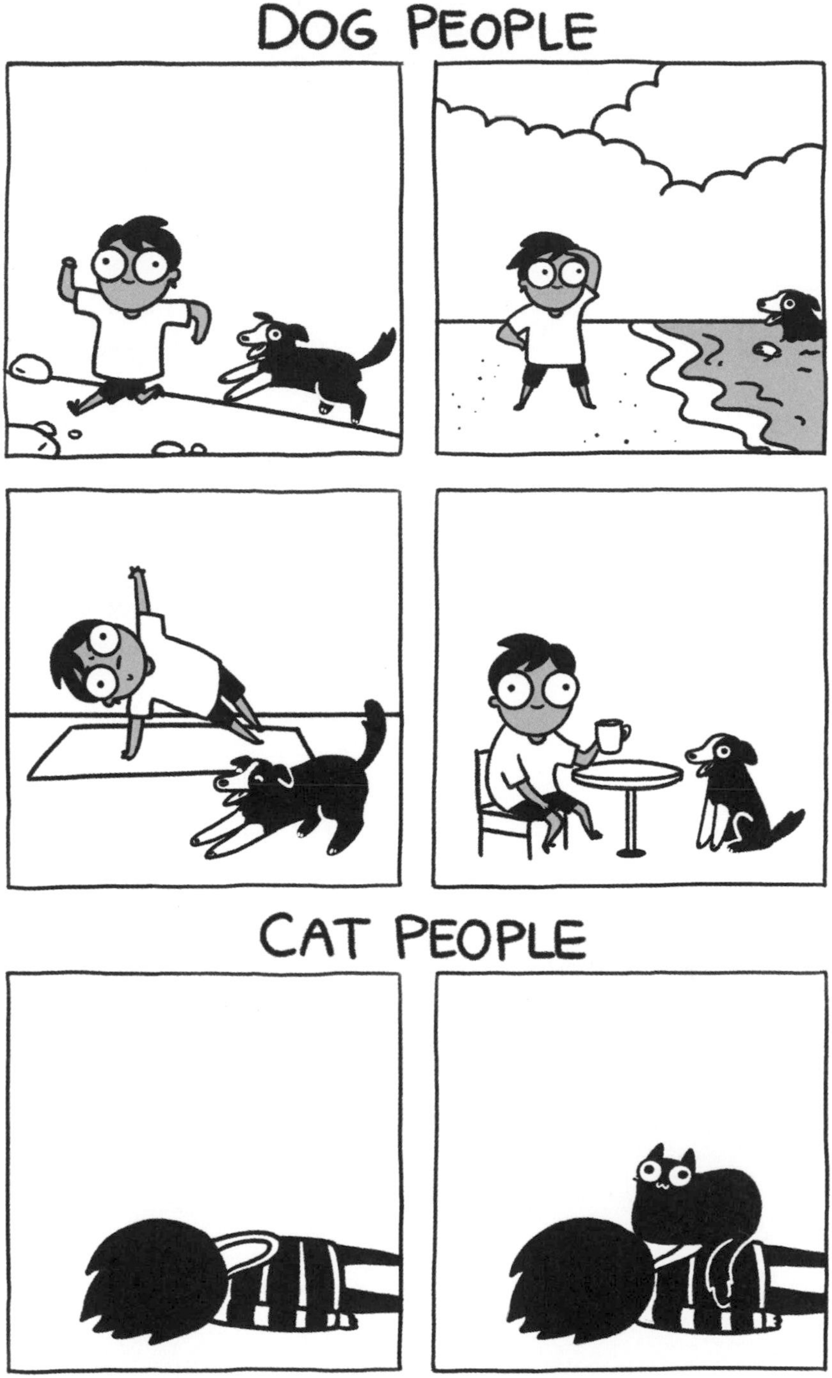
DOG PEOPLE
CAT PEOPLE

THROUGHOUT THE DAY

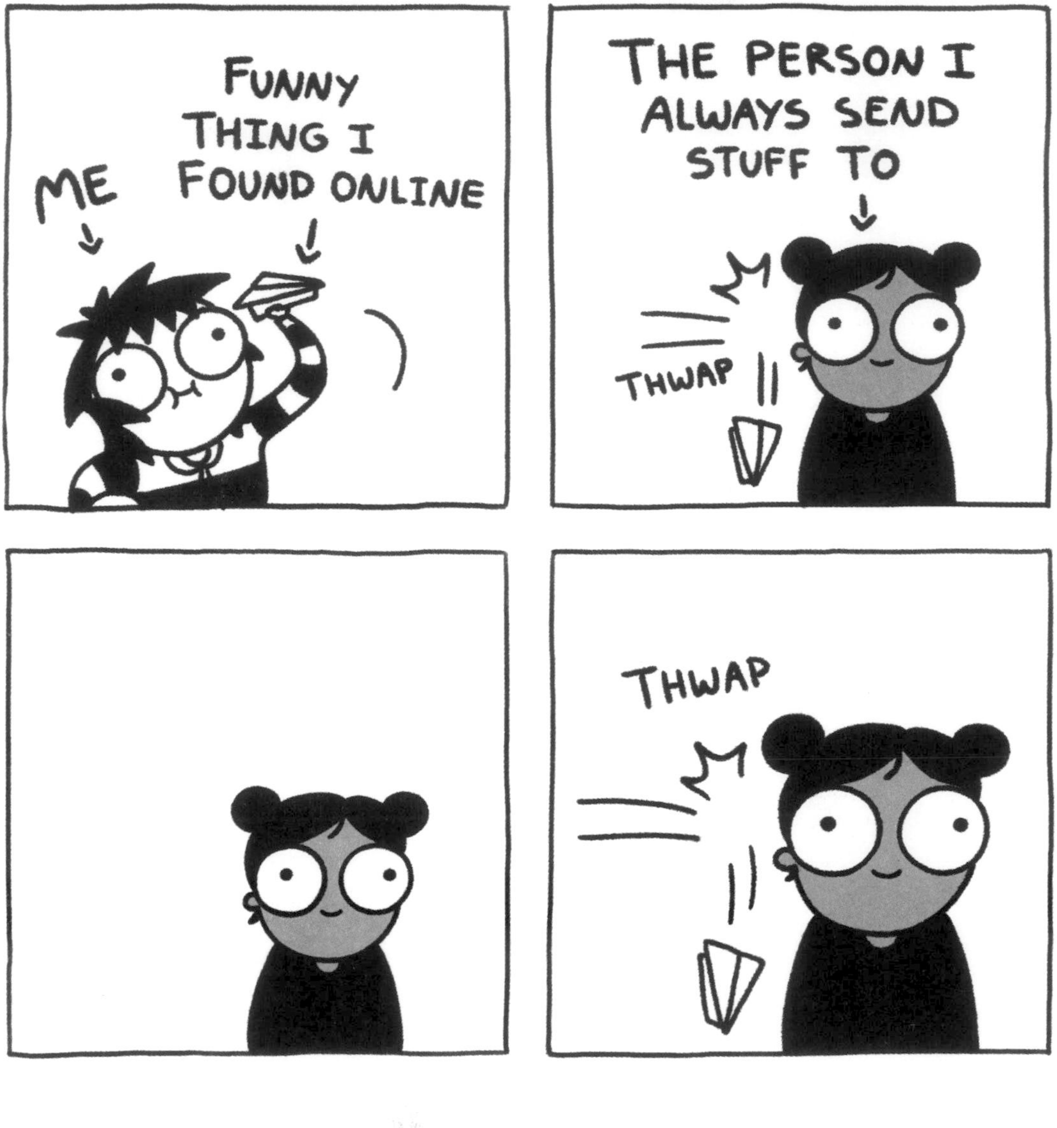
ME
FUNNY THING I FOUND ONLINE
THE PERSON I ALWAYS SEND STUFF TO
THWAP
THWAP

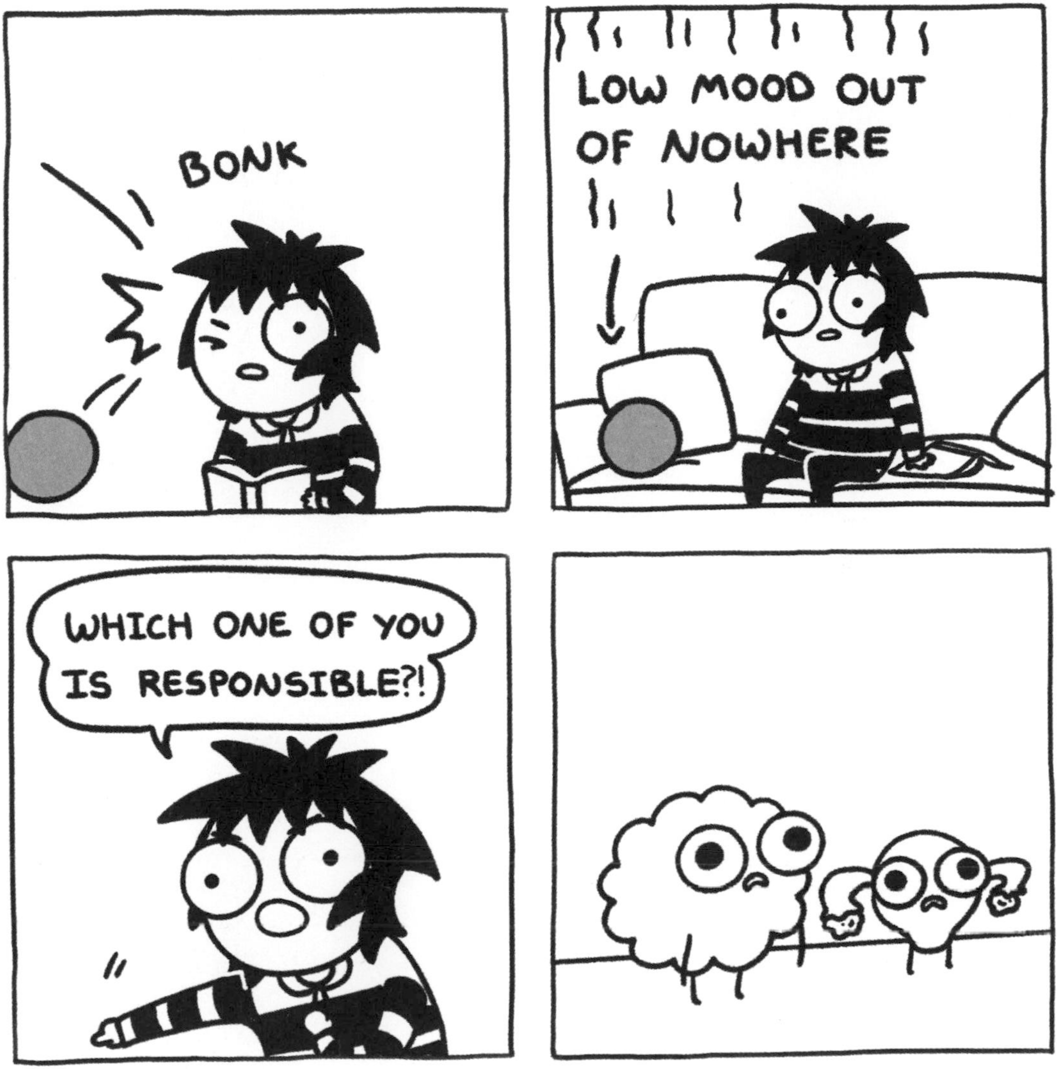
BONK
LOW MOOD OUT OF NOWHERE
WHICH ONE OF YOU IS RESPONSIBLE?!

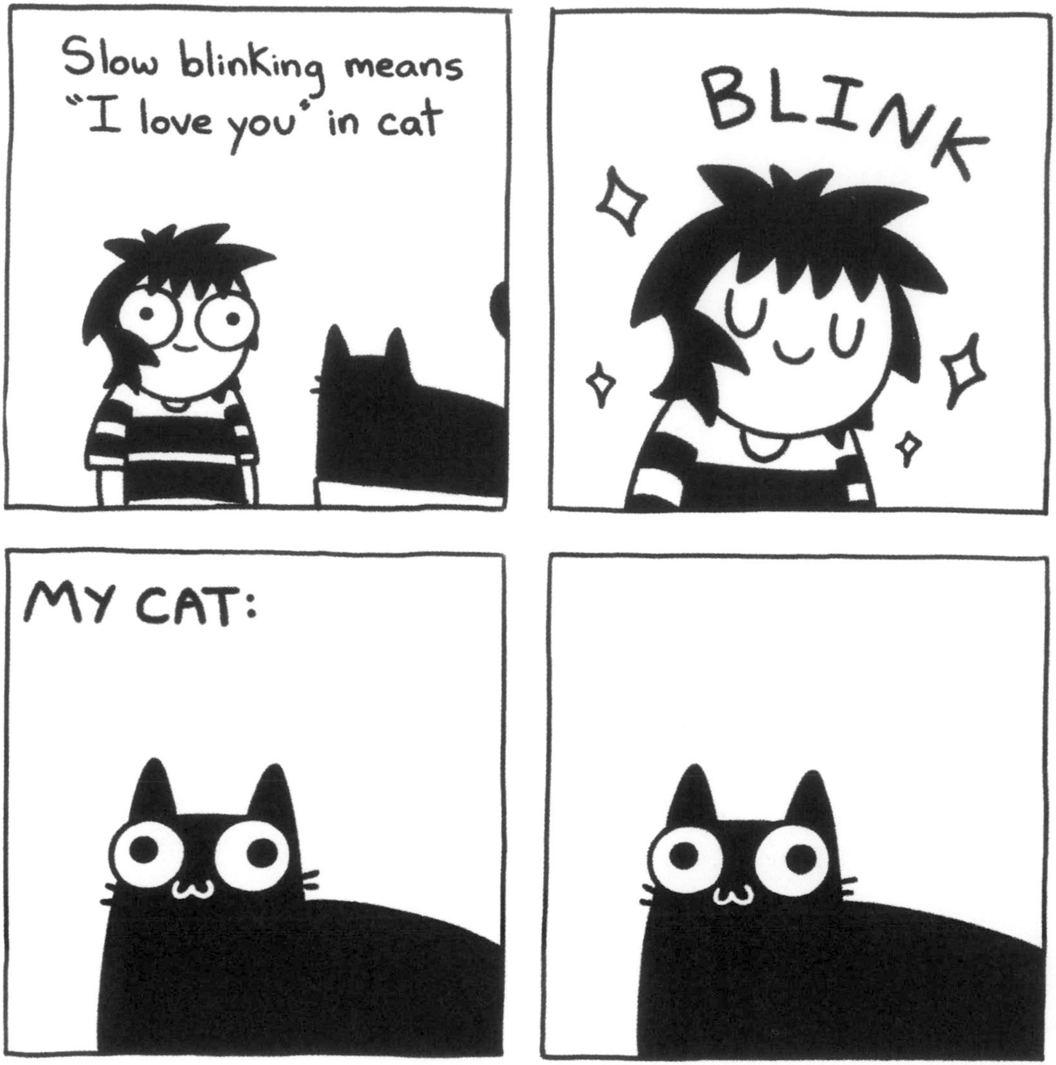
Slow blinking means "I love you" in cat
BLINK
MY CAT:

CARRYING A CONVERSATION

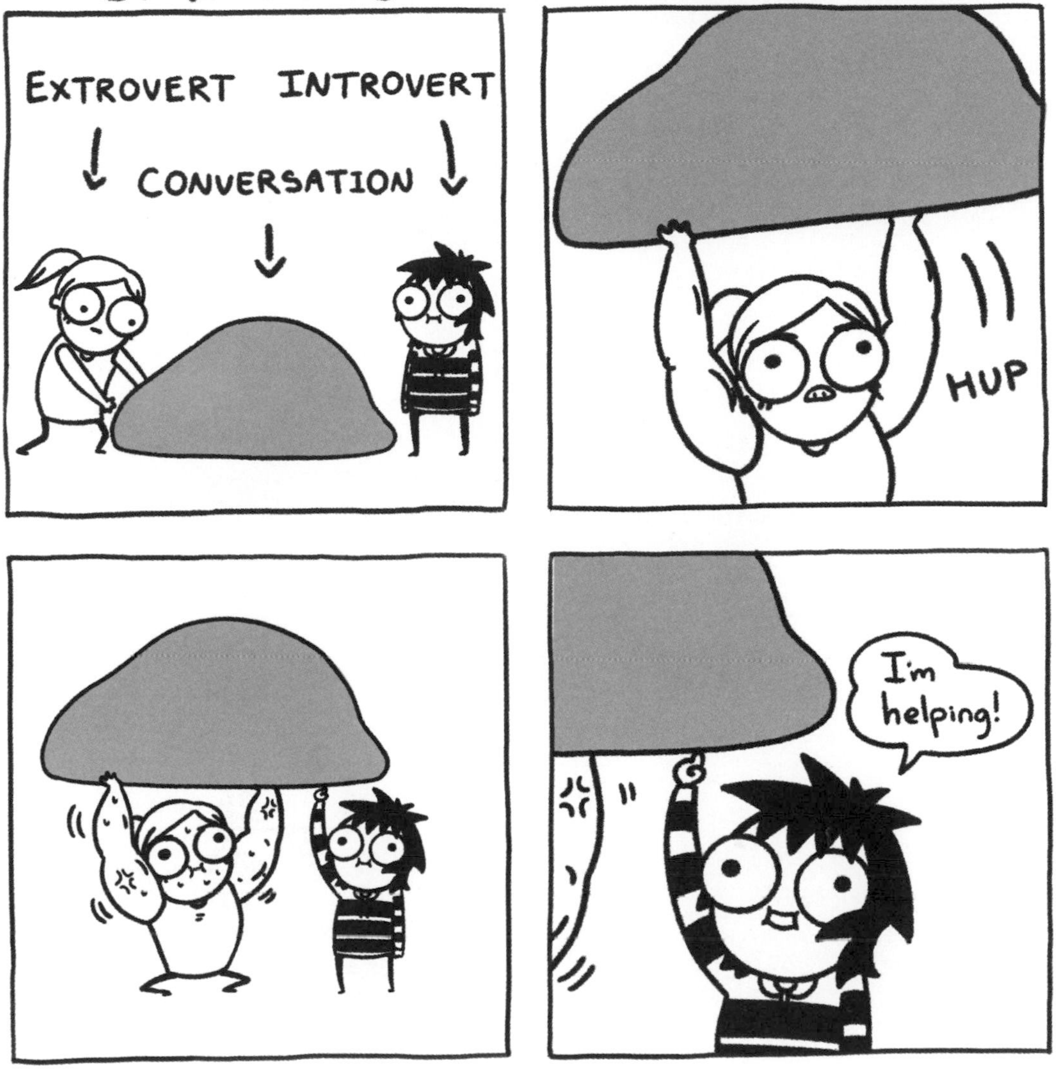
EXTROVERT
INTROVERT
CONVERSATION
HUP
I'm helping!

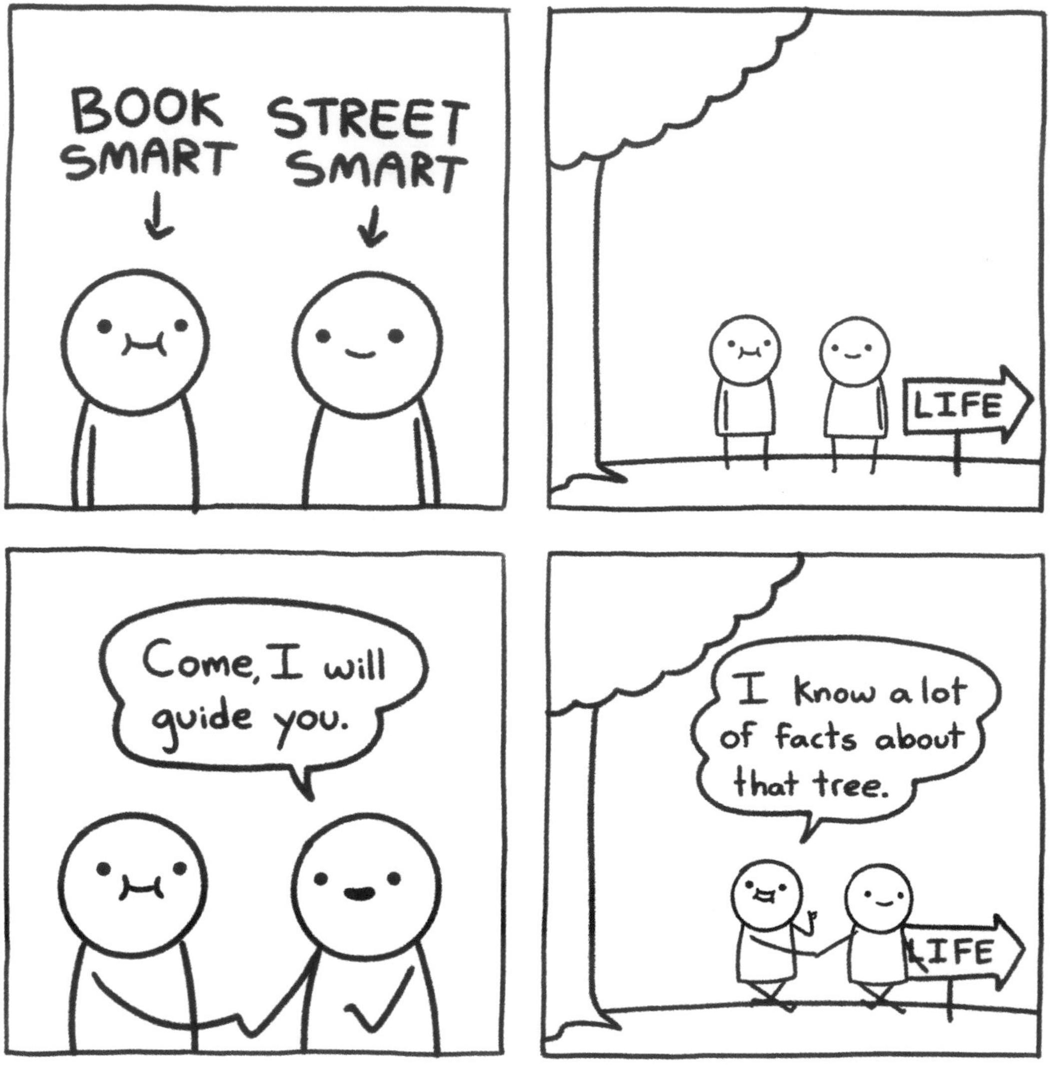
BOOK SMART
STREET SMART
LIFE
Come, I will guide you.
I know a lot of facts about that tree.
LIFE

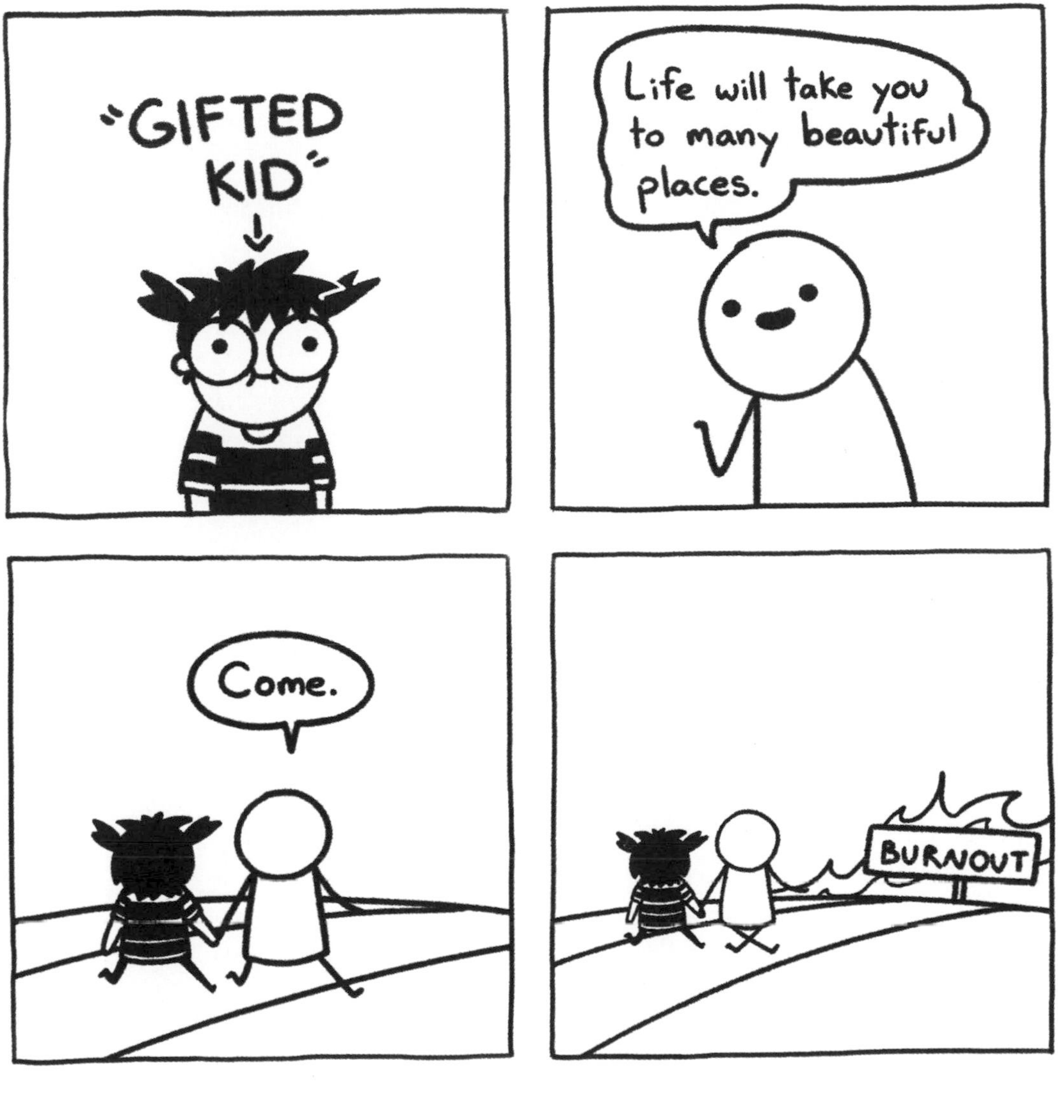
"GIFTED KID"
Life will take you to many beautiful places.
Come.
BURNOUT

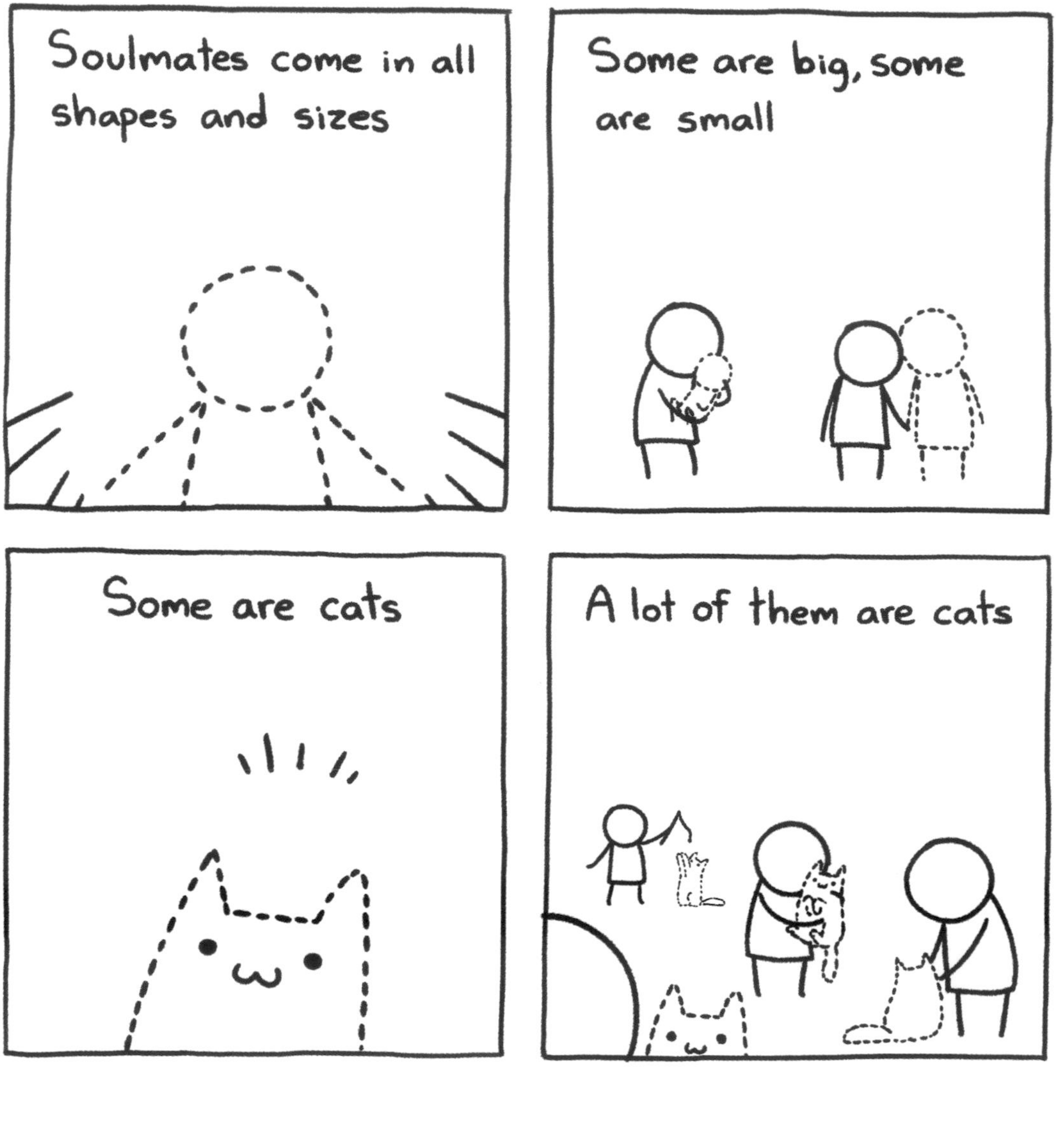
Soulmates come in all shapes and sizes
Some are big, some are small
Some are cats
A lot of them are cats

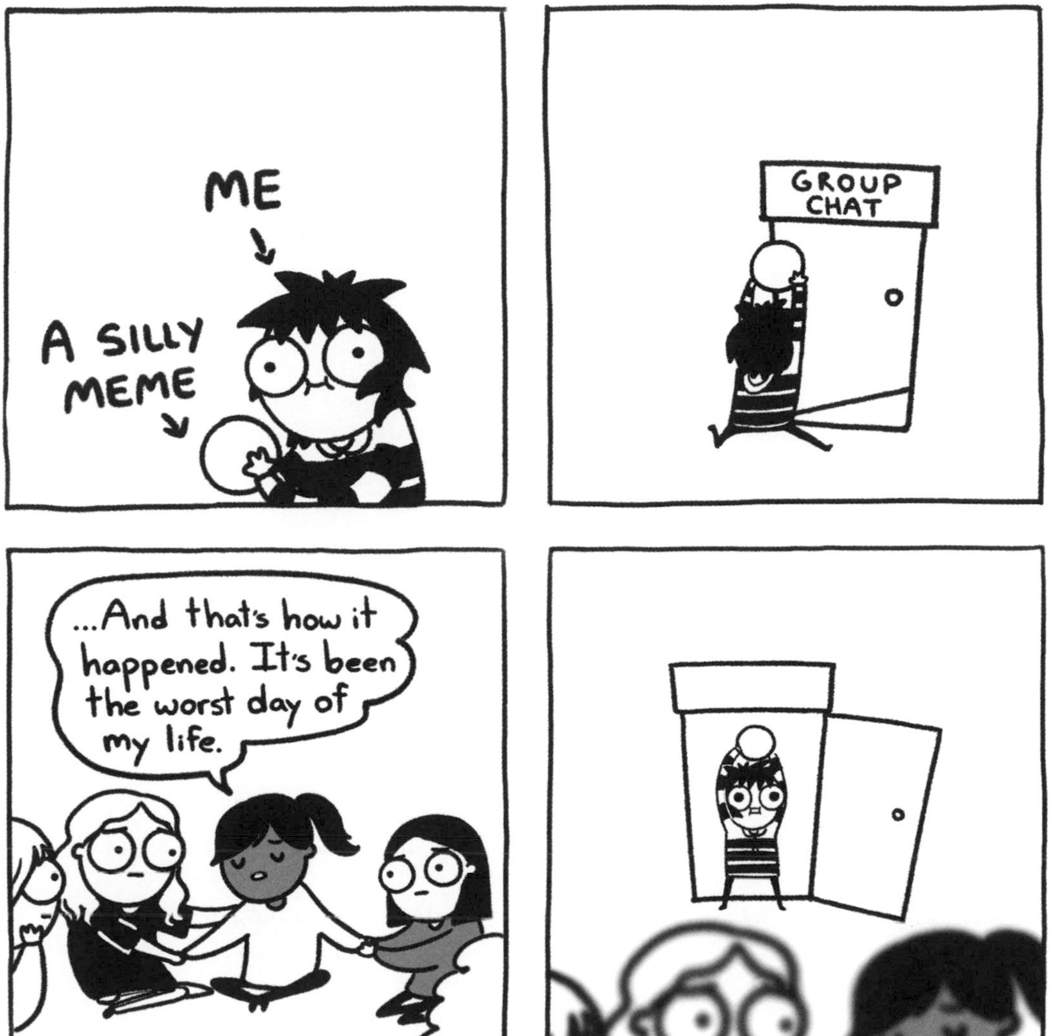
ME
A SILLY MEME
GROUP CHAT
...And that's how it happened. It's been the worst day of my life.

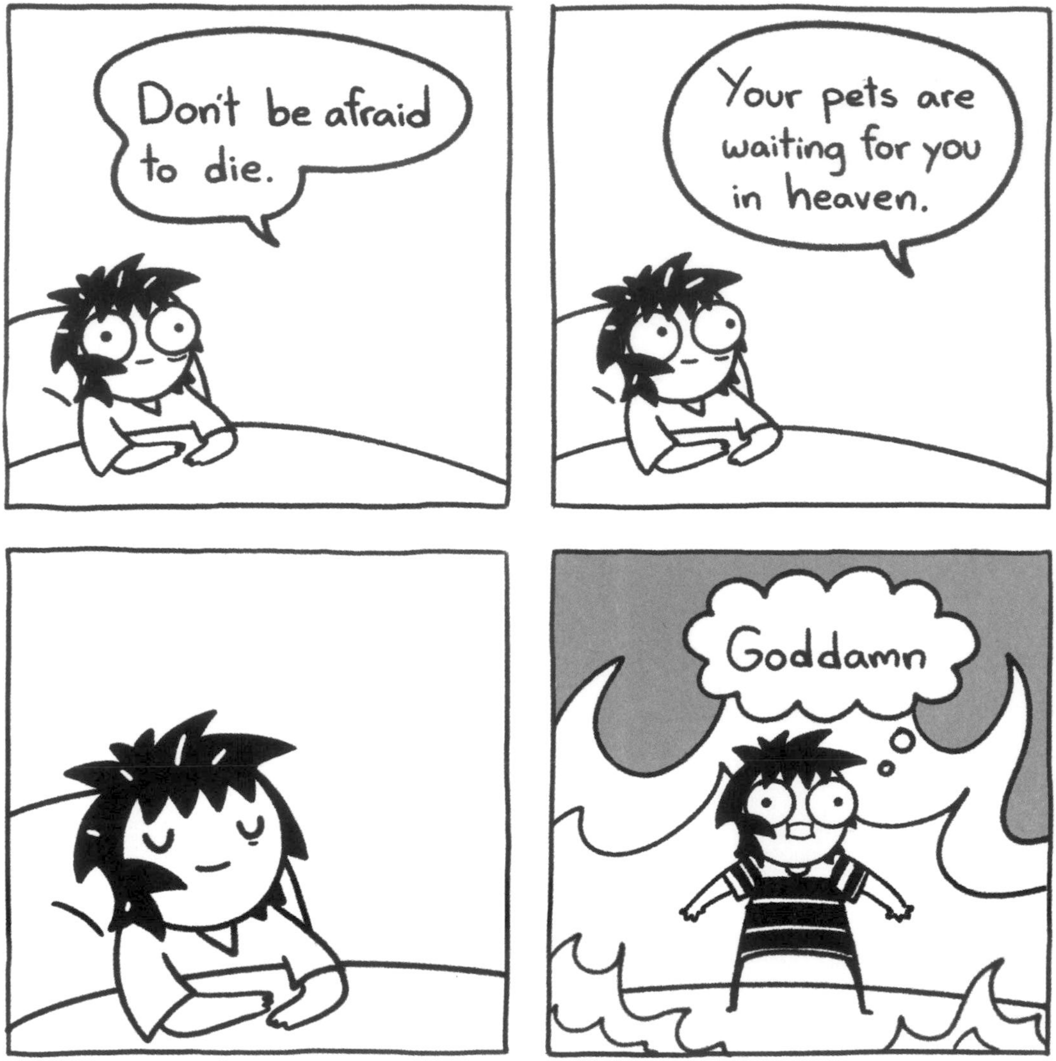
Don't be afraid to die.
Your pets are waiting for you in heaven.
Goddamn

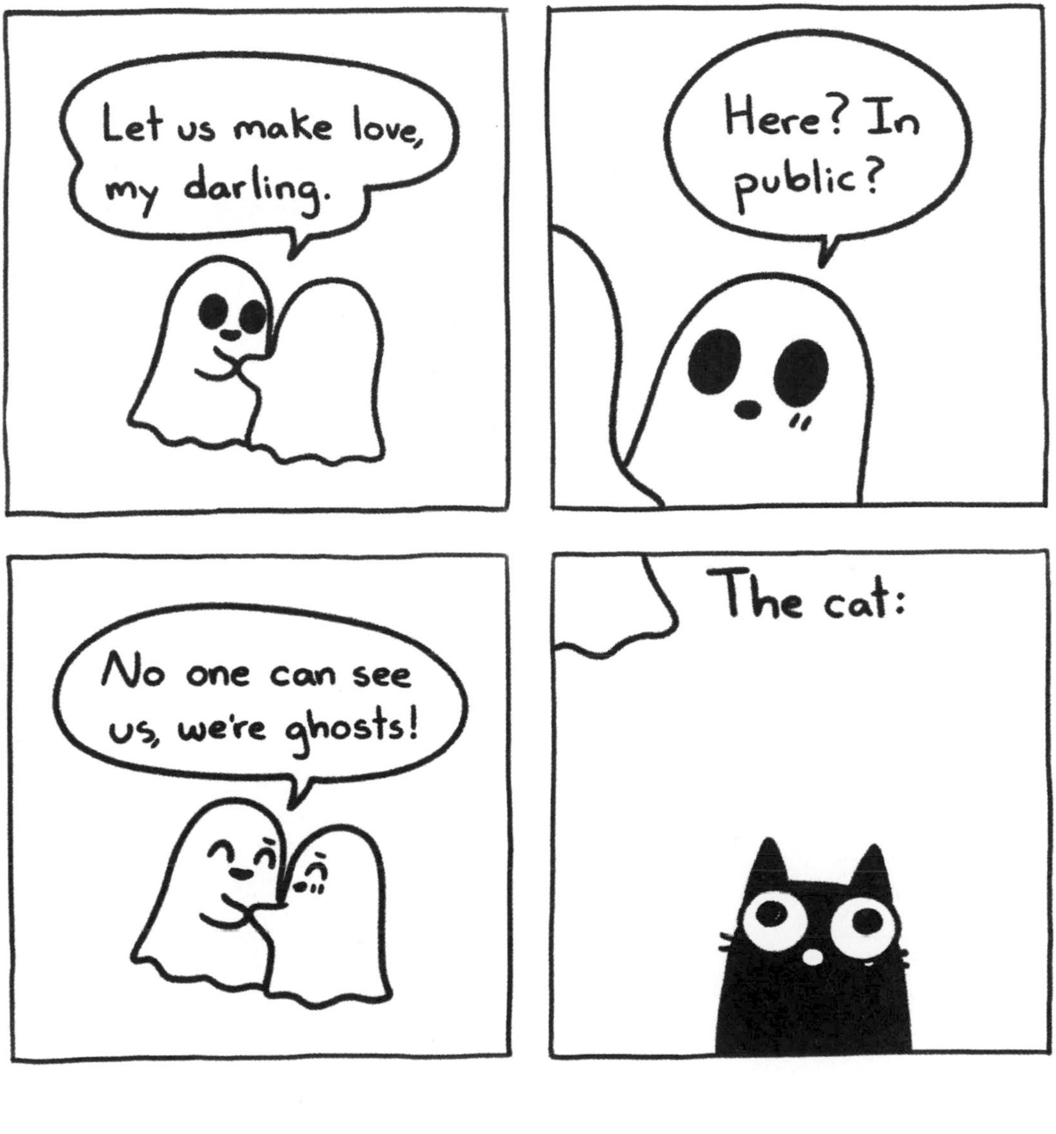
Let us make love, my darling.
Here? In public?
No one can see us, we're ghosts!
The cat:

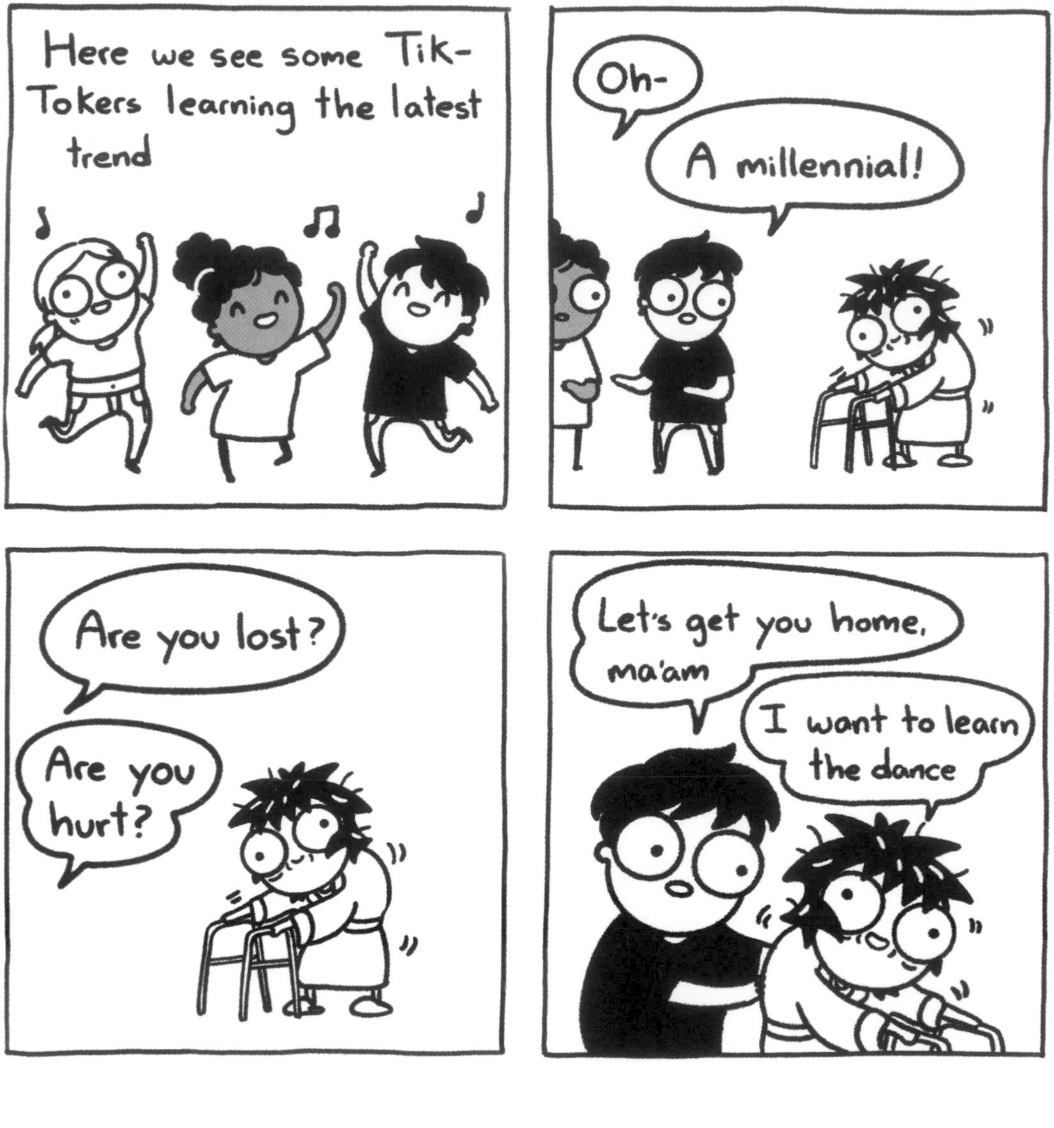
Here we see some Tik-Tokers learning the latest trend
Oh-
A millennial!
Are you lost?
Are you hurt?
Let's get you home, ma'am
I want to learn the dance

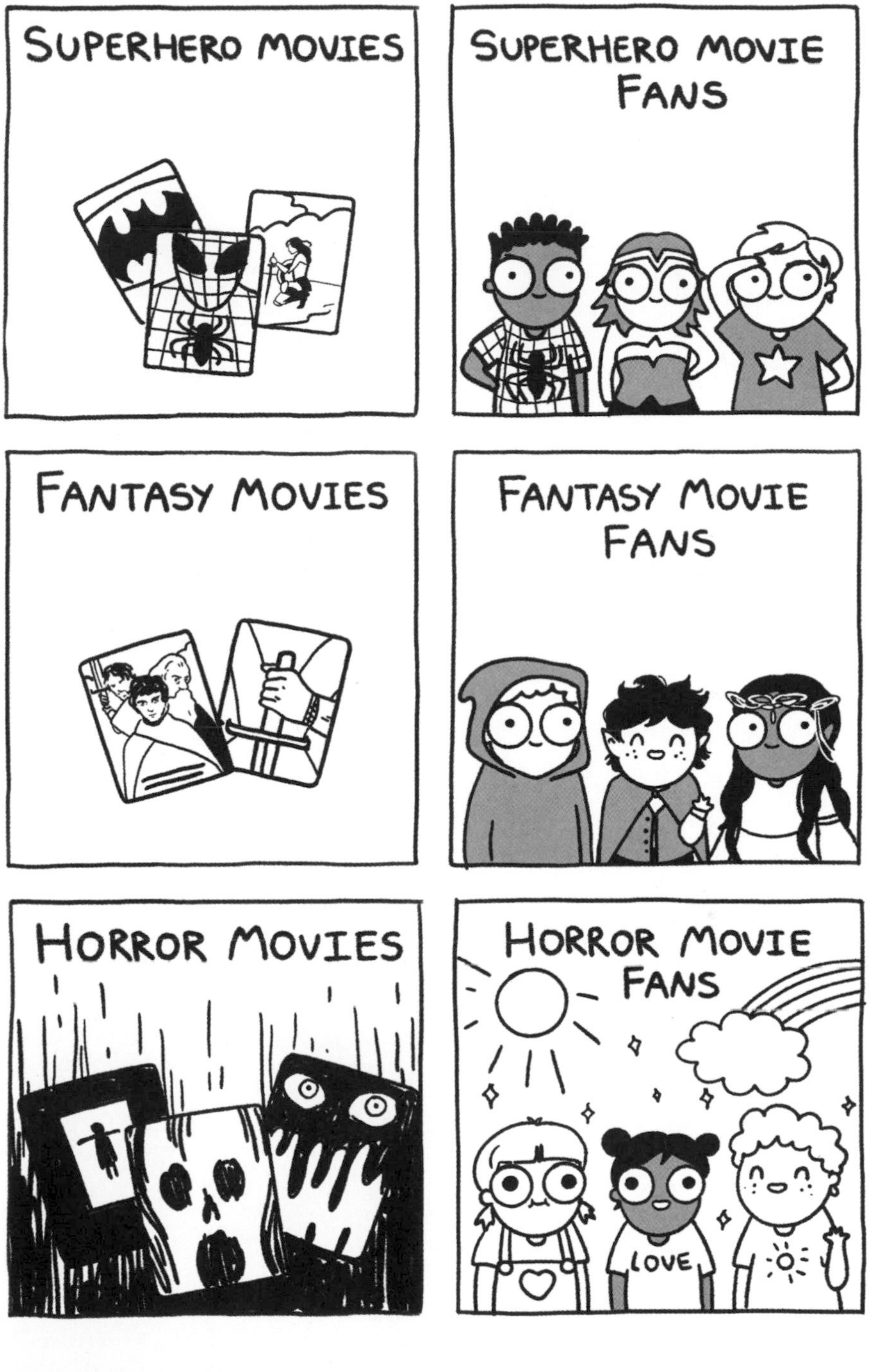
SUPERHERO MOVIES
SUPERHERO MOVIE FANS
FANTASY MOVIES
FANTASY MOVIE FANS
HORROR MOVIES
HORROR MOVIE FANS
LOVE

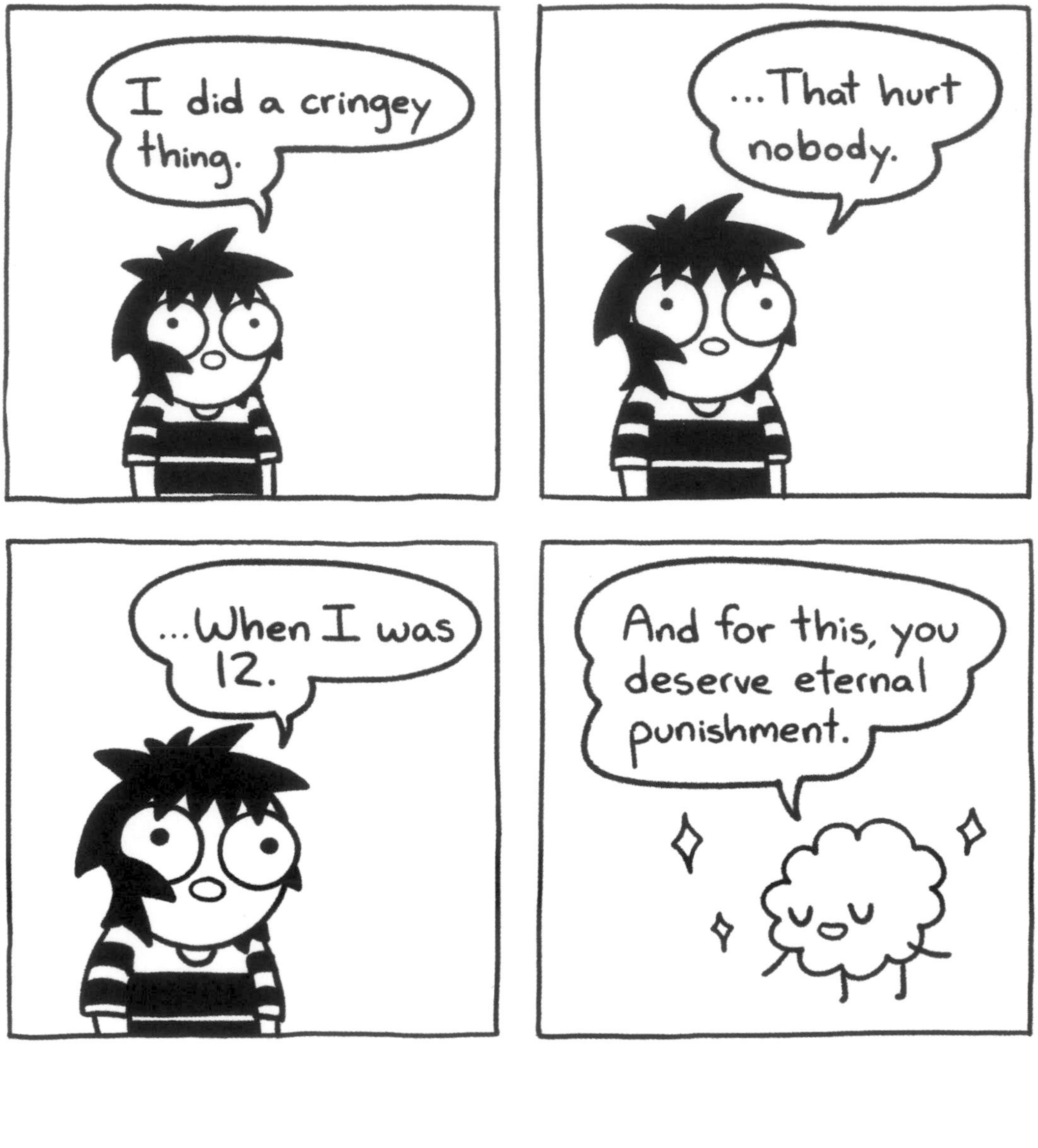
I did a cringey thing.
...That hurt nobody.
...When I was 12.
And for this, you deserve eternal punishment.

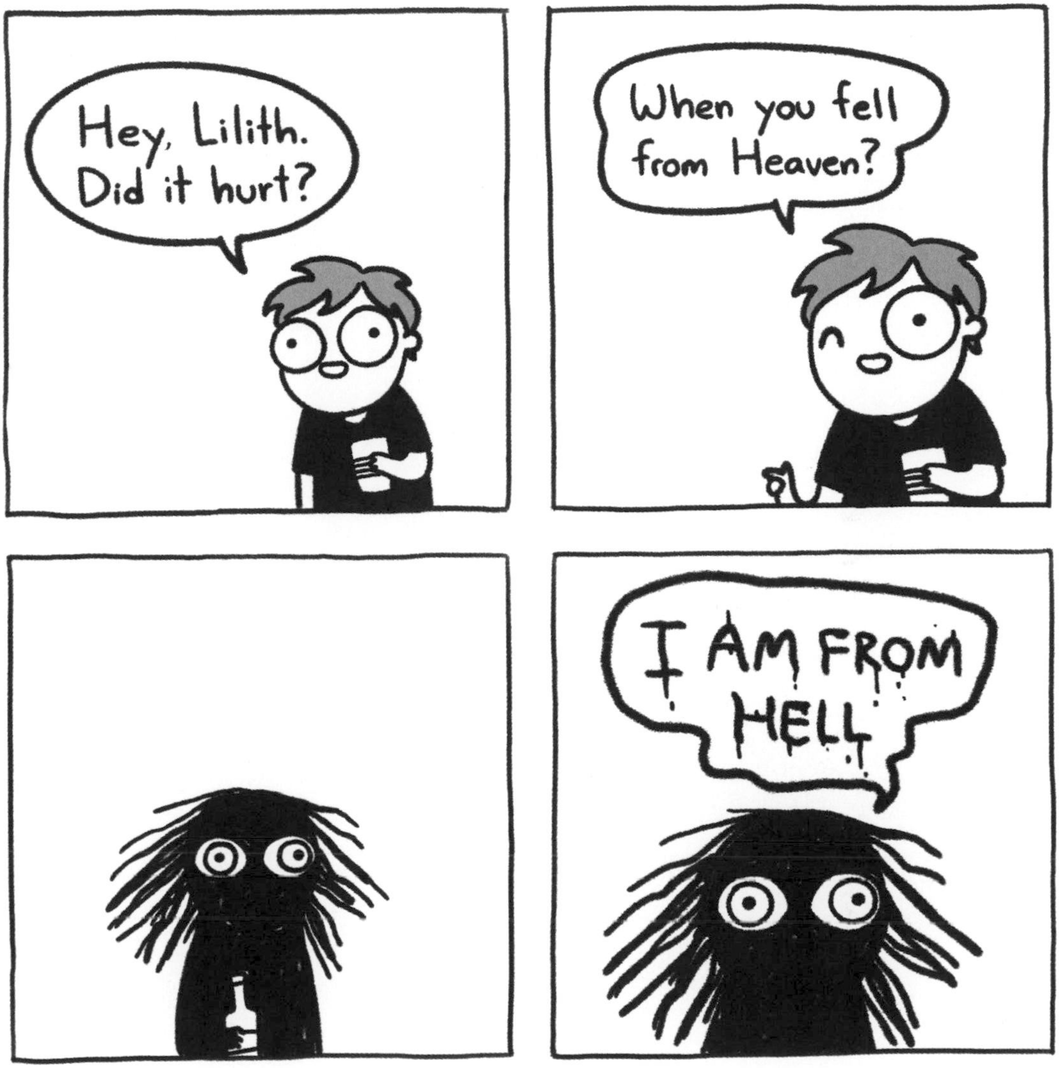
Hey, Lilith.
Did it hurt?
When you fell
from Heaven?
I AM FROM
HELL

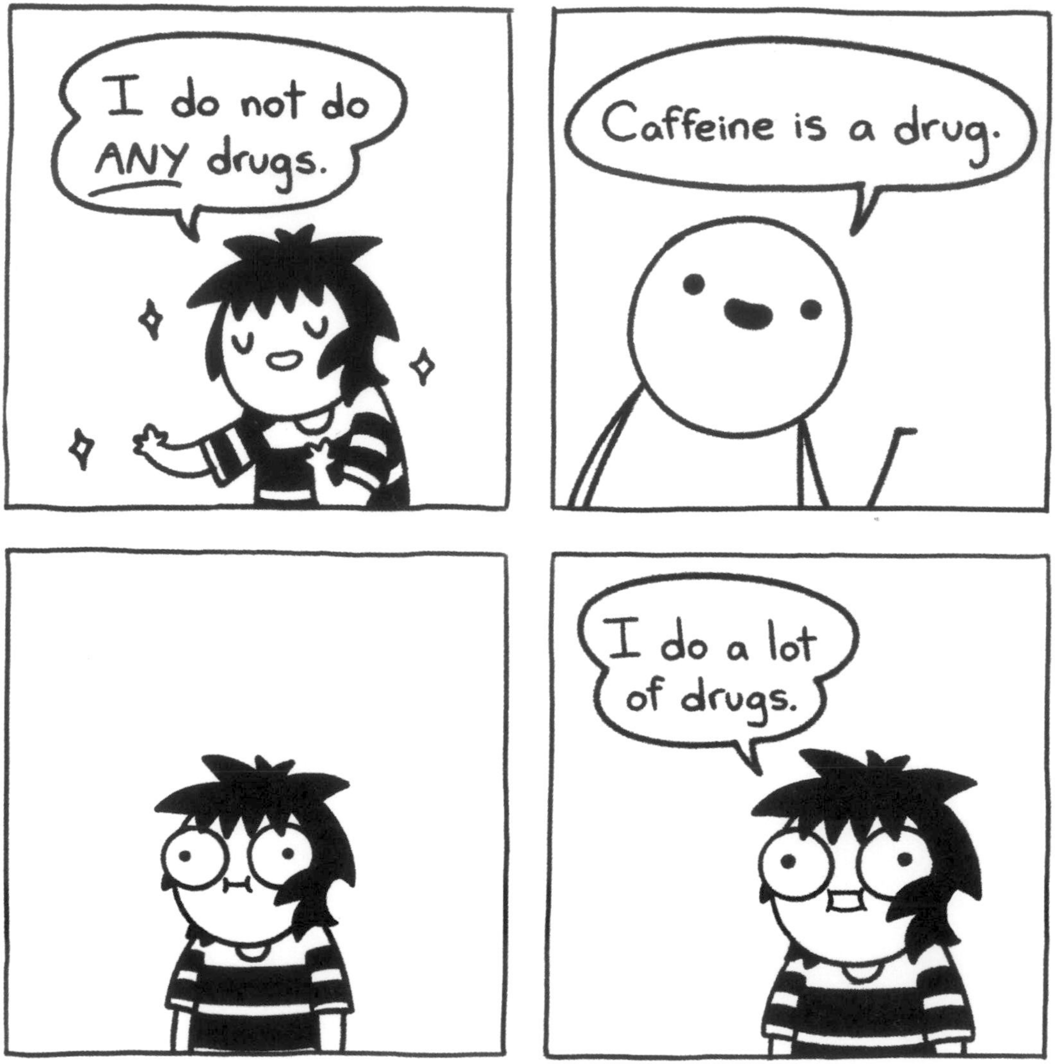
I do not do ANY drugs.
Caffeine is a drug.
I do a lot of drugs.

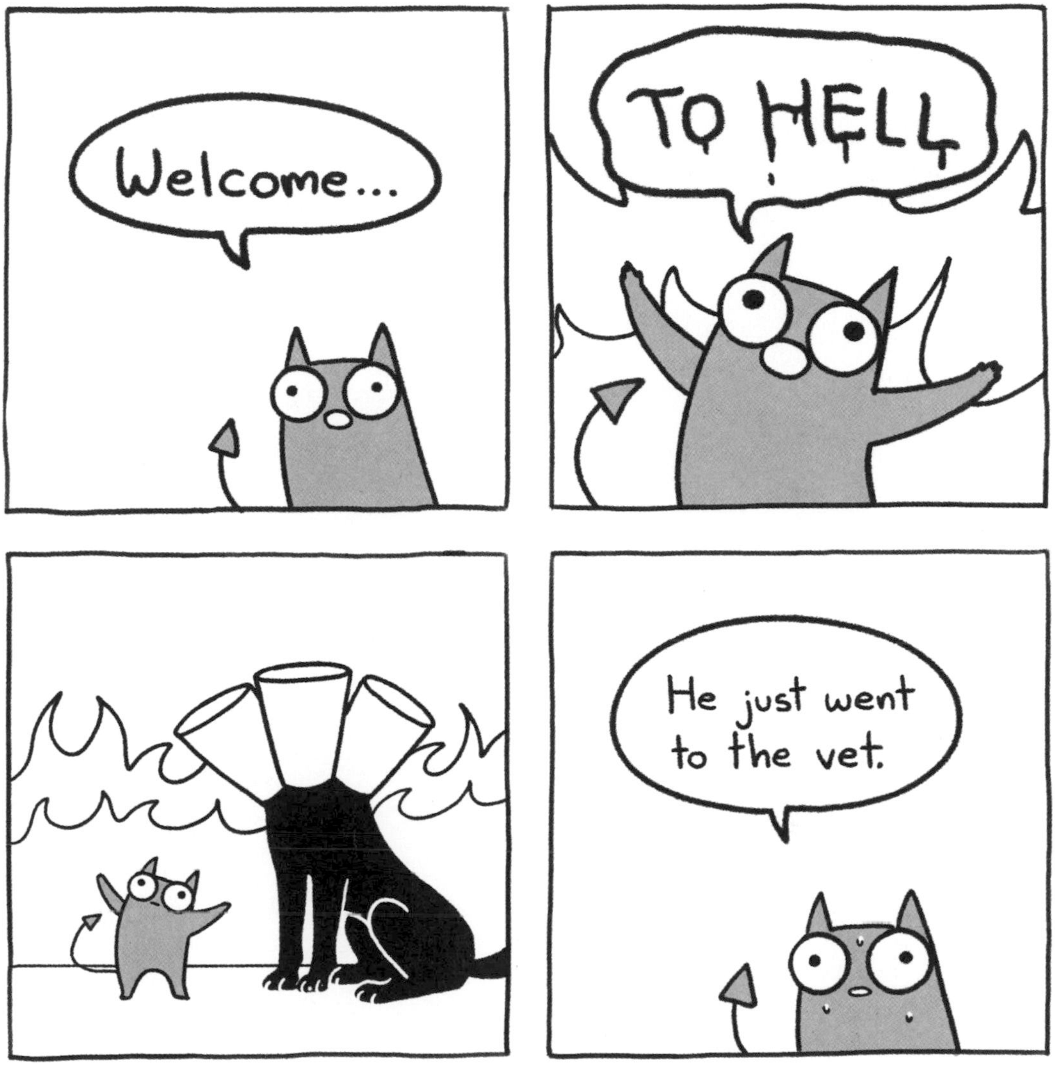
Welcome...
TO HELL
He just went to the vet.

NATURE WATCHING

The beach is beautiful in summer.
GASP
It's a Goth!
These are very, very rare this time of year!

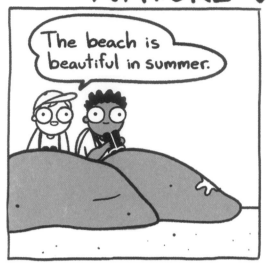

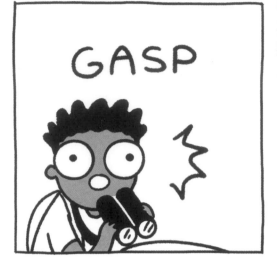

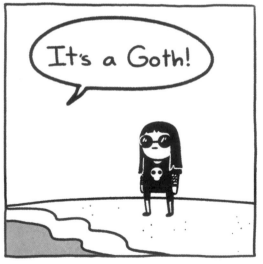

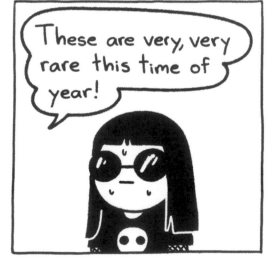

I want to heal my inner child.
PAST
Hello, past me.
I am a wolf

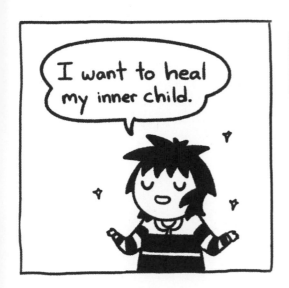

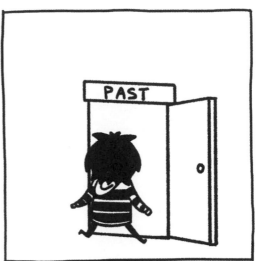

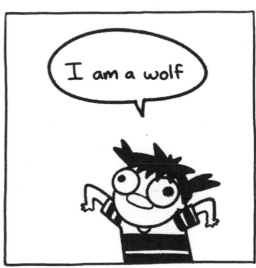

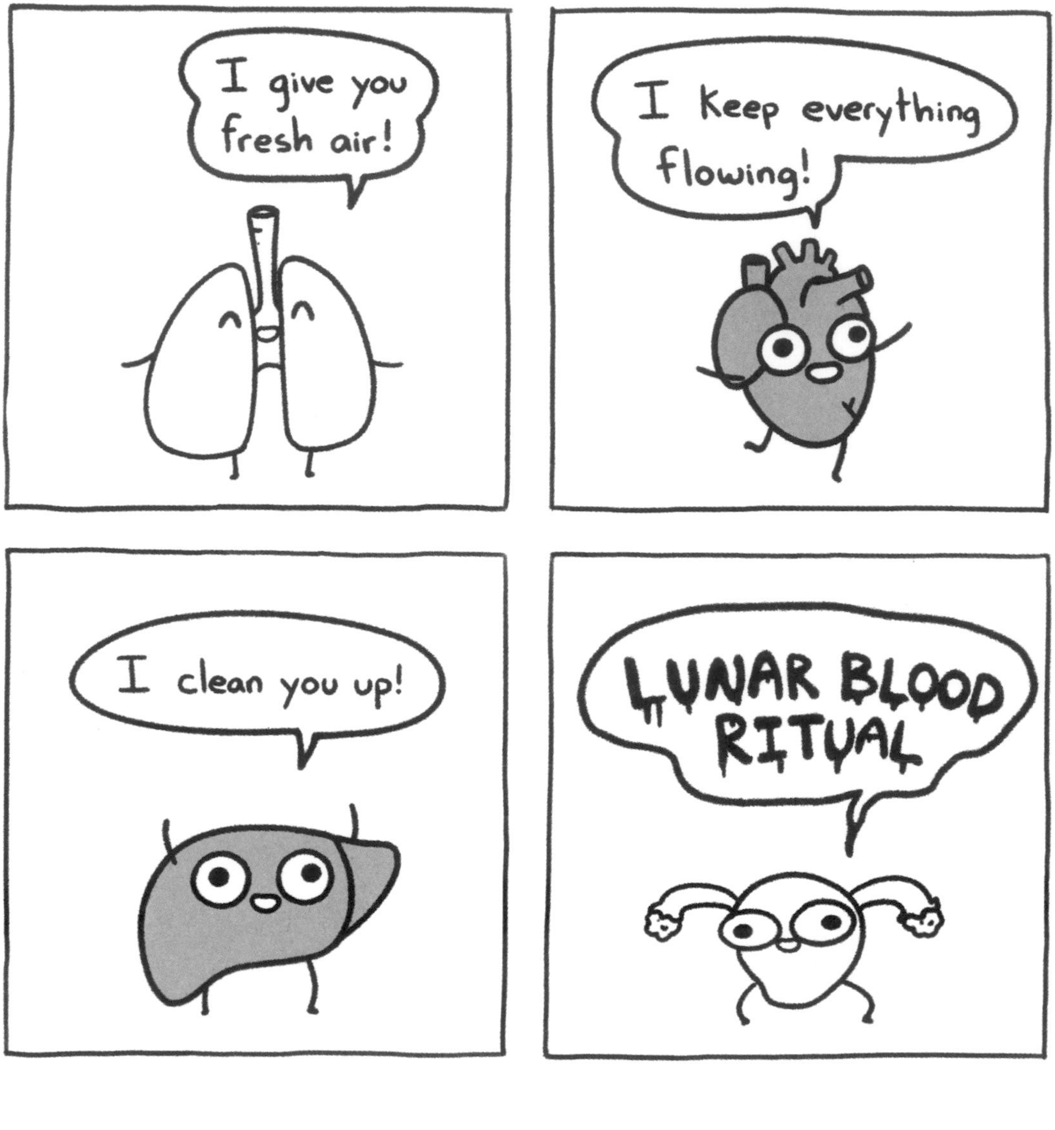
I give you fresh air!
I keep everything flowing!
I clean you up!
LUNAR BLOOD RITUAL

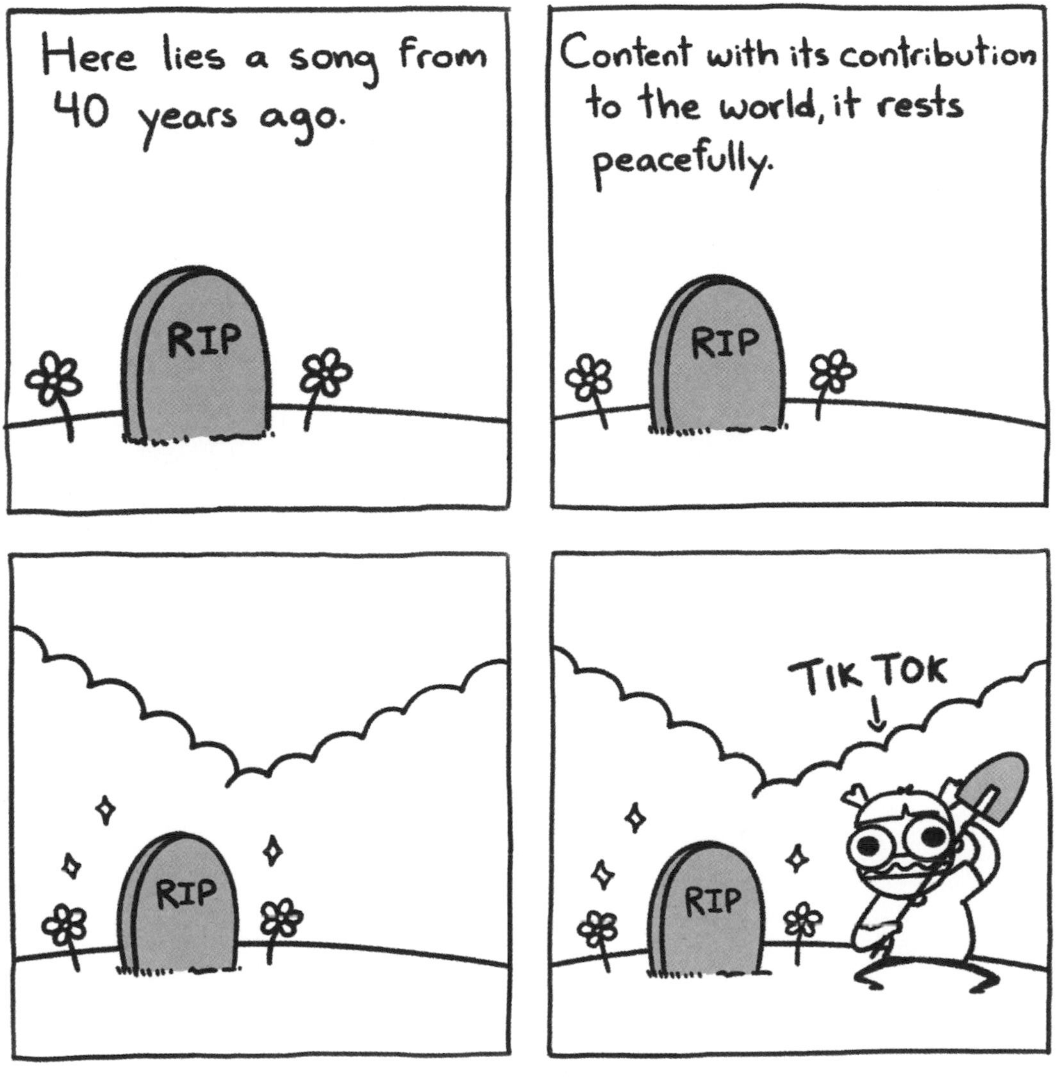
Here lies a song from 40 years ago.
RIP
Content with its contribution to the world, it rests peacefully.
RIP
RIP
TIK TOK
RIP

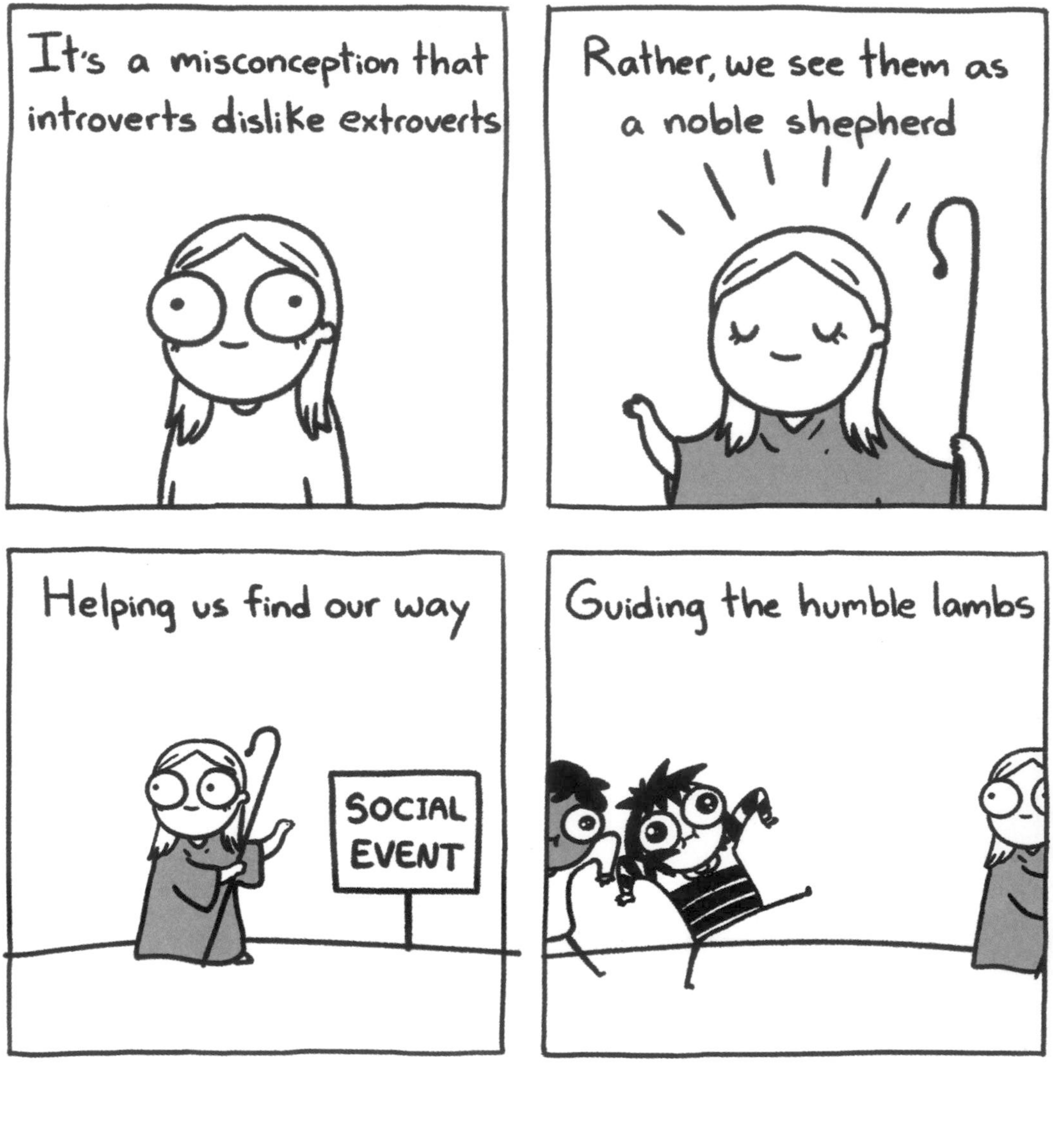
It's a misconception that introverts dislike extroverts
Rather, we see them as a noble shepherd
Helping us find our way
SOCIAL EVENT
Guiding the humble lambs

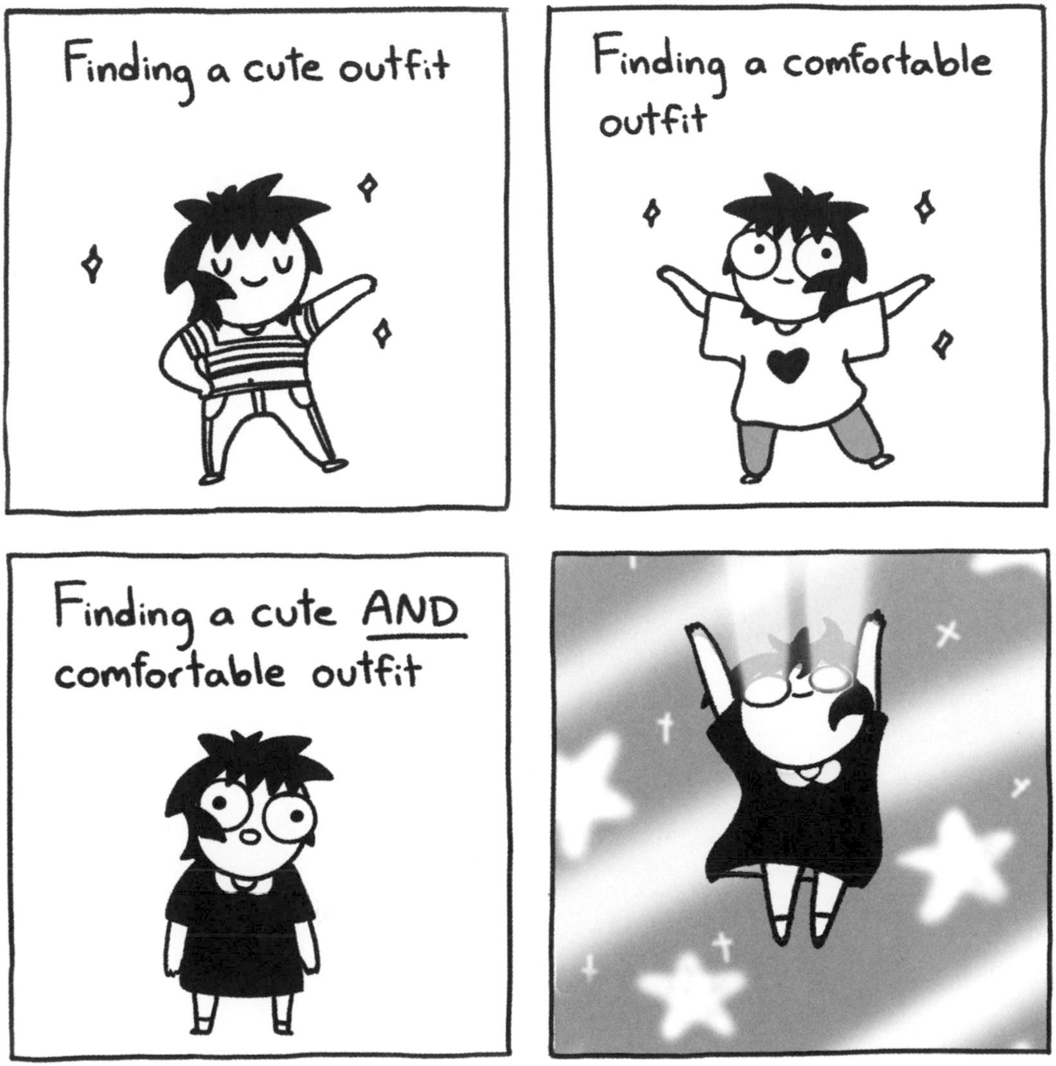
Finding a cute outfit
Finding a comfortable outfit
Finding a cute AND comfortable outfit

THE ORGANS ARE A TEAM

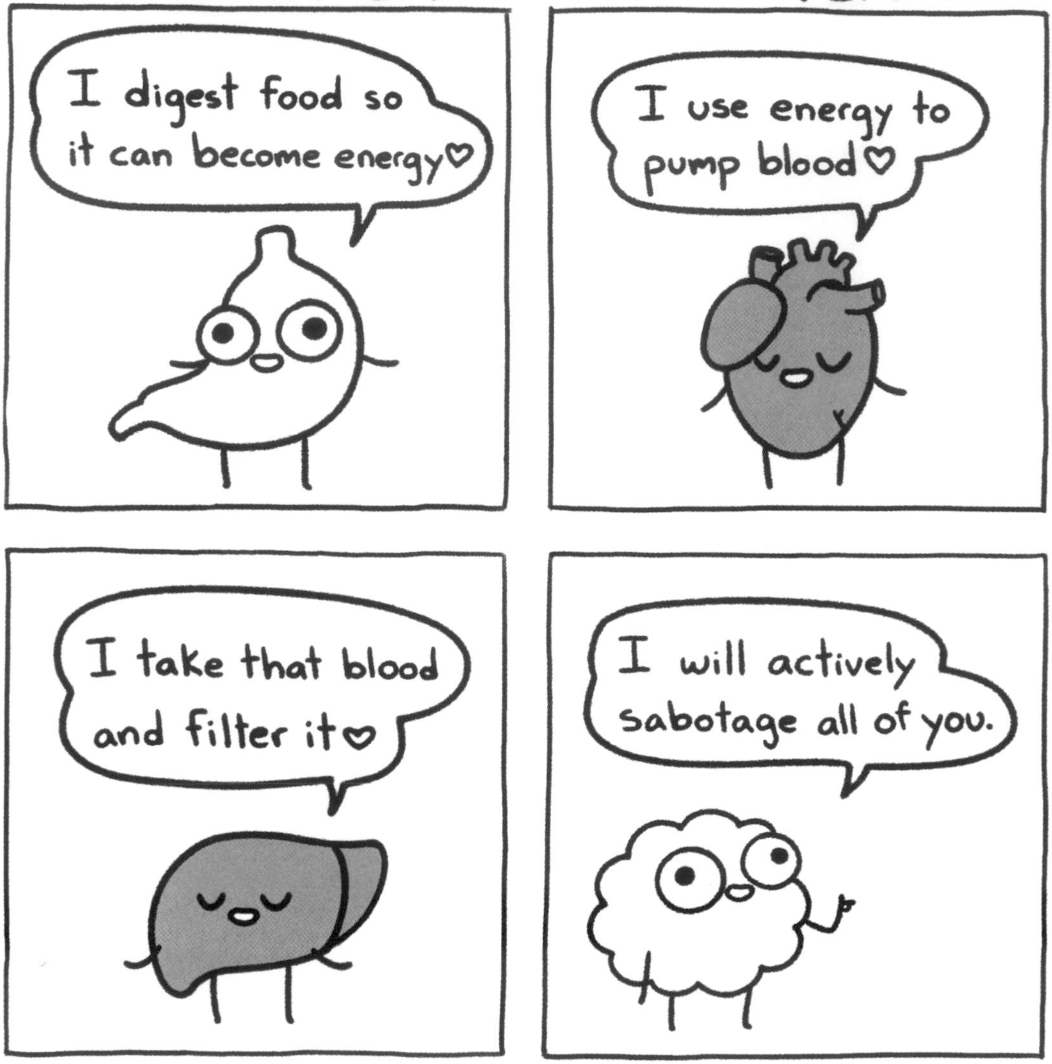
I digest food so it can become energy♡
I use energy to pump blood♡
I take that blood and filter it♡
I will actively sabotage all of you.

ADOPTING A DOG

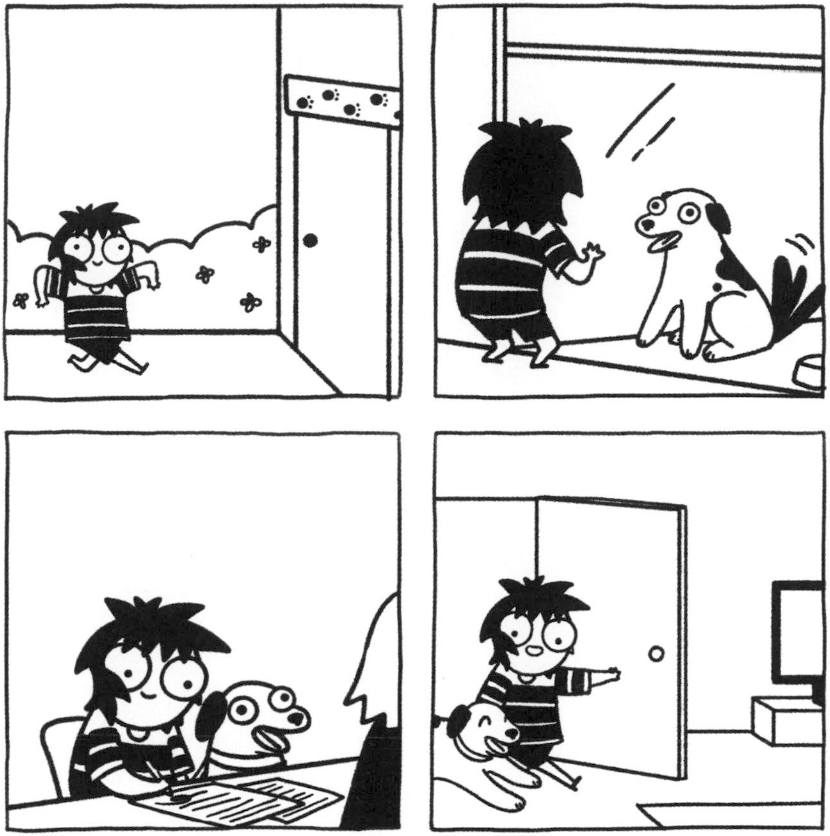

ADOPTING A CAT

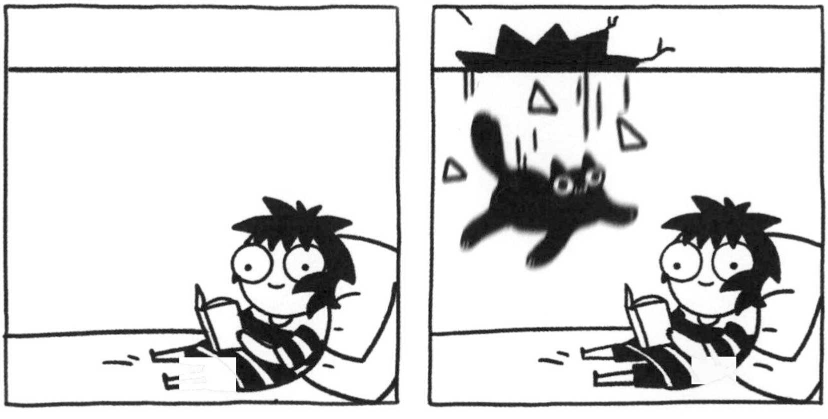

GROUP CHATS

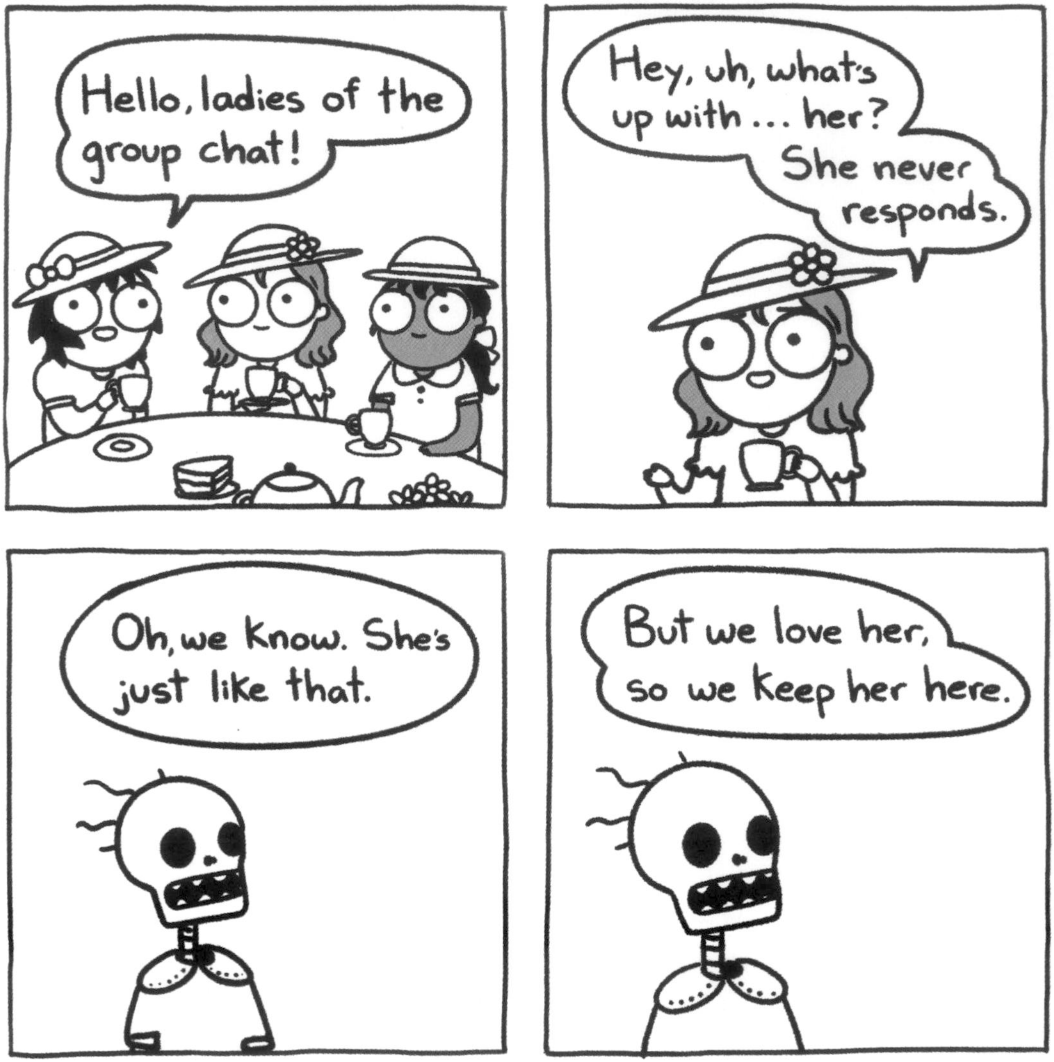
Hello, ladies of the group chat!
Hey, uh, what's up with... her?
She never responds.
Oh, we know. She's just like that.
But we love her, so we keep her here.

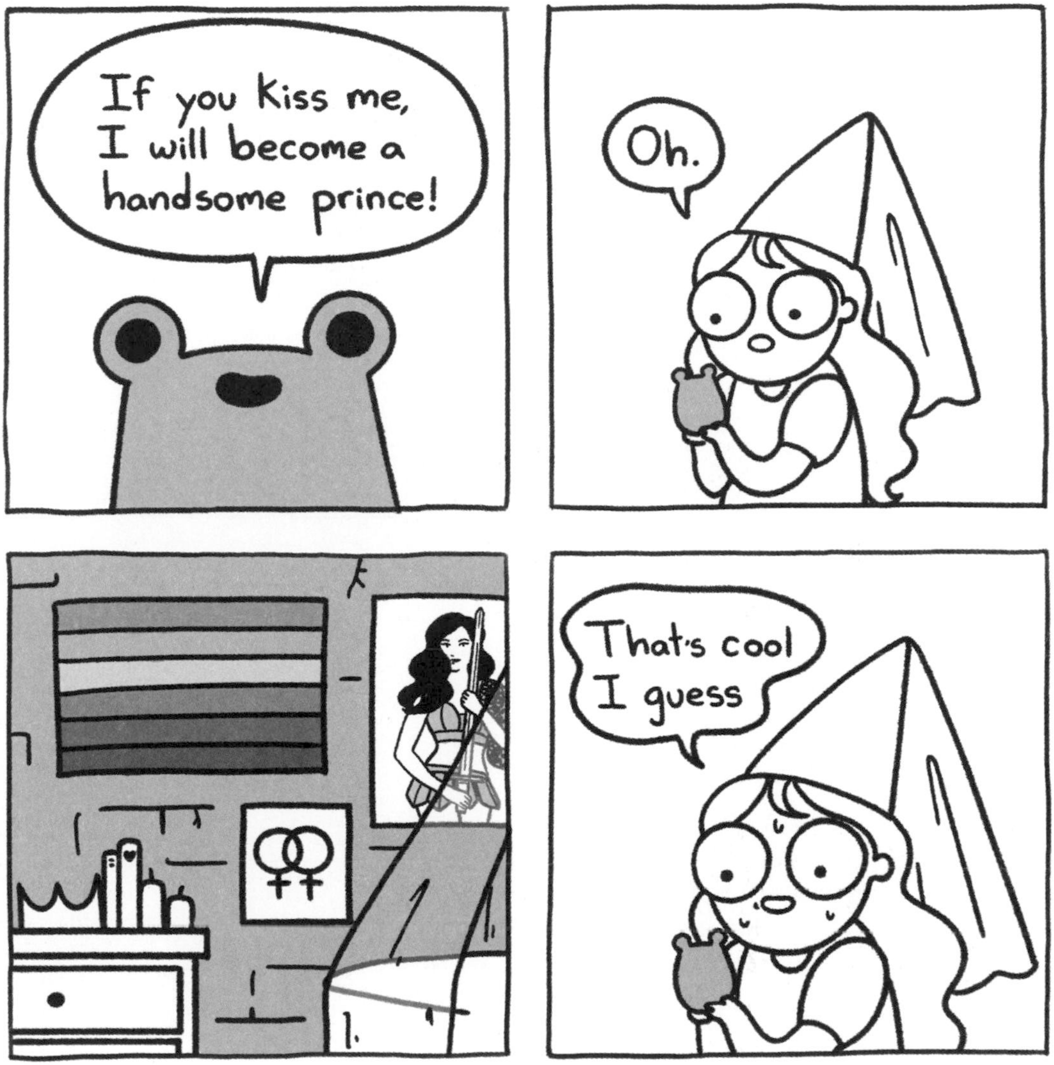
If you Kiss me, I will become a handsome prince!
Oh.
That's cool I guess

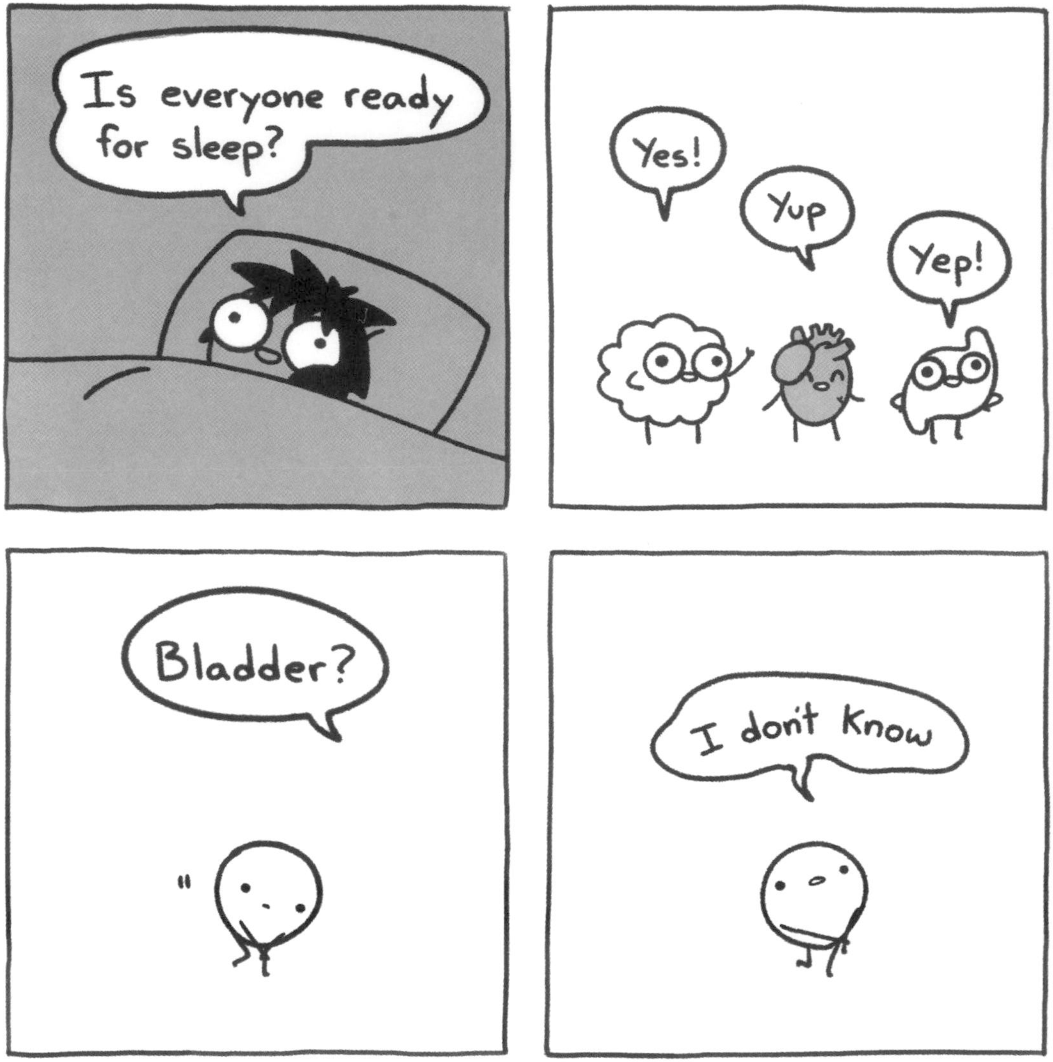

Is everyone ready for sleep?
Yes!
Yup
Yep!
Bladder?
I don't know

The human has shown Kindness
I shall complete the ancient ritual
And bestow a gift from our Elder Gods
Cool, a shiny rock!

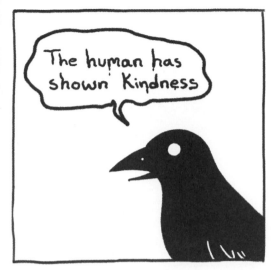

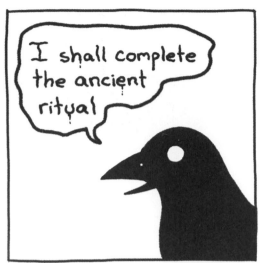

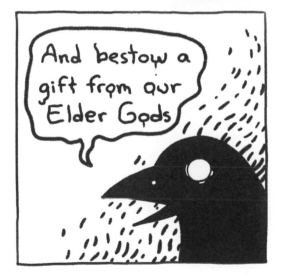

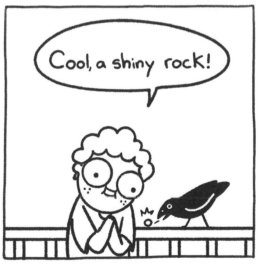

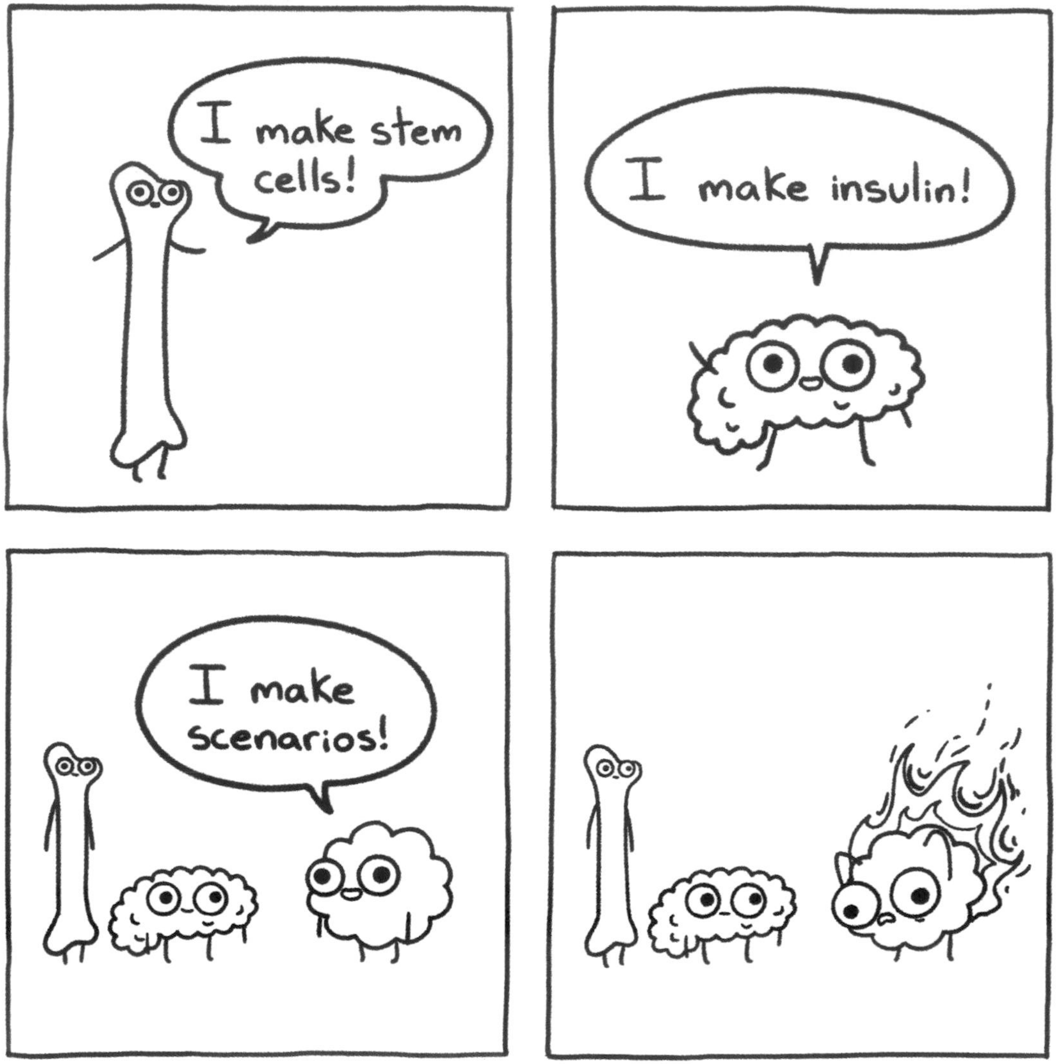
I make stem cells!
I make insulin!
I make scenarios!

EVERYBODY HAS A ROLE

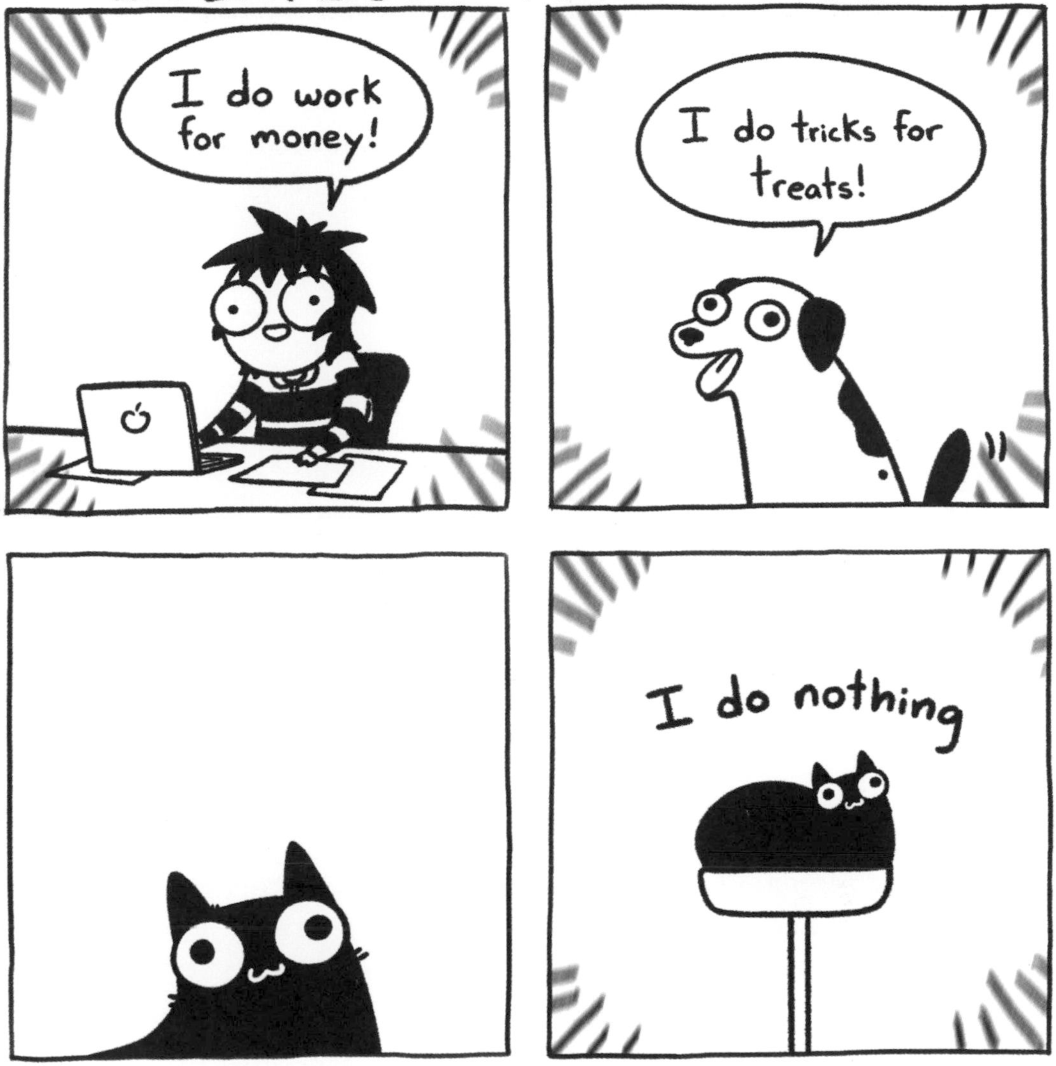
I do work for money!
I do tricks for treats!
I do nothing

DISHES

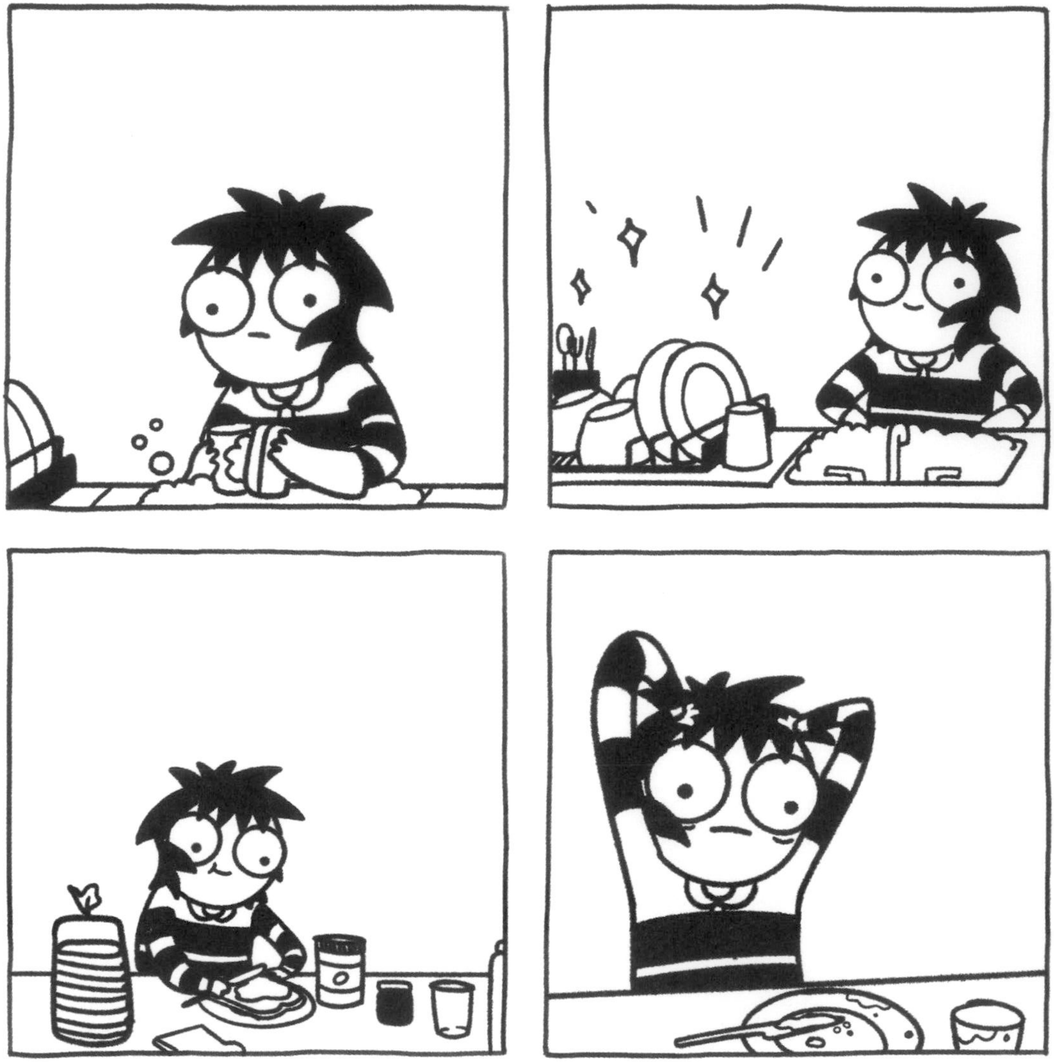

SWAN PRINCESS

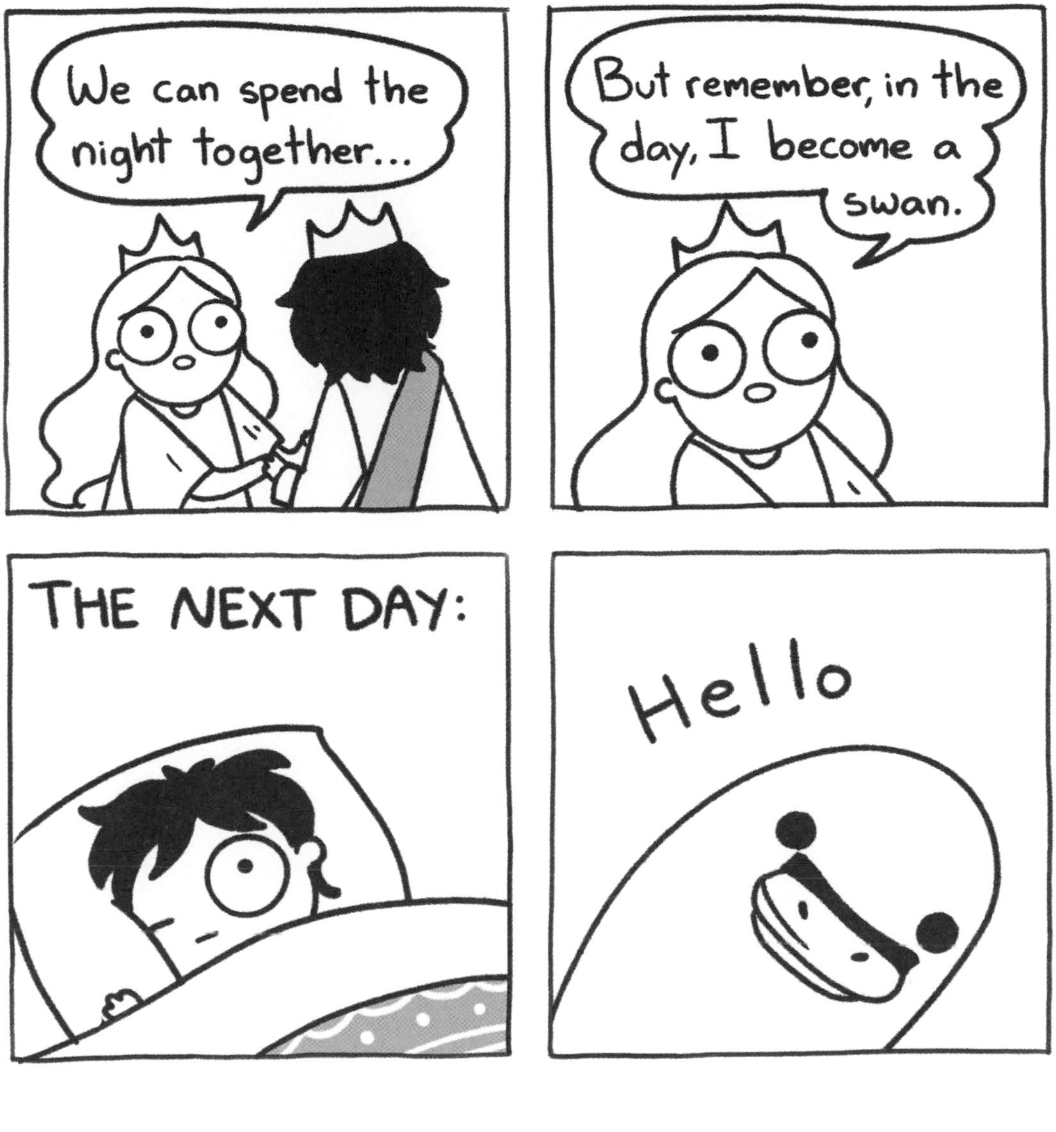
We can spend the night together...
But remember, in the day, I become a swan.
THE NEXT DAY:
Hello

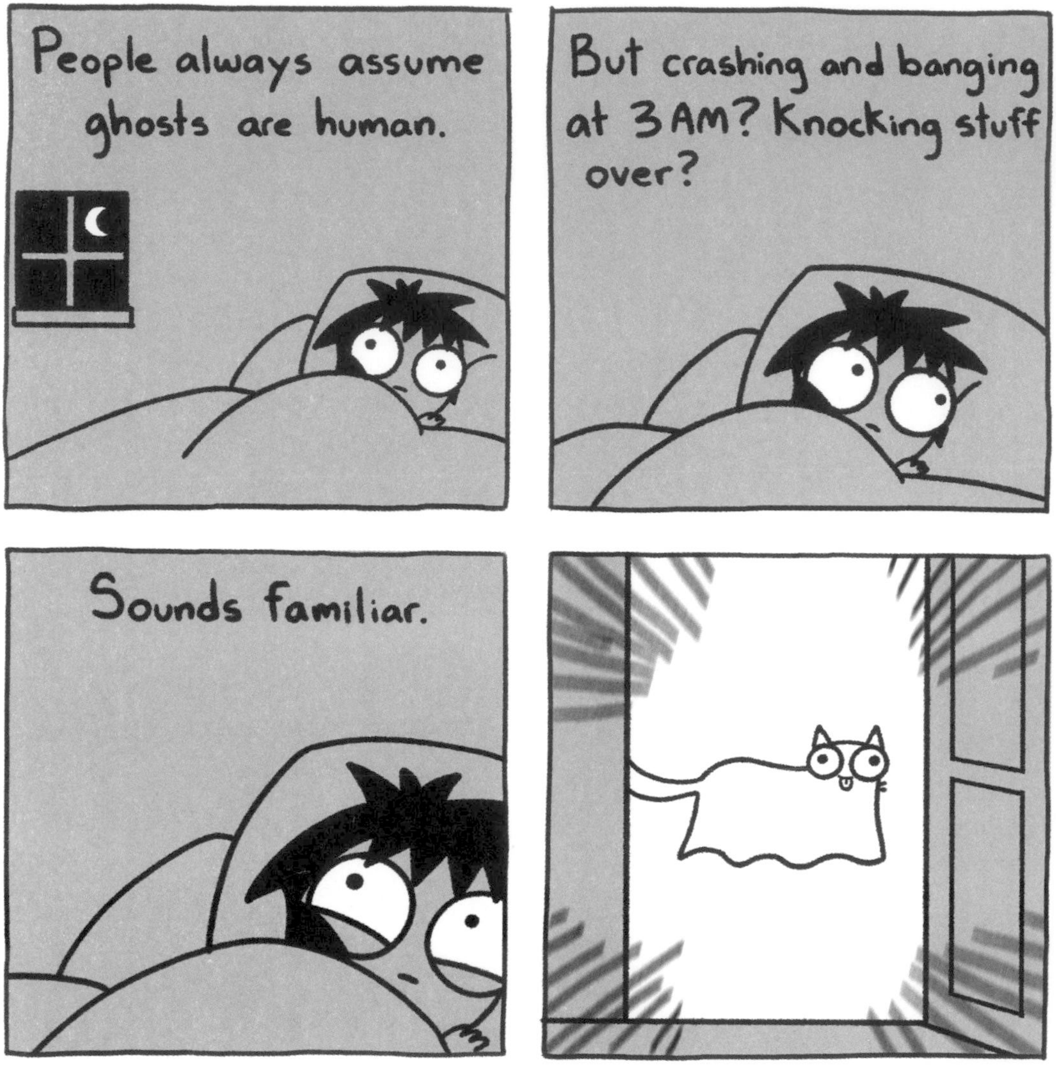
People always assume ghosts are human.
But crashing and banging at 3 AM? Knocking stuff over?
Sounds familiar.

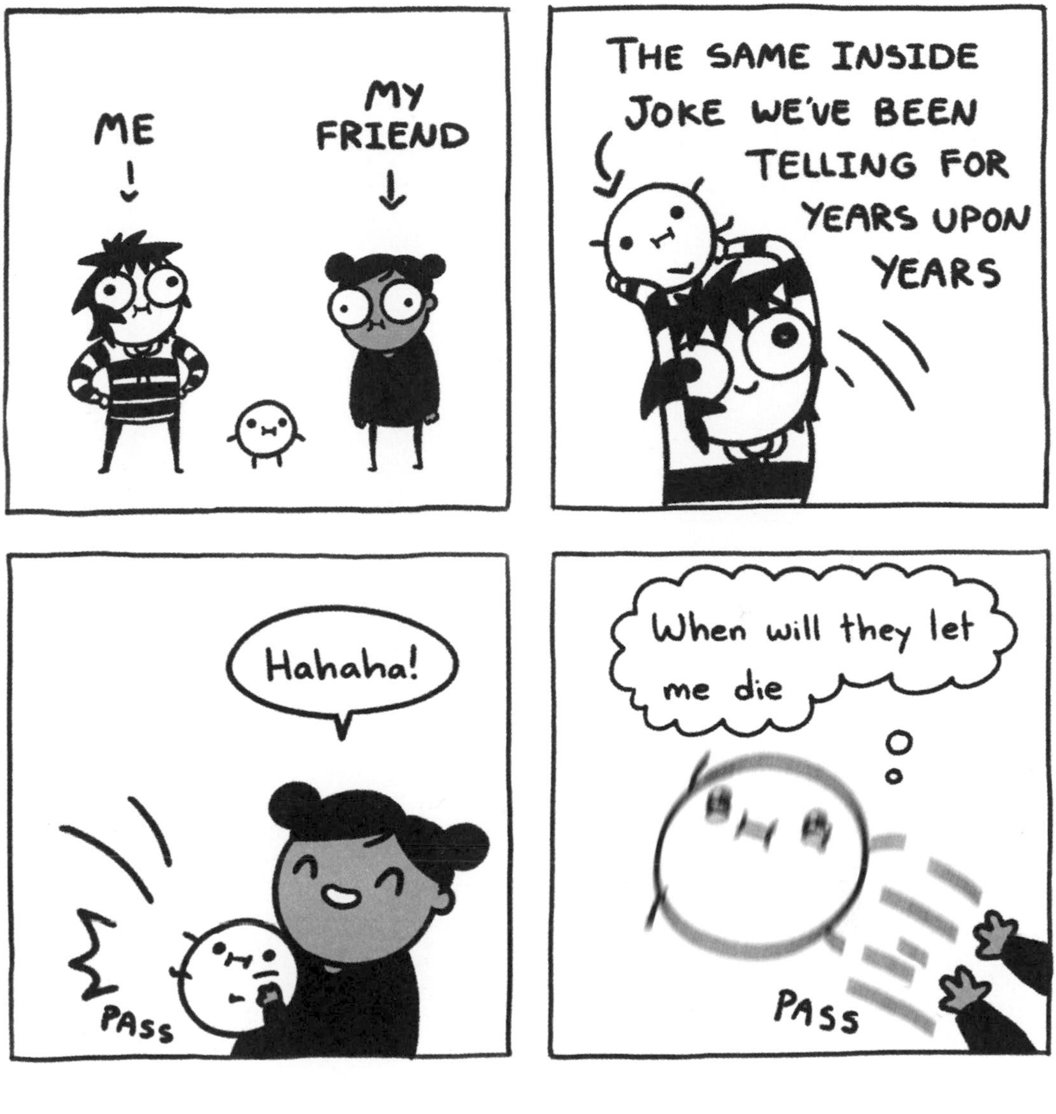
ME
MY FRIEND
THE SAME INSIDE JOKE WE'VE BEEN TELLING FOR YEARS UPON YEARS
Hahaha!
PASS
When will they let me die
PASS

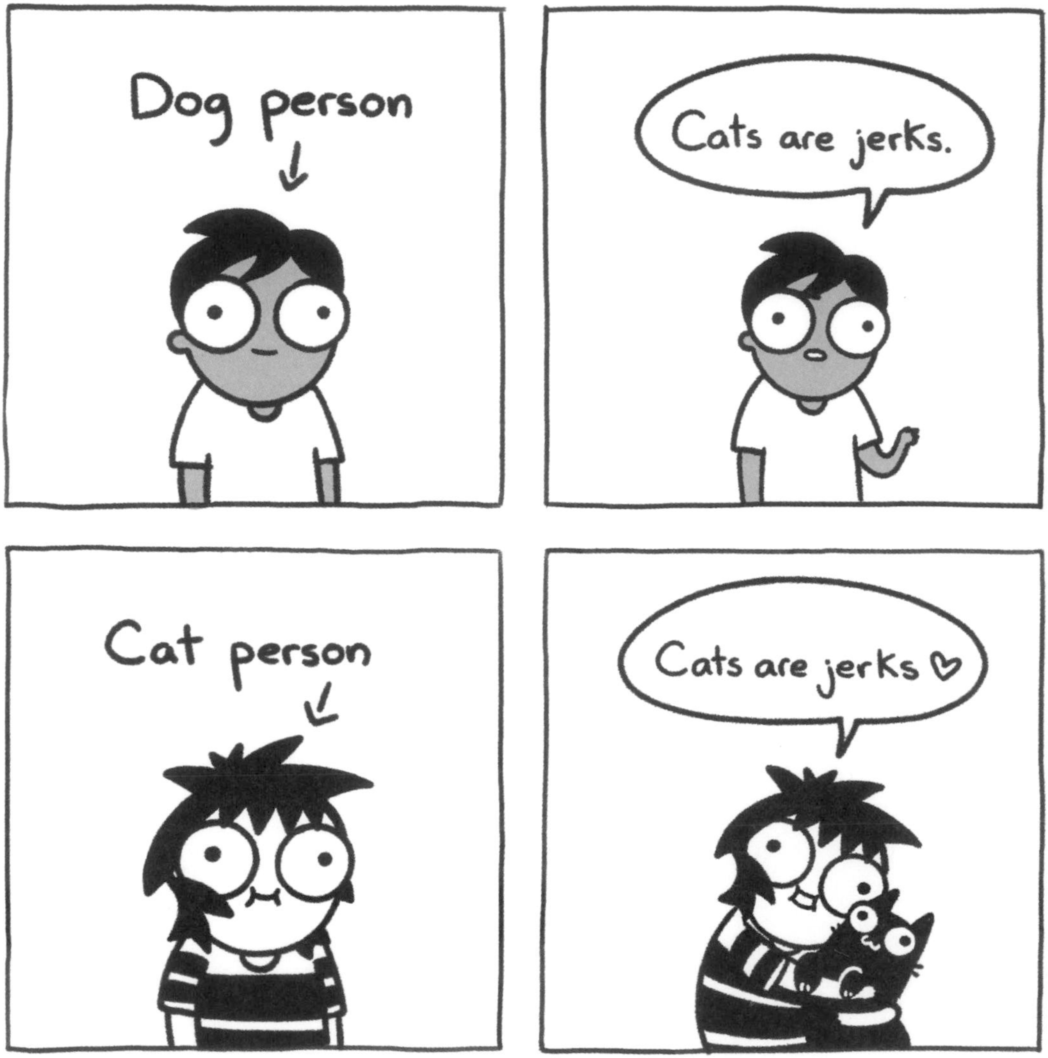
Dog person
Cats are jerks.
Cat person
Cats are jerks ♡

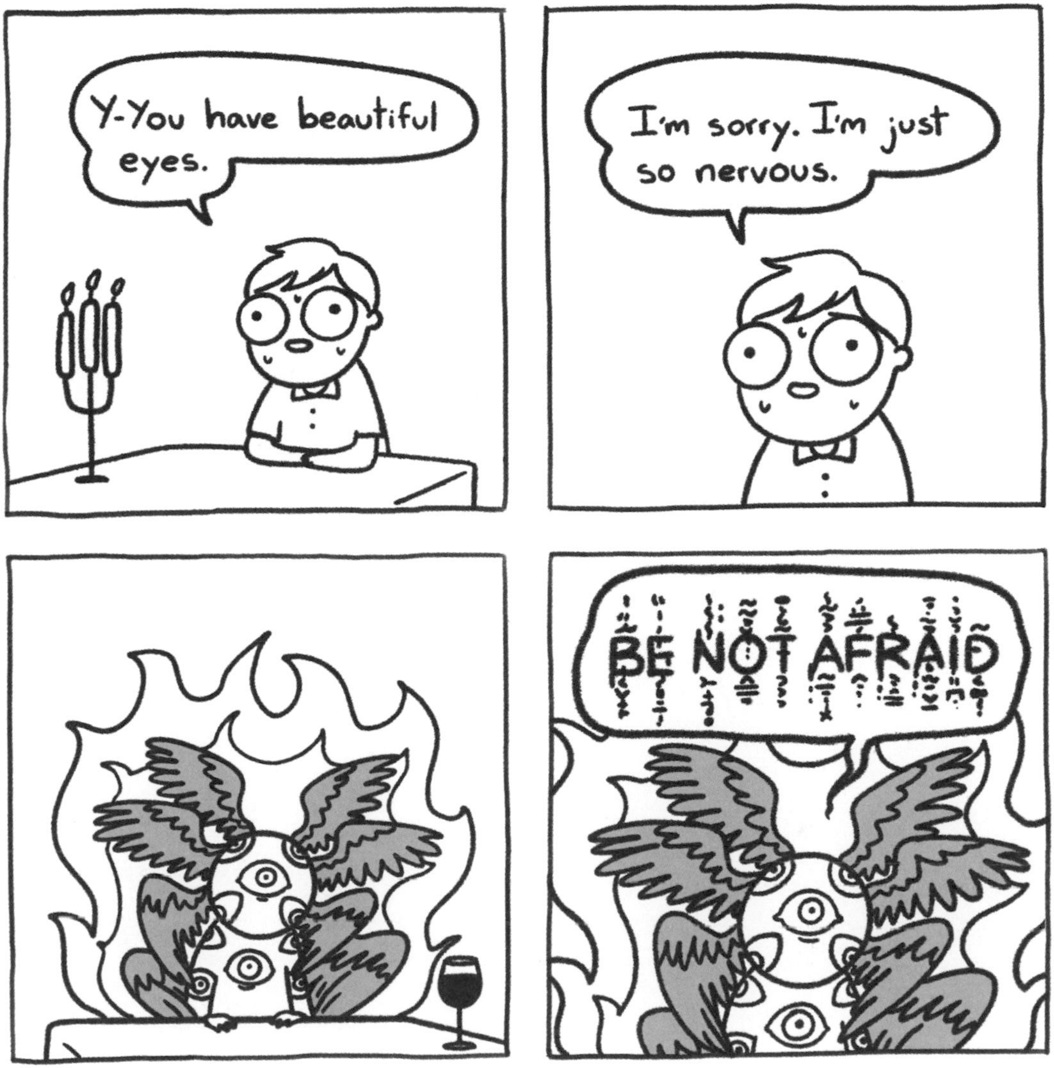
Y-You have beautiful eyes.
I'm sorry. I'm just so nervous.
BE NOT AFRAID

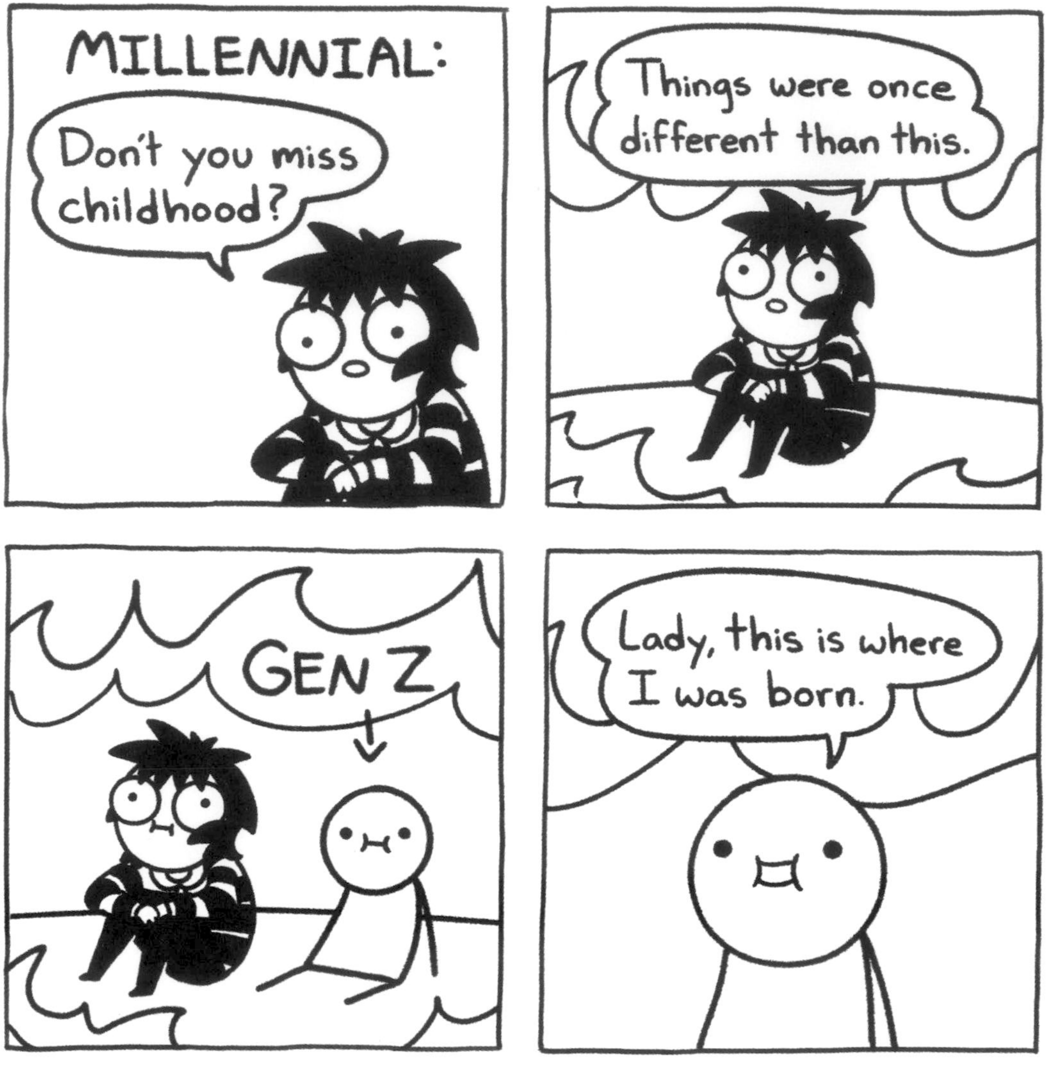
MILLENNIAL:
Don't you miss childhood?
Things were once different than this.
GEN Z
Lady, this is where I was born.

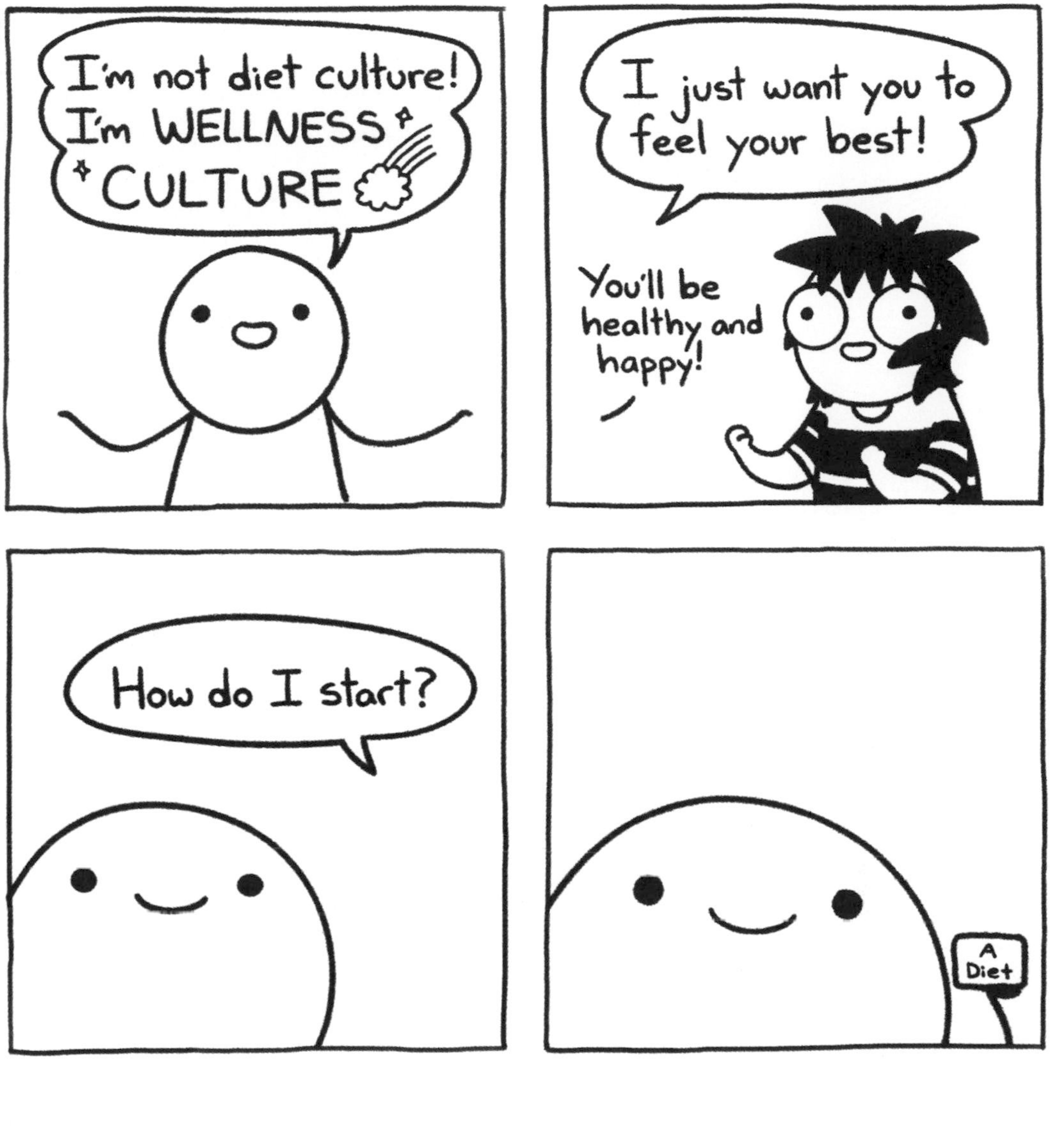
I'm not diet culture! I'm WELLNESS CULTURE
I just want you to feel your best!
You'll be healthy and happy!
How do I start?
A Diet

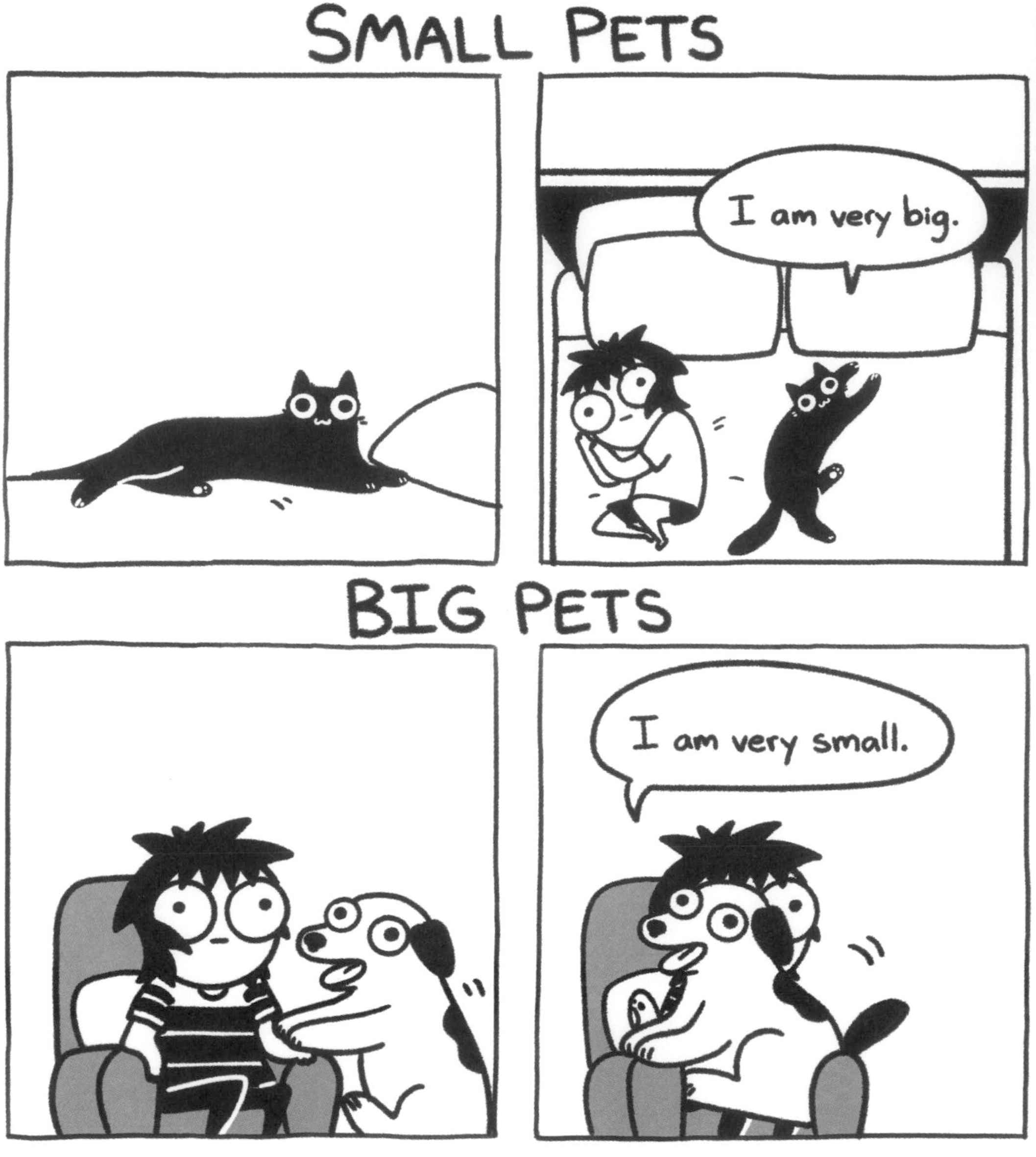
SMALL PETS
I am very big.
BIG PETS
I am very small.

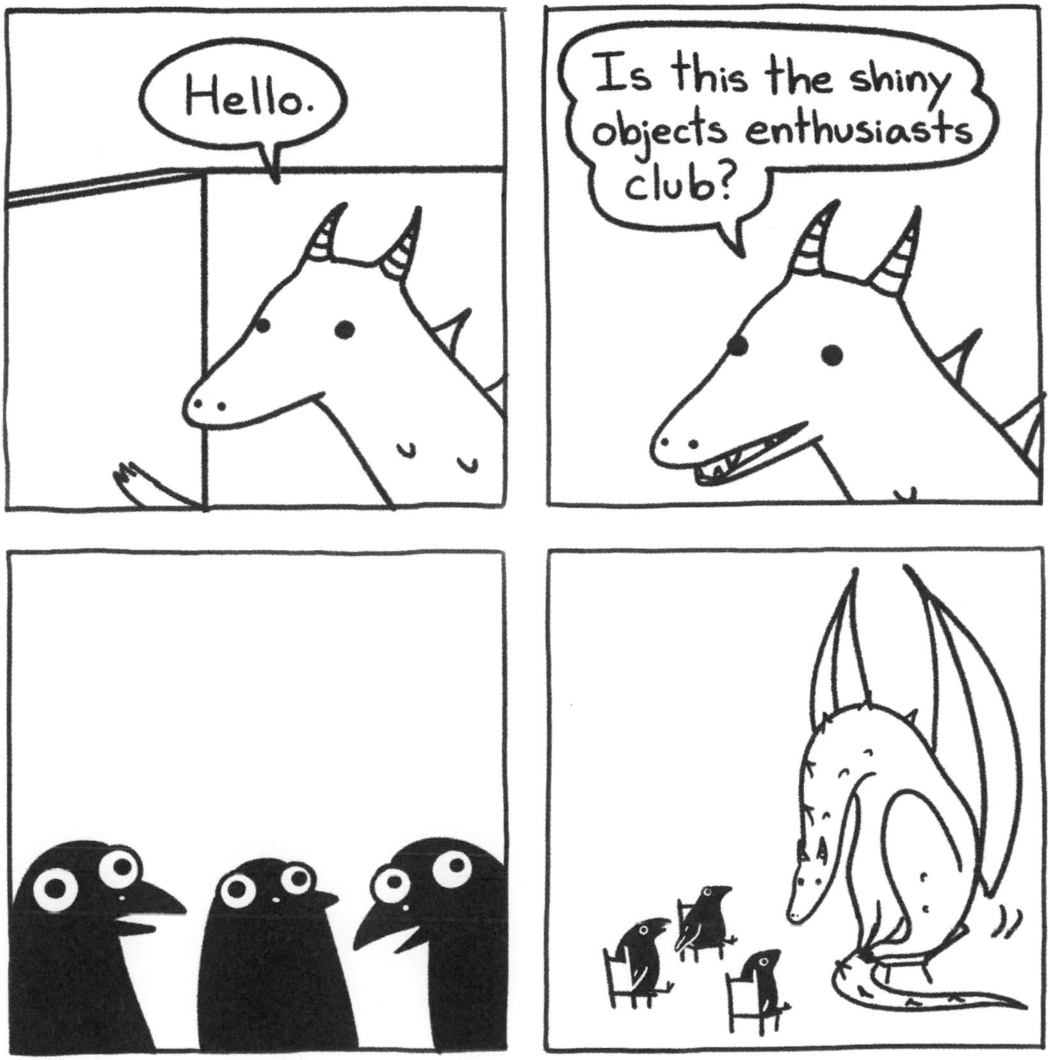
Hello.
Is this the shiny objects enthusiasts club?

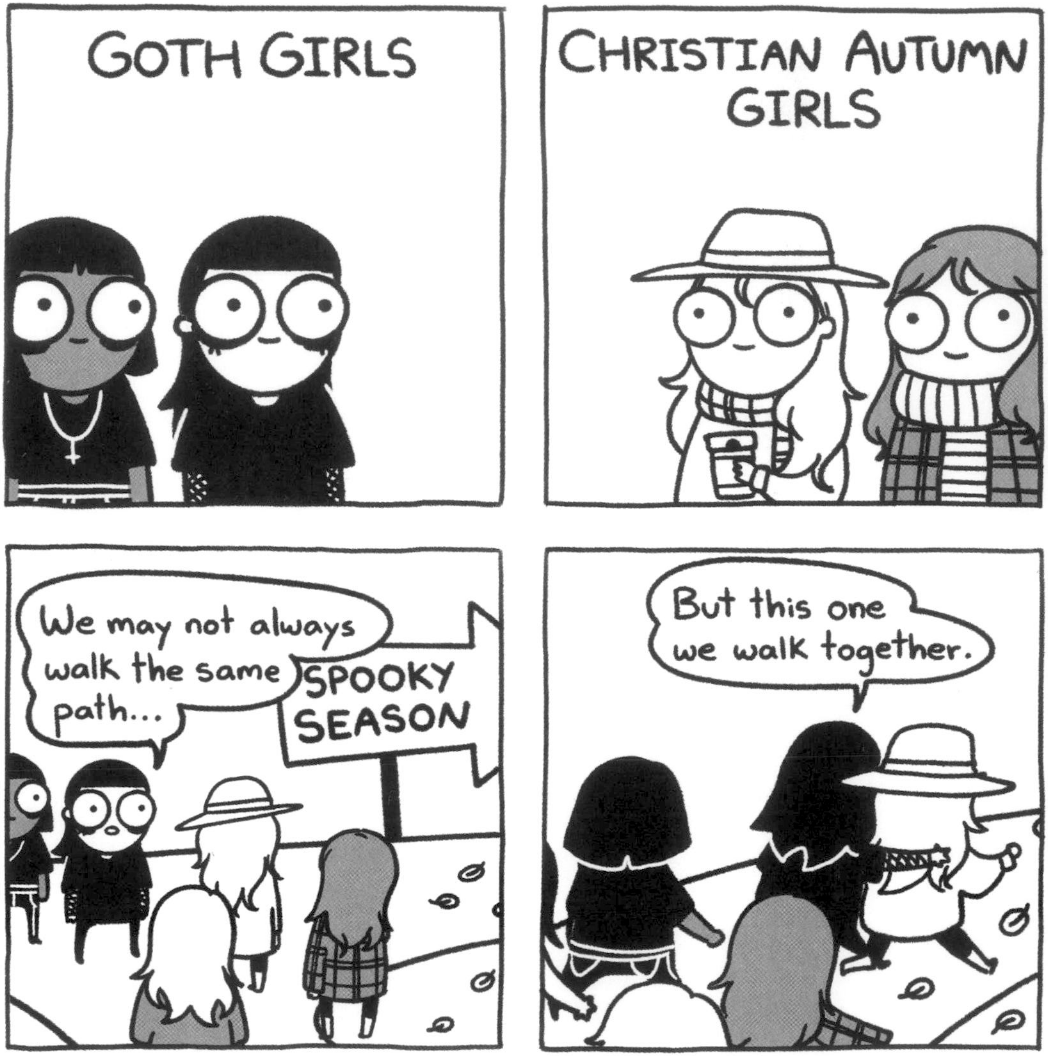
GOTH GIRLS
CHRISTIAN AUTUMN GIRLS
We may not always walk the same path...
SPOOKY SEASON
But this one we walk together.

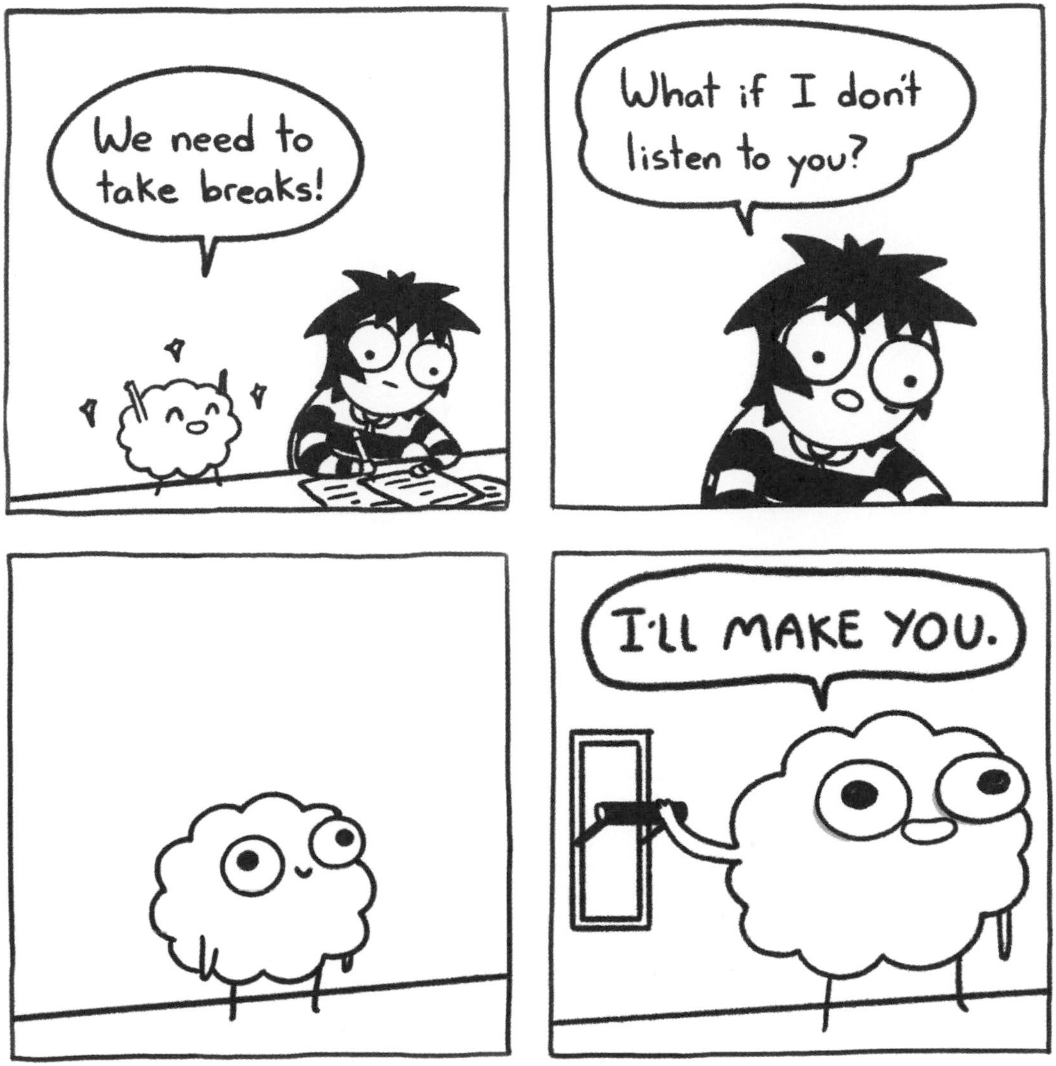
We need to take breaks!
What if I don't listen to you?
I'LL MAKE YOU.

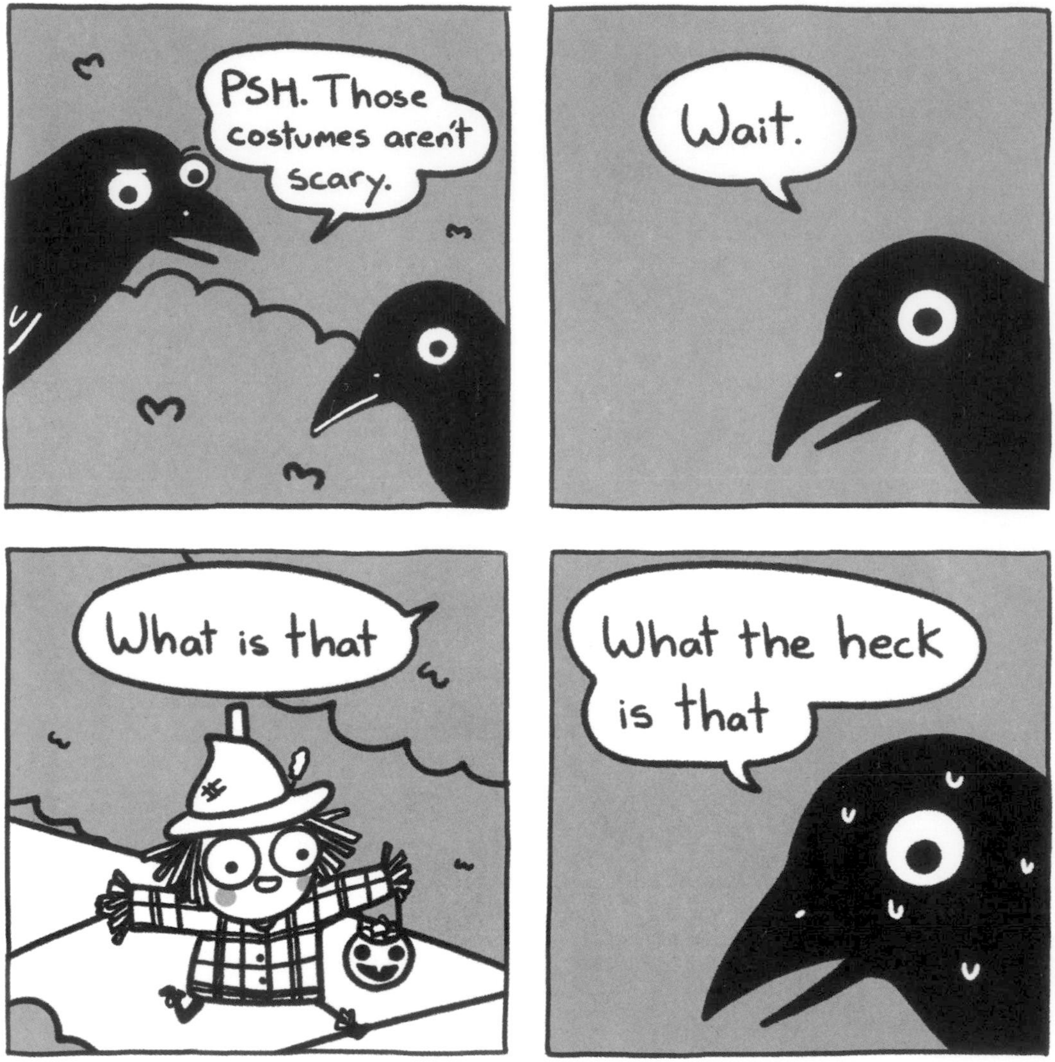
PSH. Those costumes aren't scary.
Wait.
What is that
What the heck is that

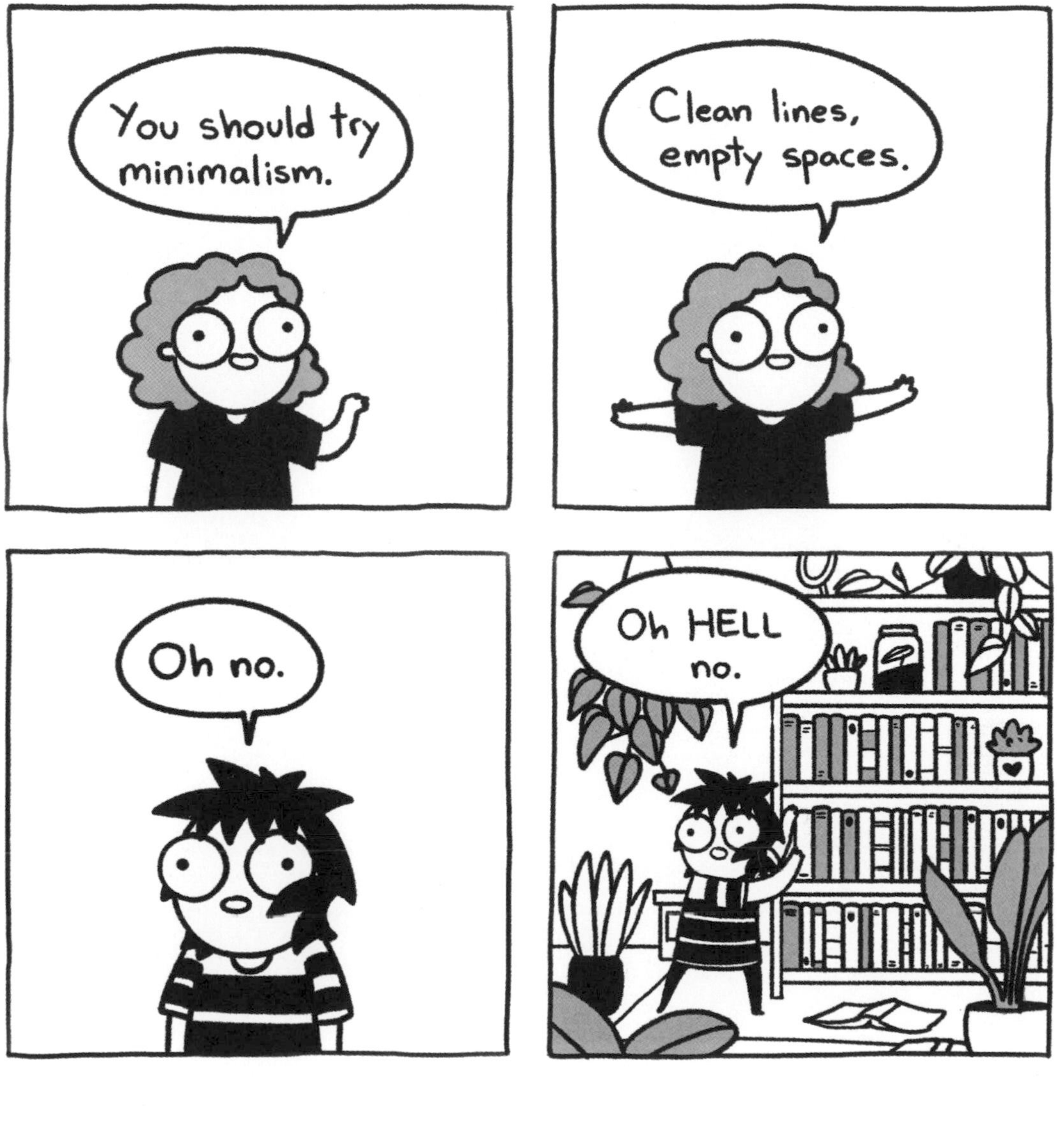
You should try minimalism.
Clean lines, empty spaces.
Oh no.
Oh HELL no.

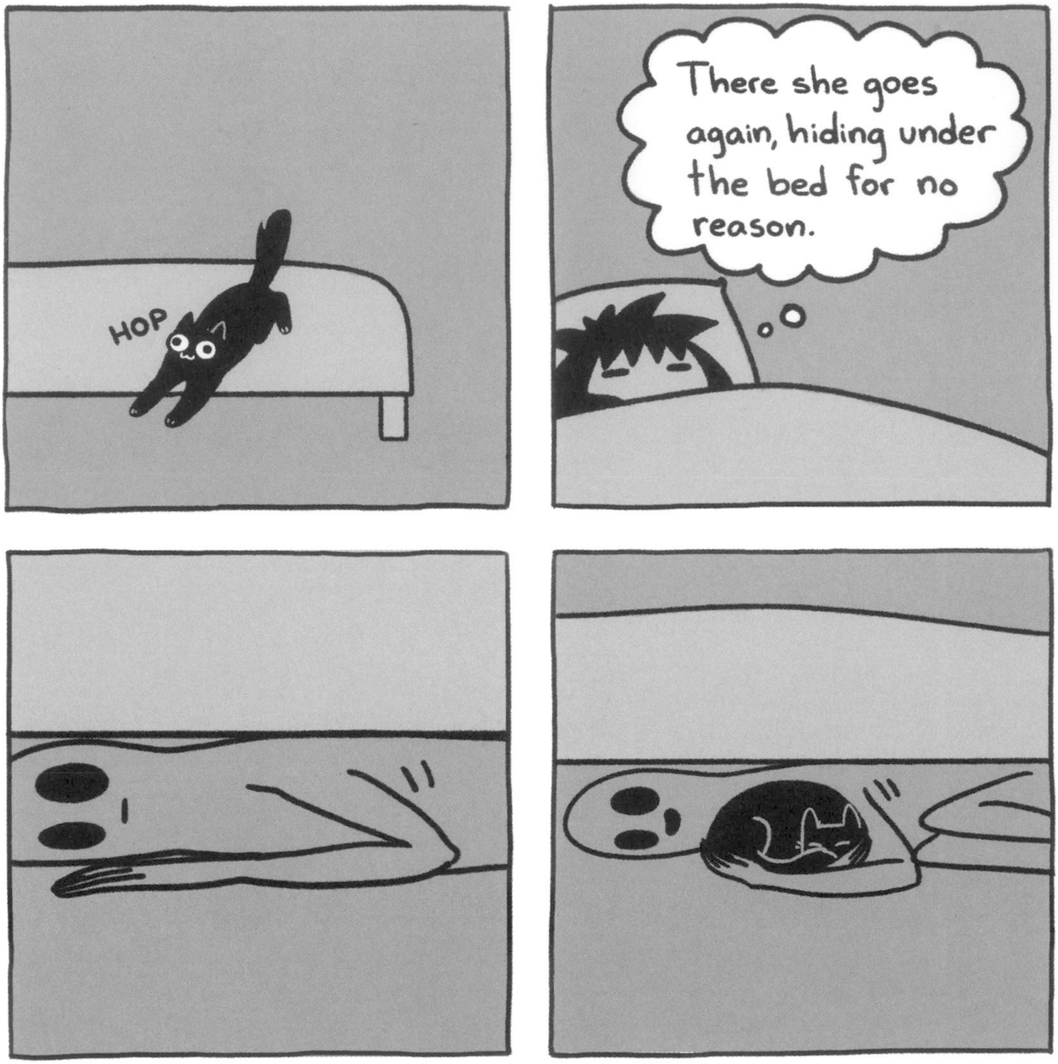
HOP
There she goes again, hiding under the bed for no reason.

DRACULA'S CAT

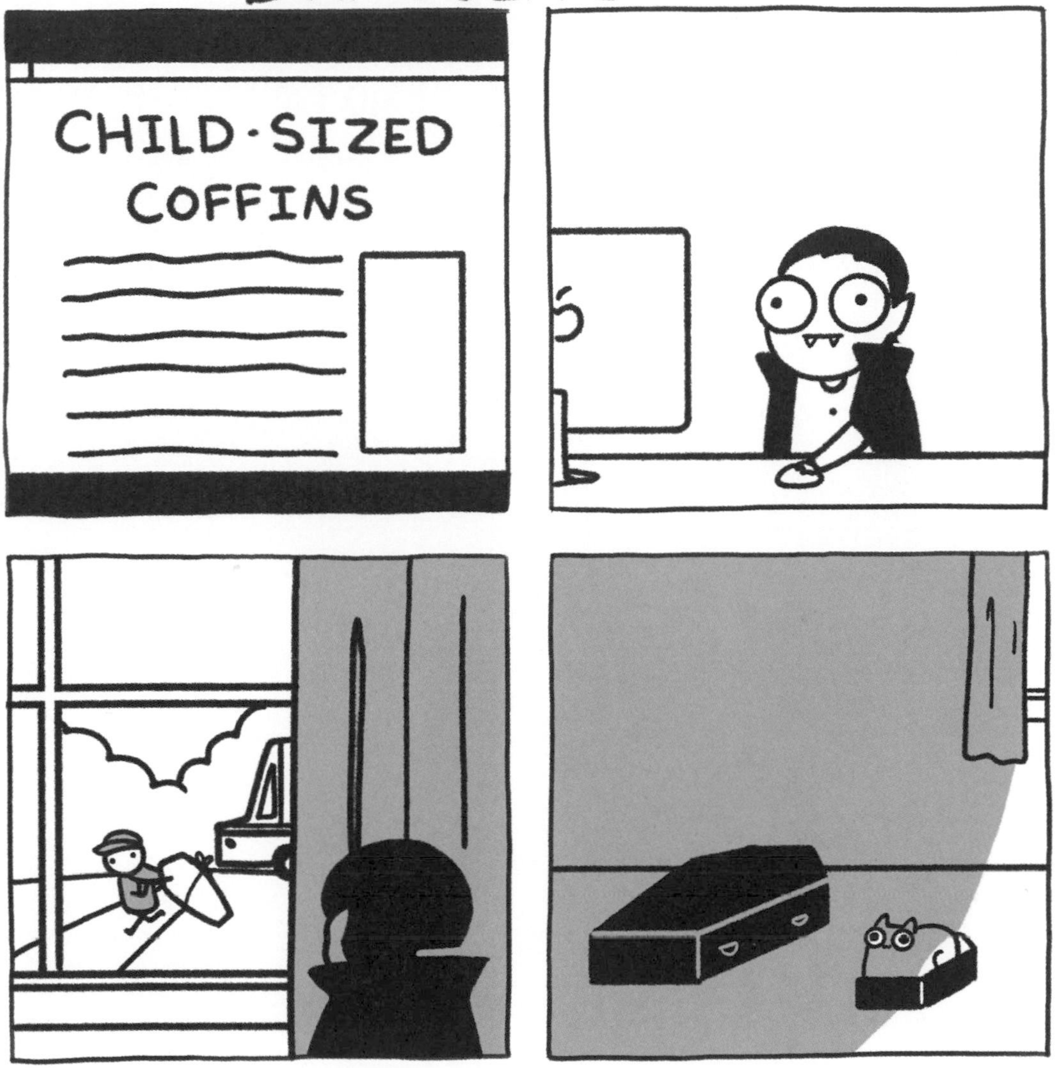
CHILD-SIZED
COFFINS

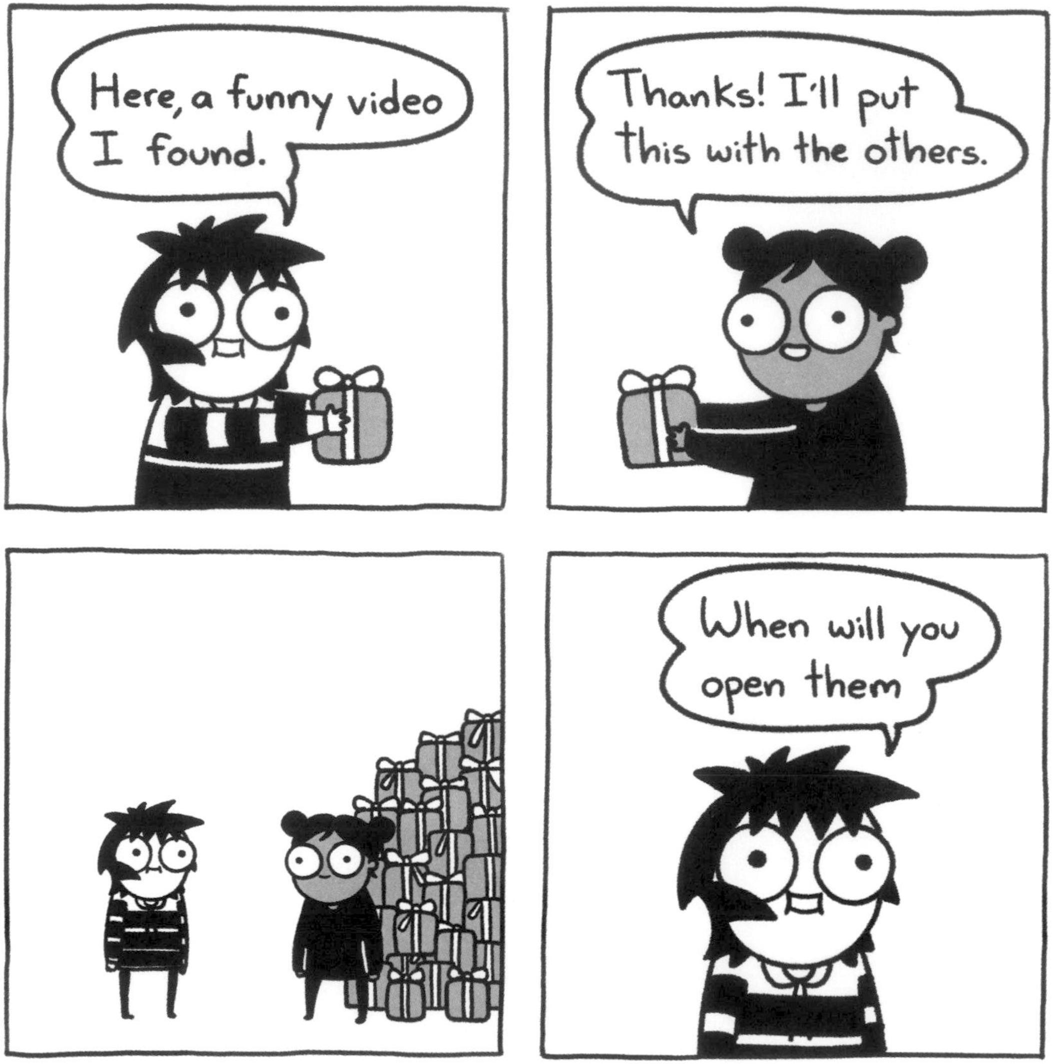
Here, a funny video I found.
Thanks! I'll put this with the others.
When will you open them

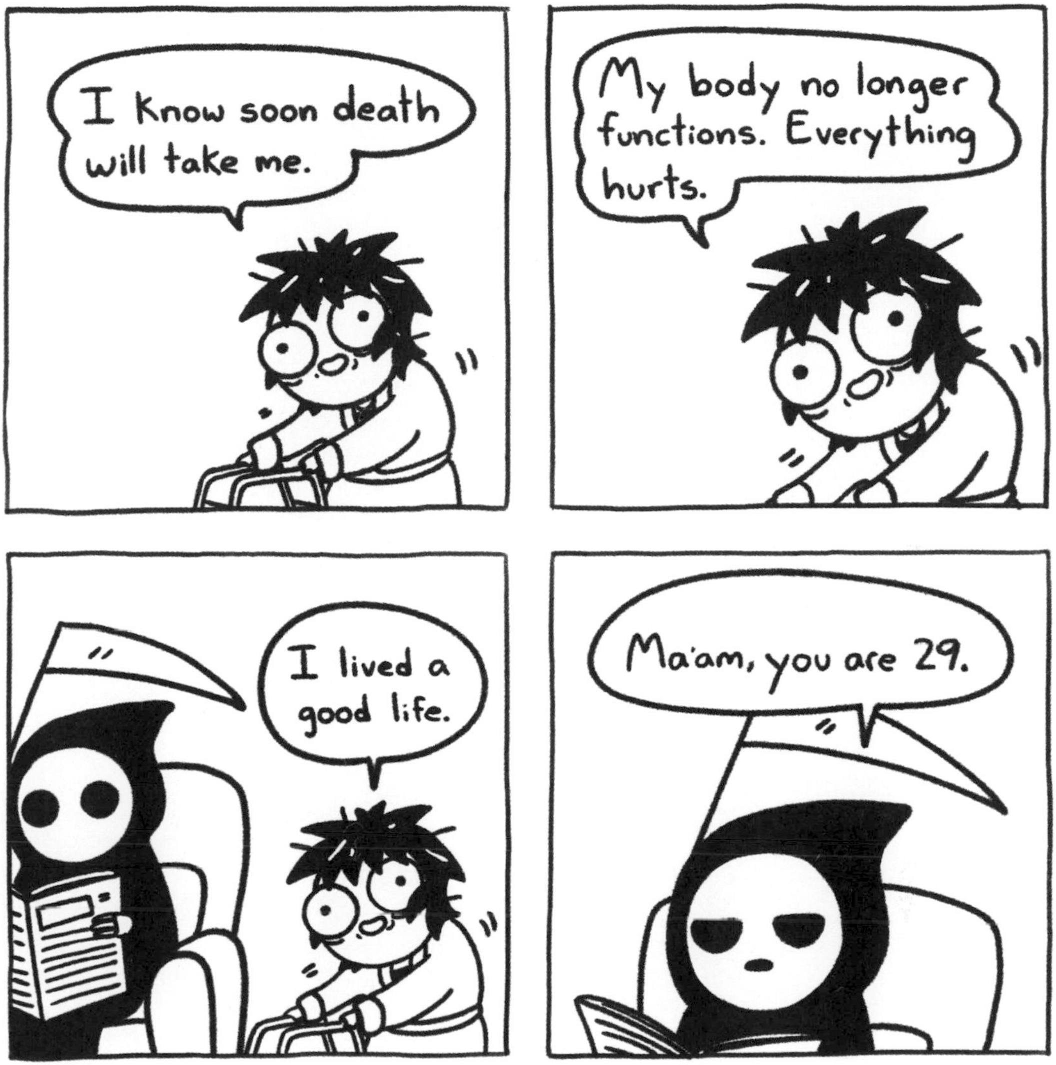
I know soon death will take me.
My body no longer functions. Everything hurts.
I lived a good life.
Ma'am, you are 29.

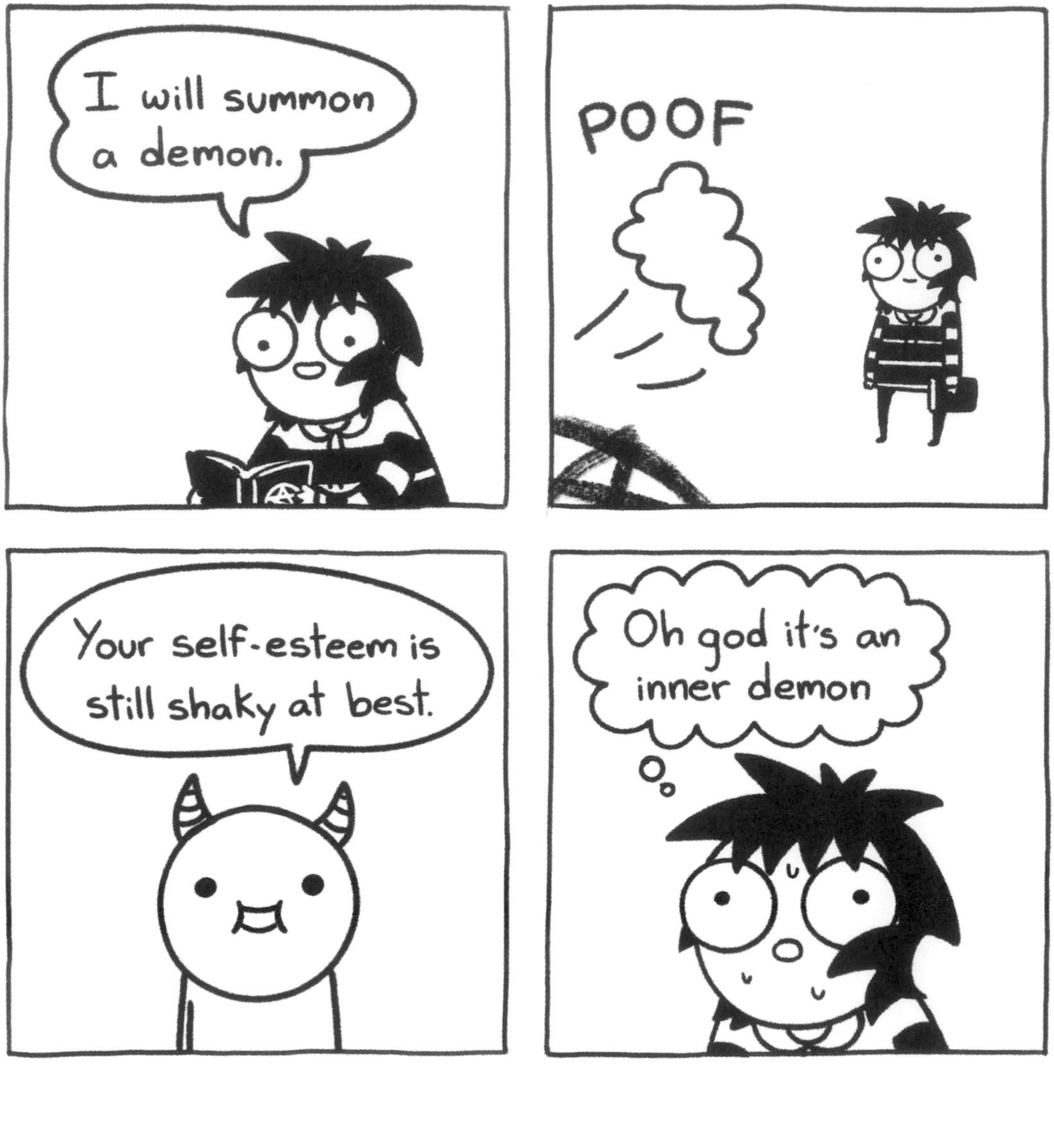
I will summon a demon.
POOF
Your self-esteem is still shaky at best.
Oh god it's an inner demon

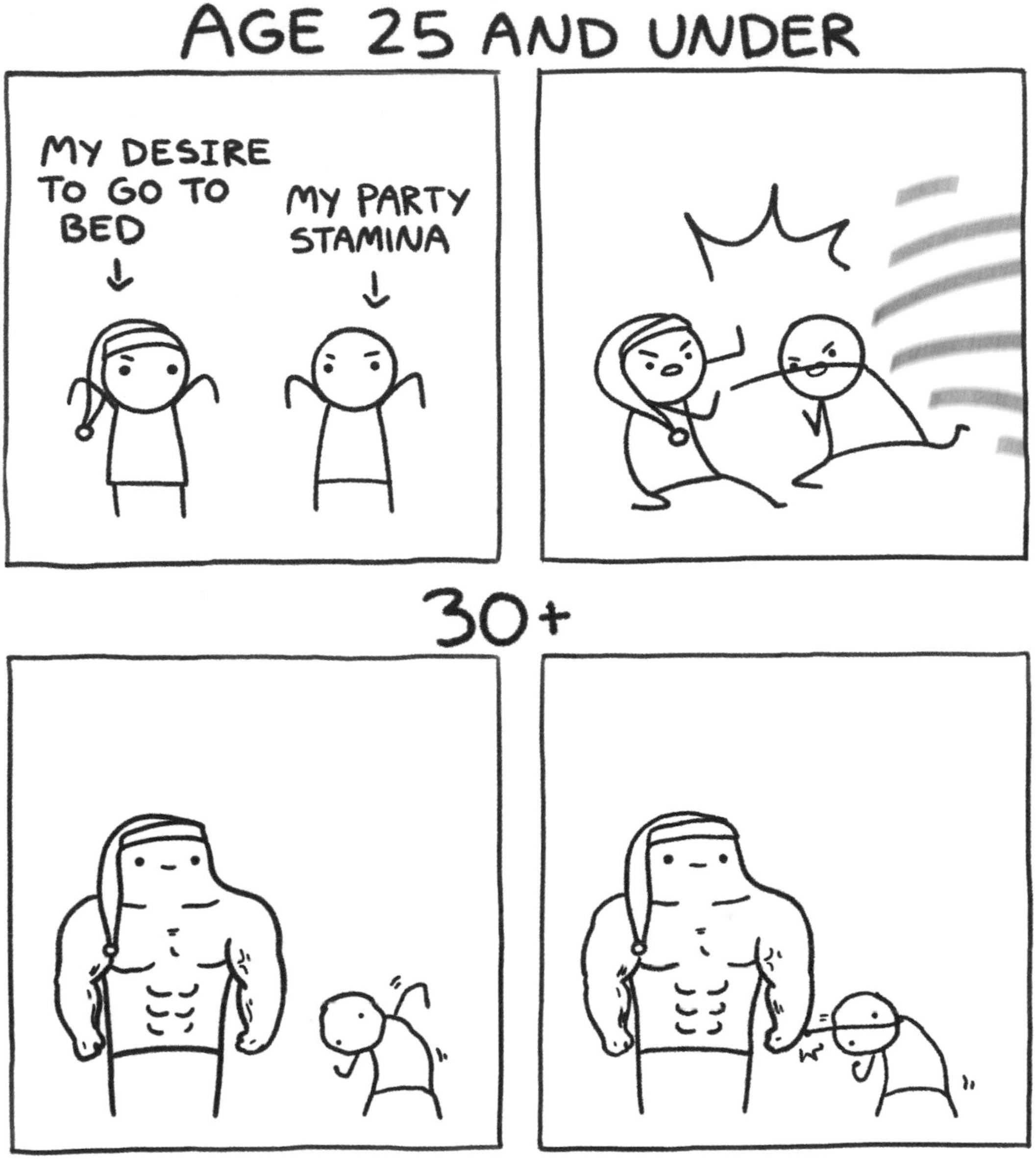
AGE 25 AND UNDER
MY DESIRE TO GO TO BED
MY PARTY STAMINA
30+

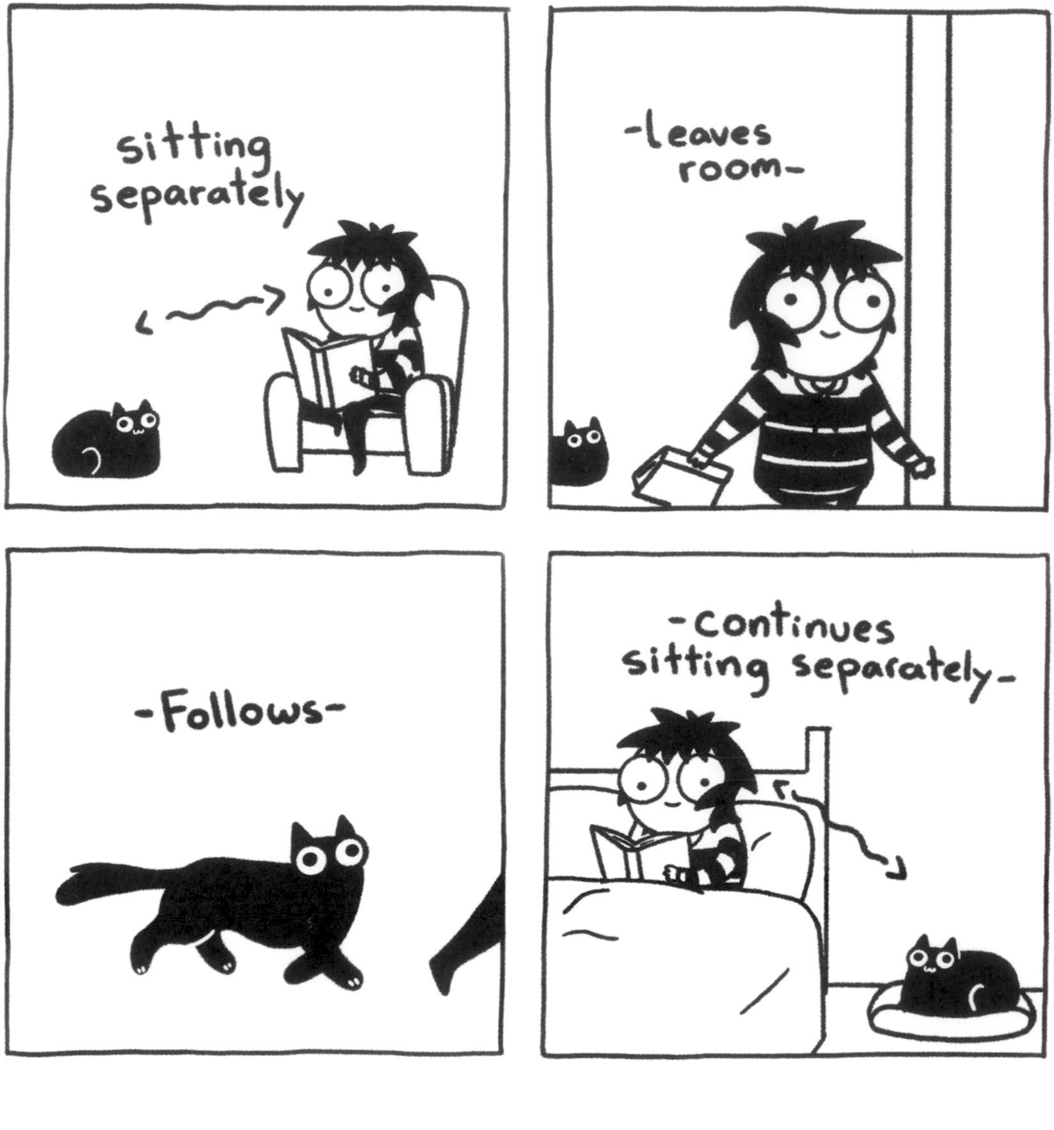
sitting separately
-leaves room-
-Follows-
-continues sitting separately-

READING ROMANCE SCENES

At last, darling, it's just you and me.

And me.

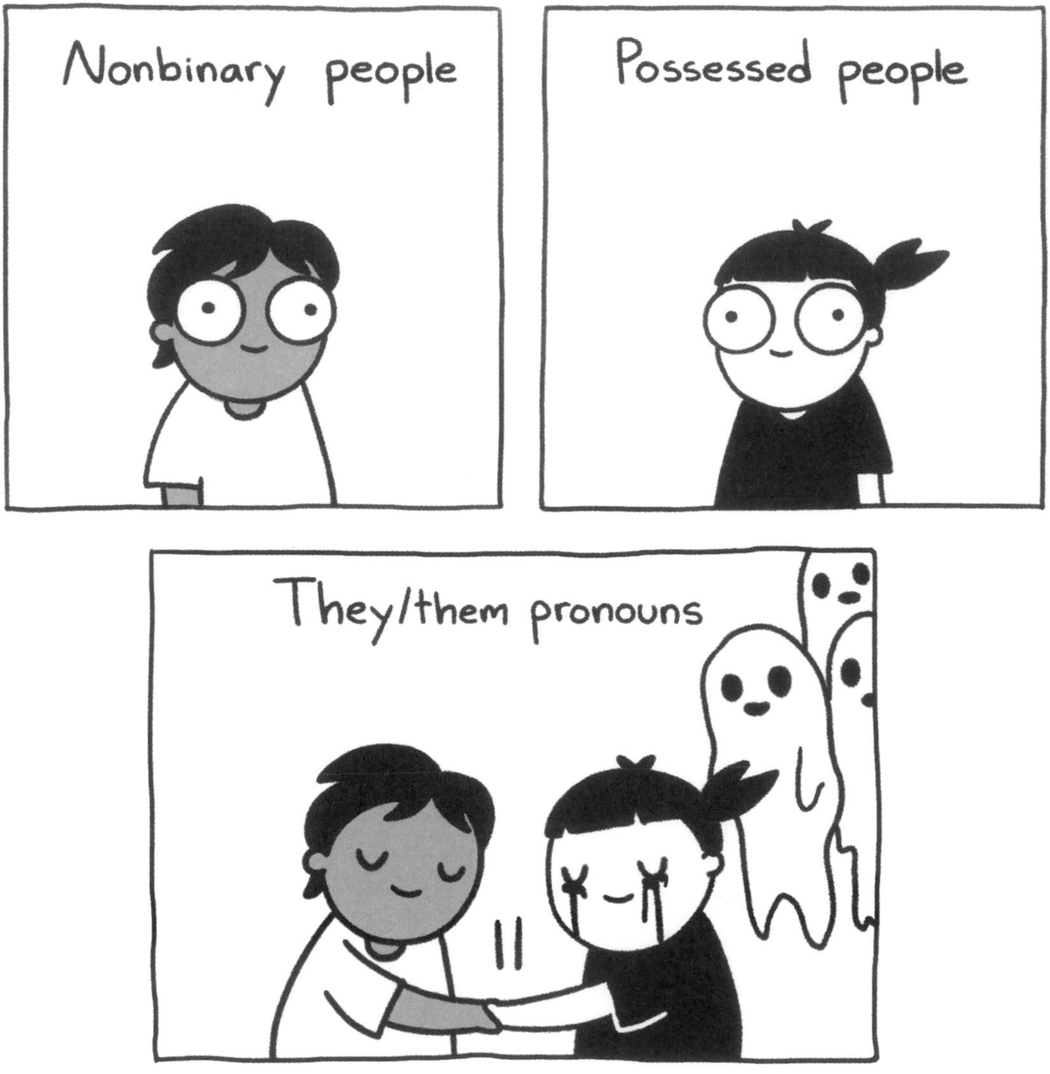
Nonbinary people
Possessed people
They/them pronouns

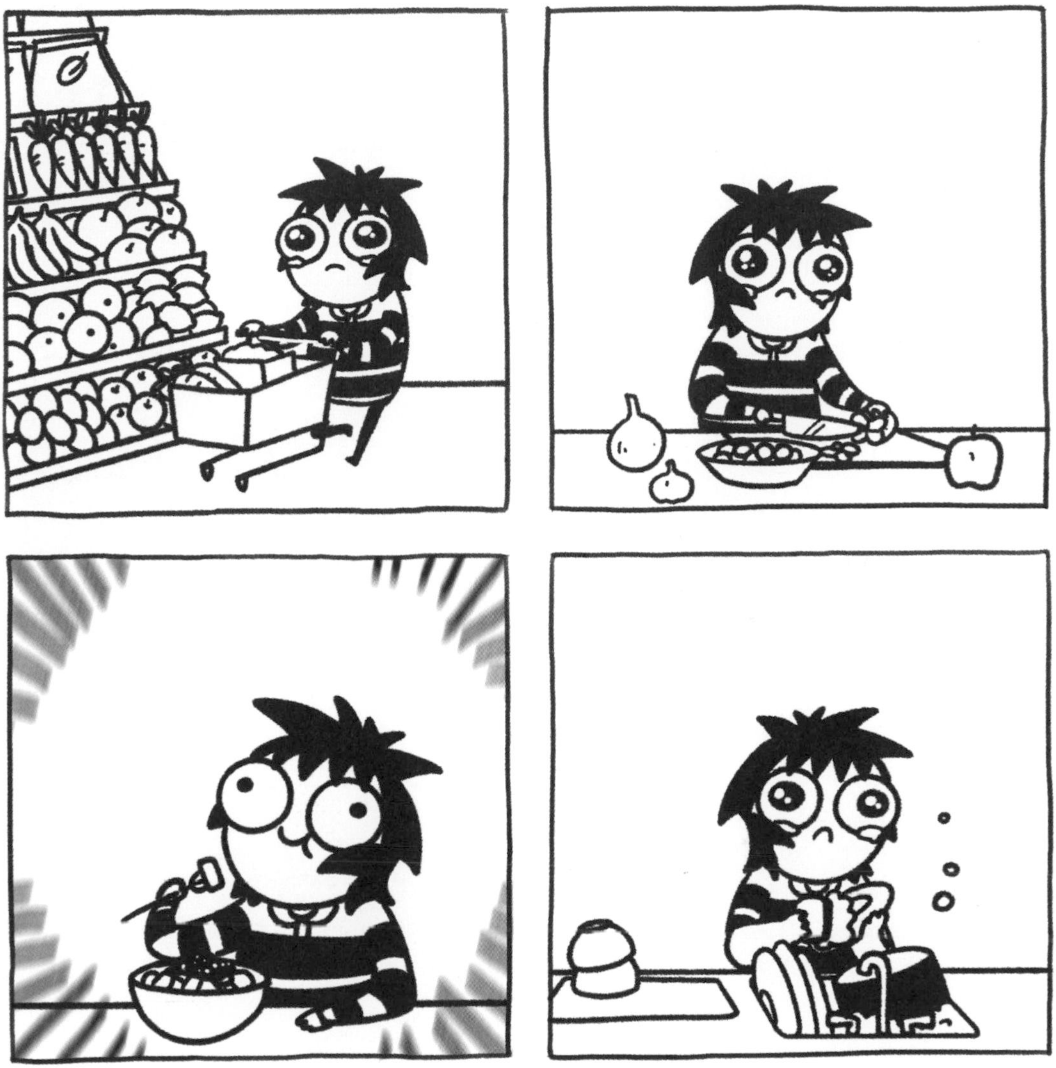

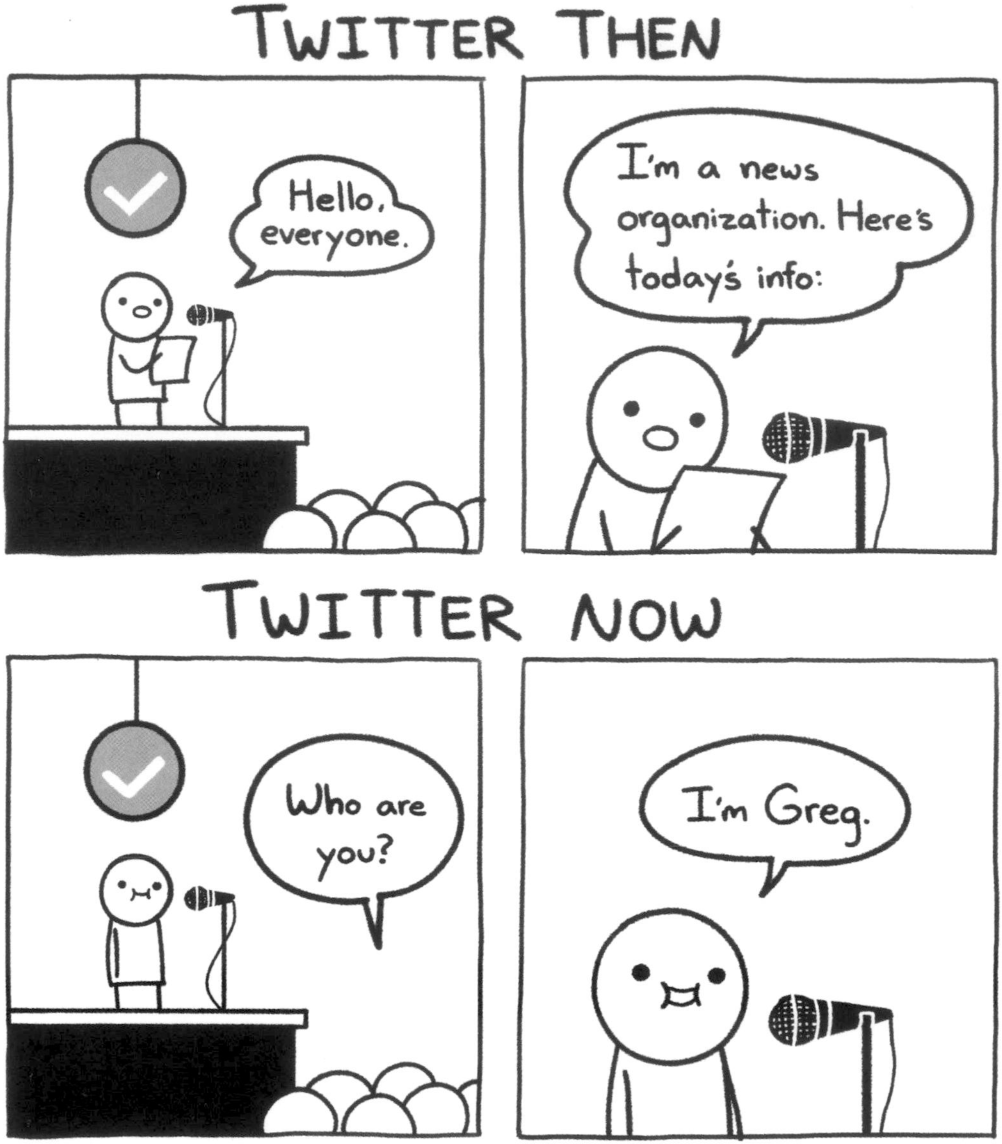
TWITTER THEN
Hello, everyone.
I'm a news organization. Here's today's info:
TWITTER NOW
Who are you?
I'm Greg.

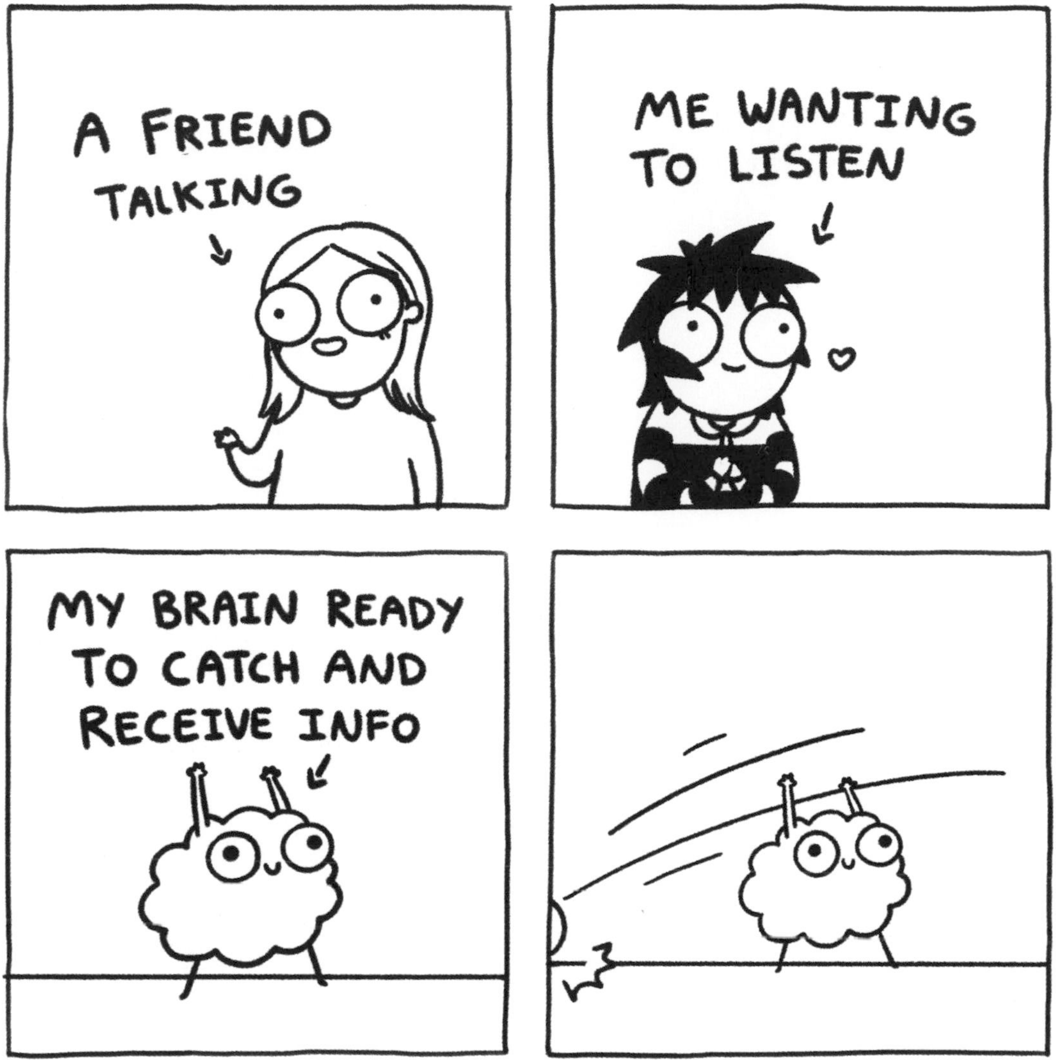
A FRIEND TALKING
ME WANTING TO LISTEN
MY BRAIN READY TO CATCH AND RECEIVE INFO

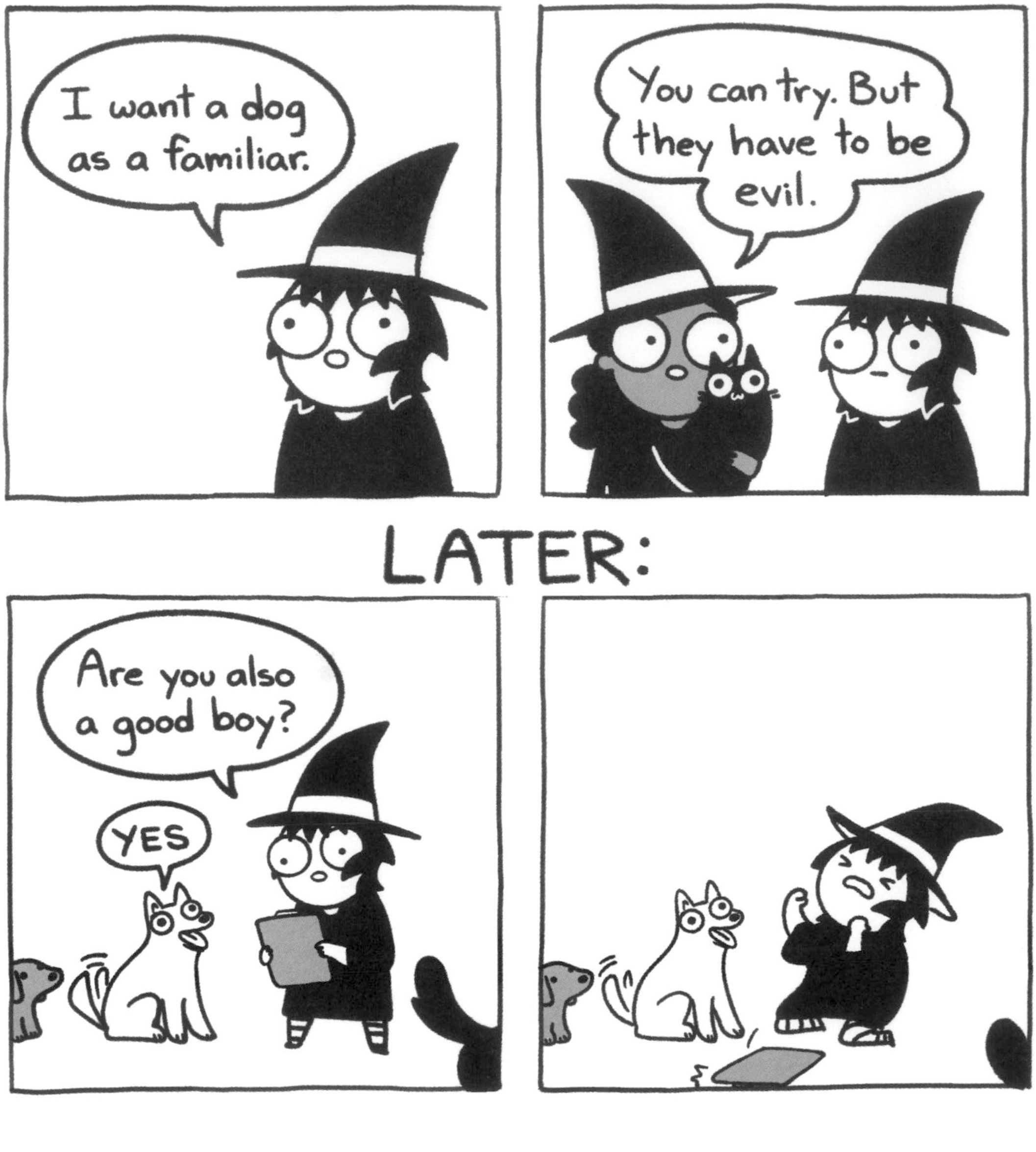
I want a dog as a familiar.
You can try. But they have to be evil.
LATER:
Are you also a good boy?
YES

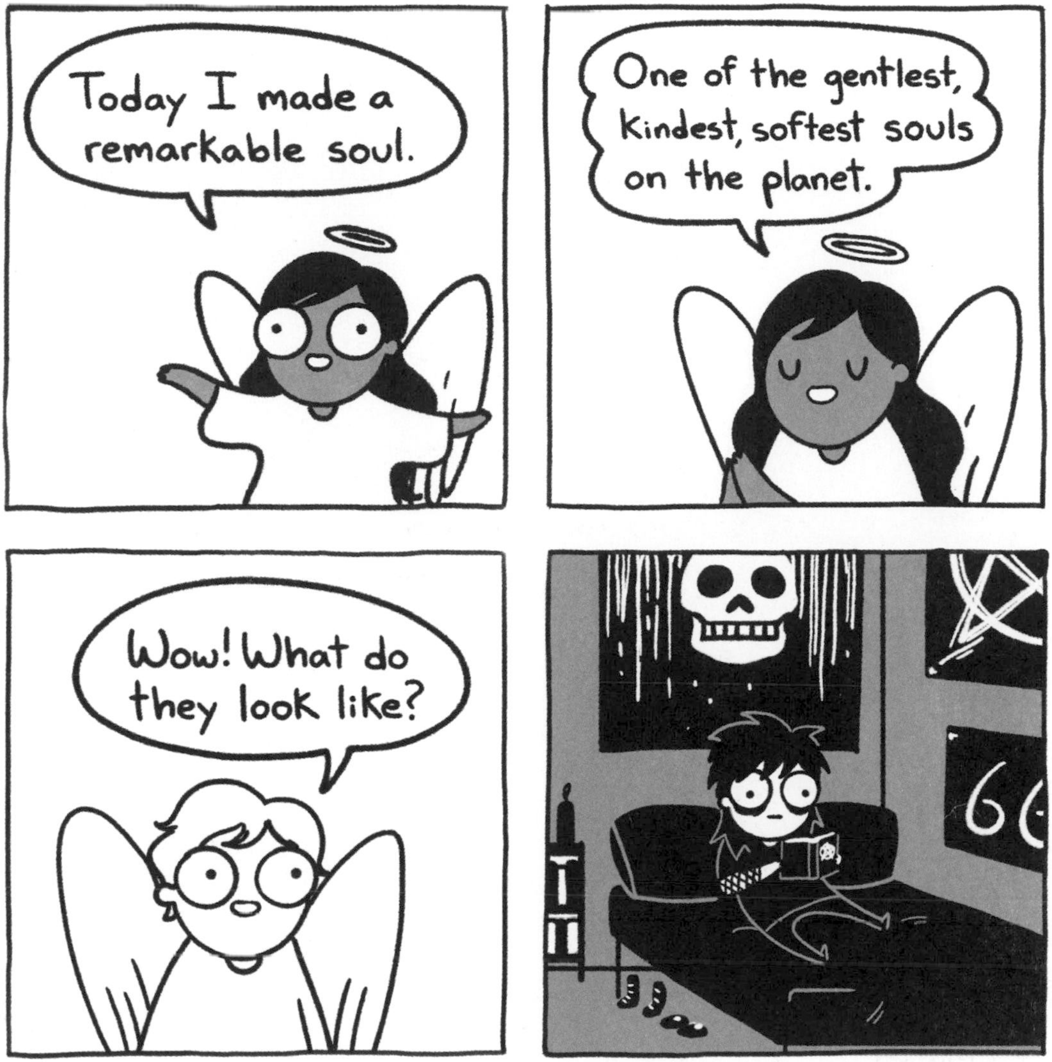
Today I made a remarkable soul.
One of the gentlest, kindest, softest souls on the planet.
Wow! What do they look like?

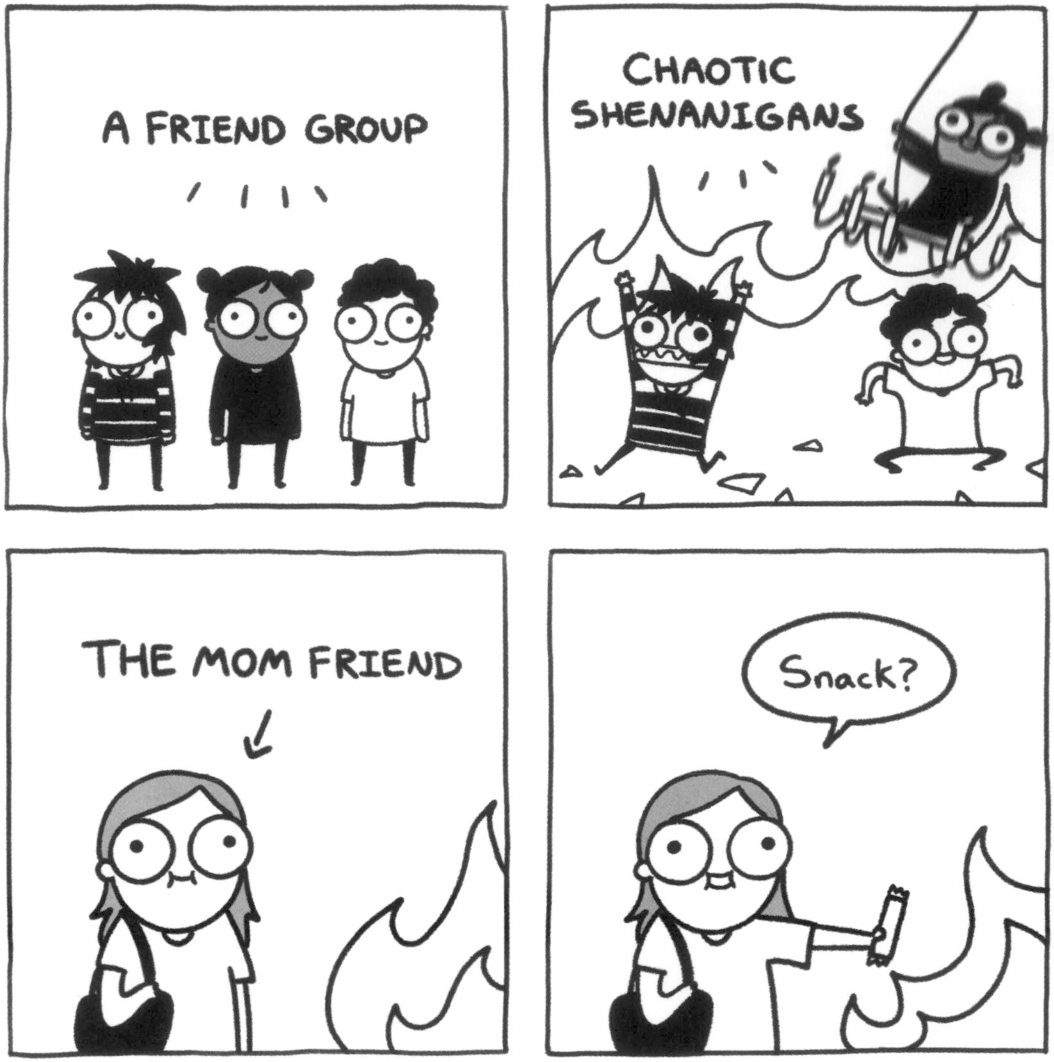
A FRIEND GROUP
CHAOTIC SHENANIGANS
THE MOM FRIEND
Snack?

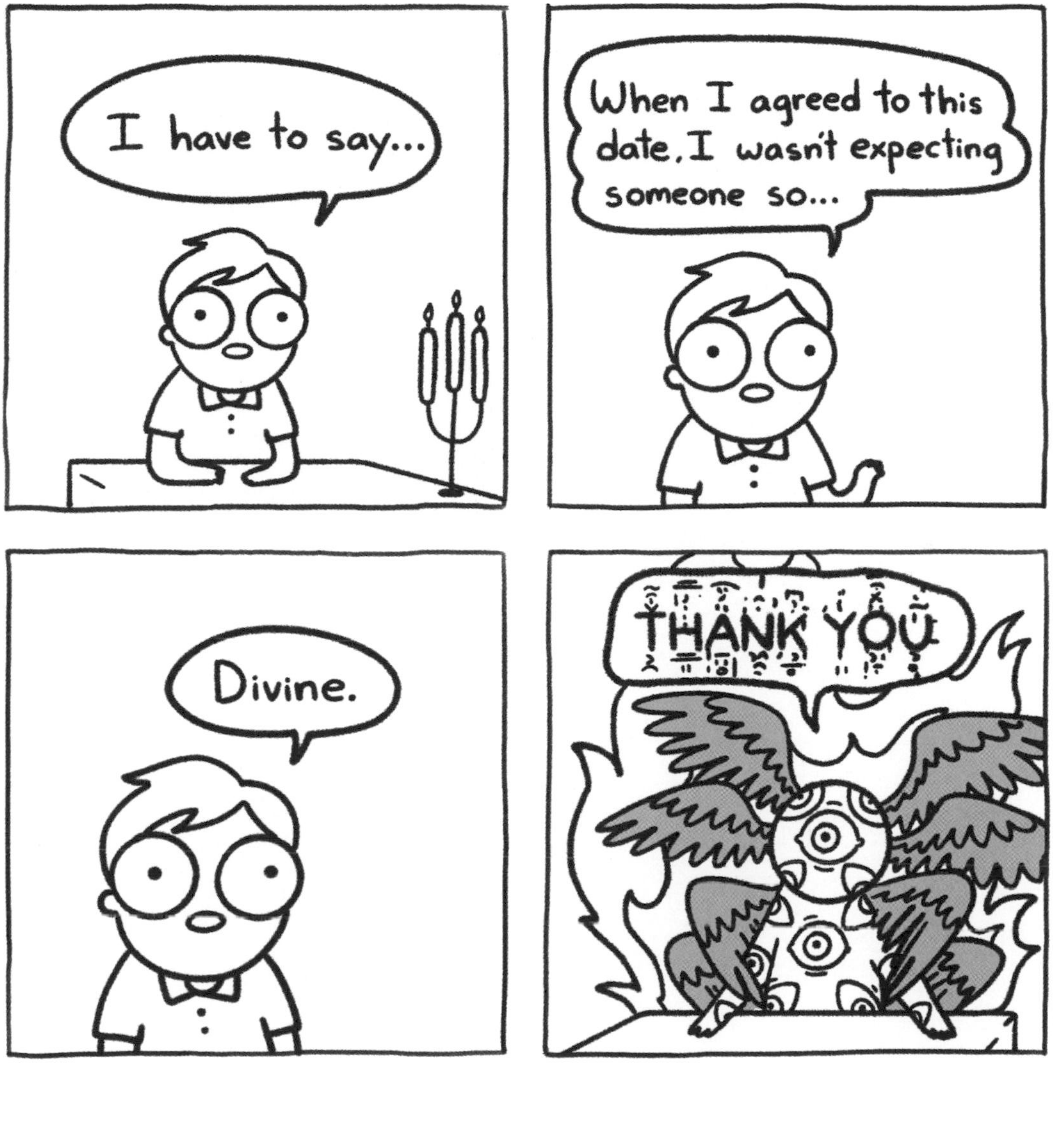
I have to say...
When I agreed to this date, I wasn't expecting someone so...
Divine.
THANK YOU

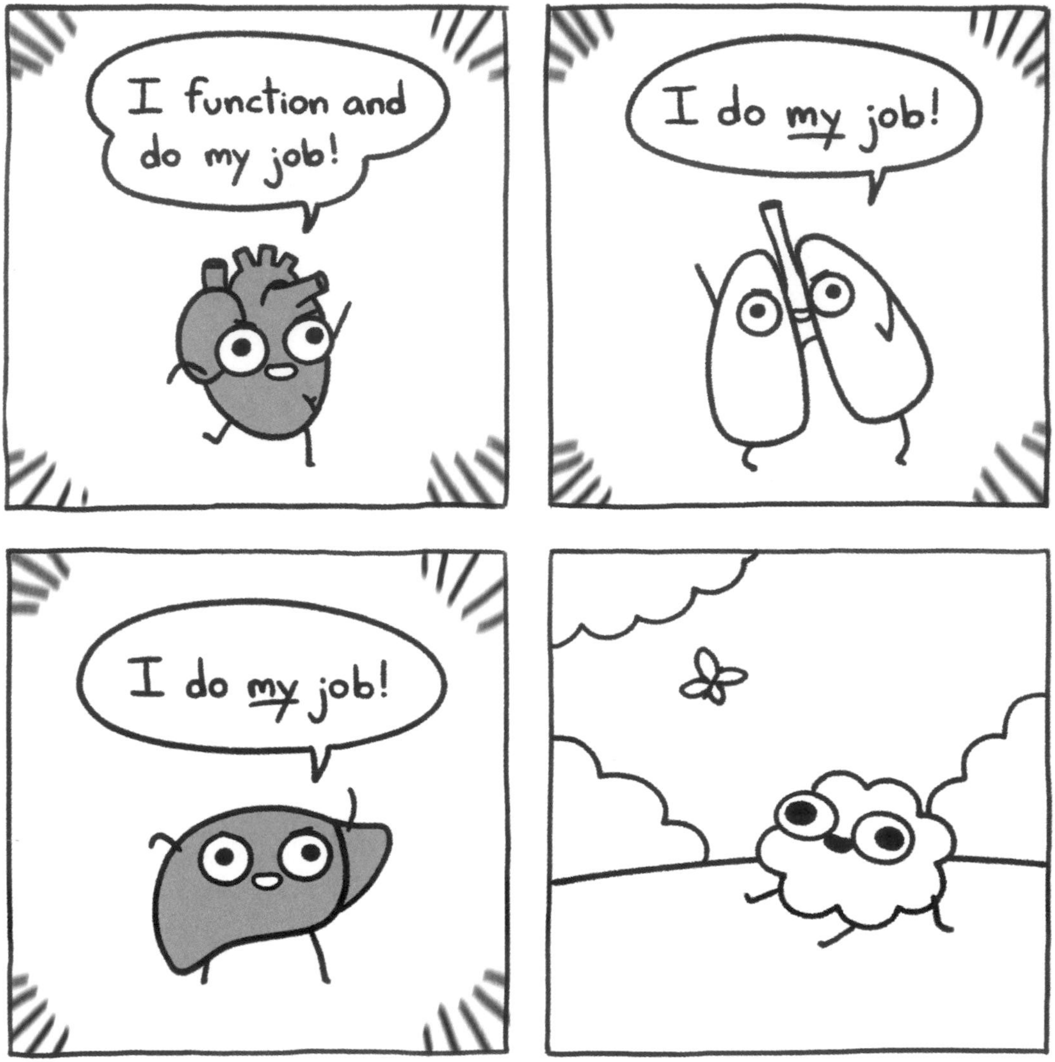
I function and do my job!
I do my job!
I do my job!

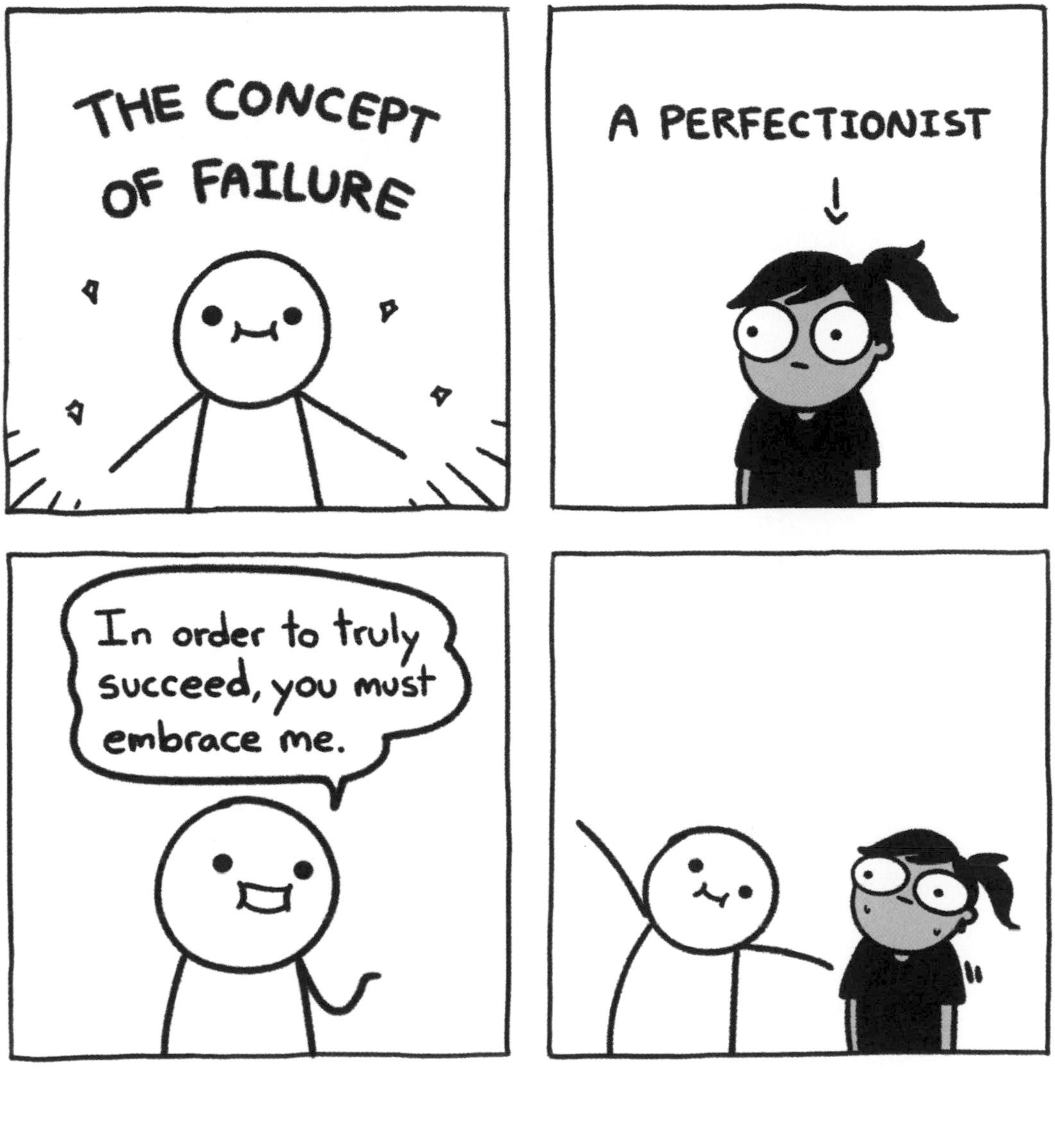
THE CONCEPT OF FAILURE
A PERFECTIONIST
In order to truly succeed, you must embrace me.

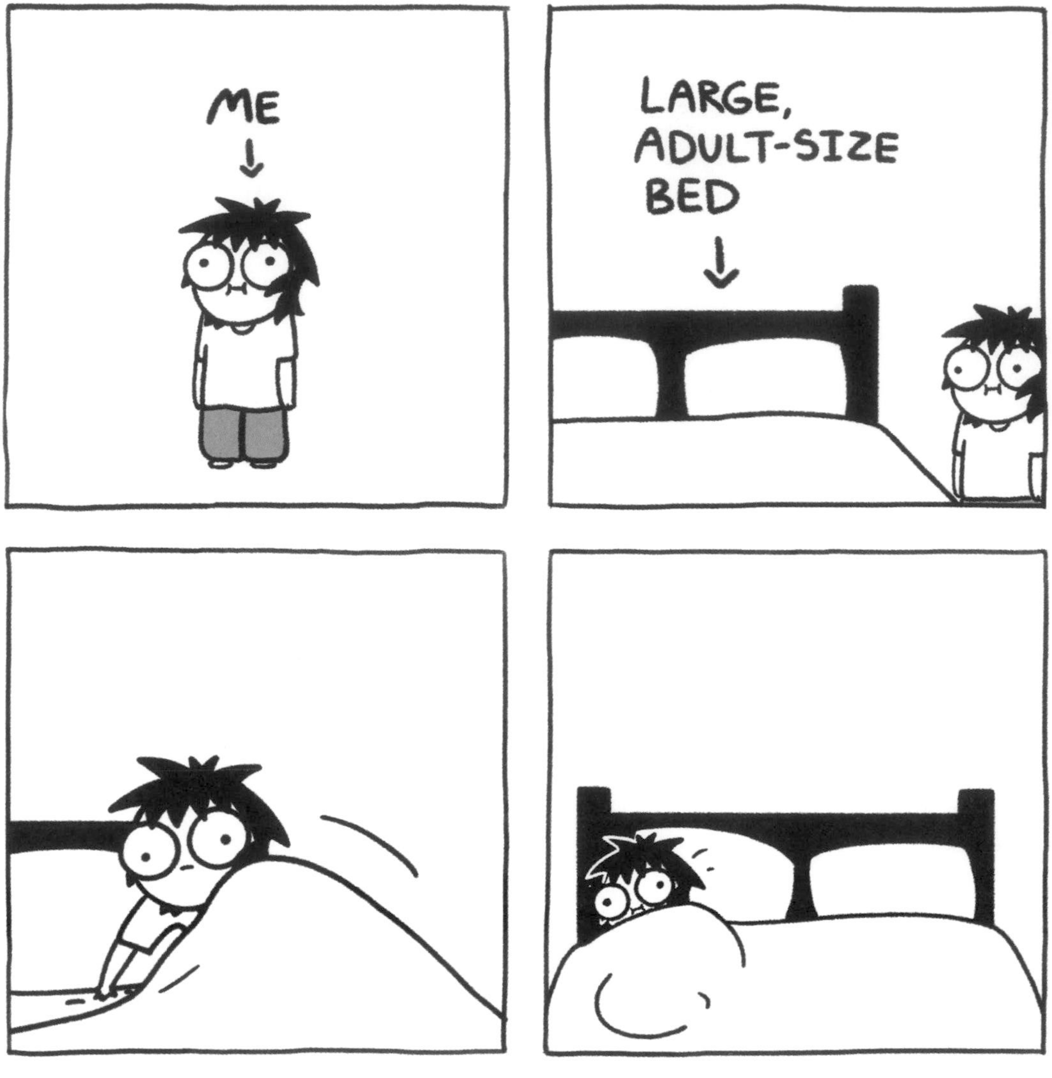
ME
LARGE, ADULT-SIZE BED

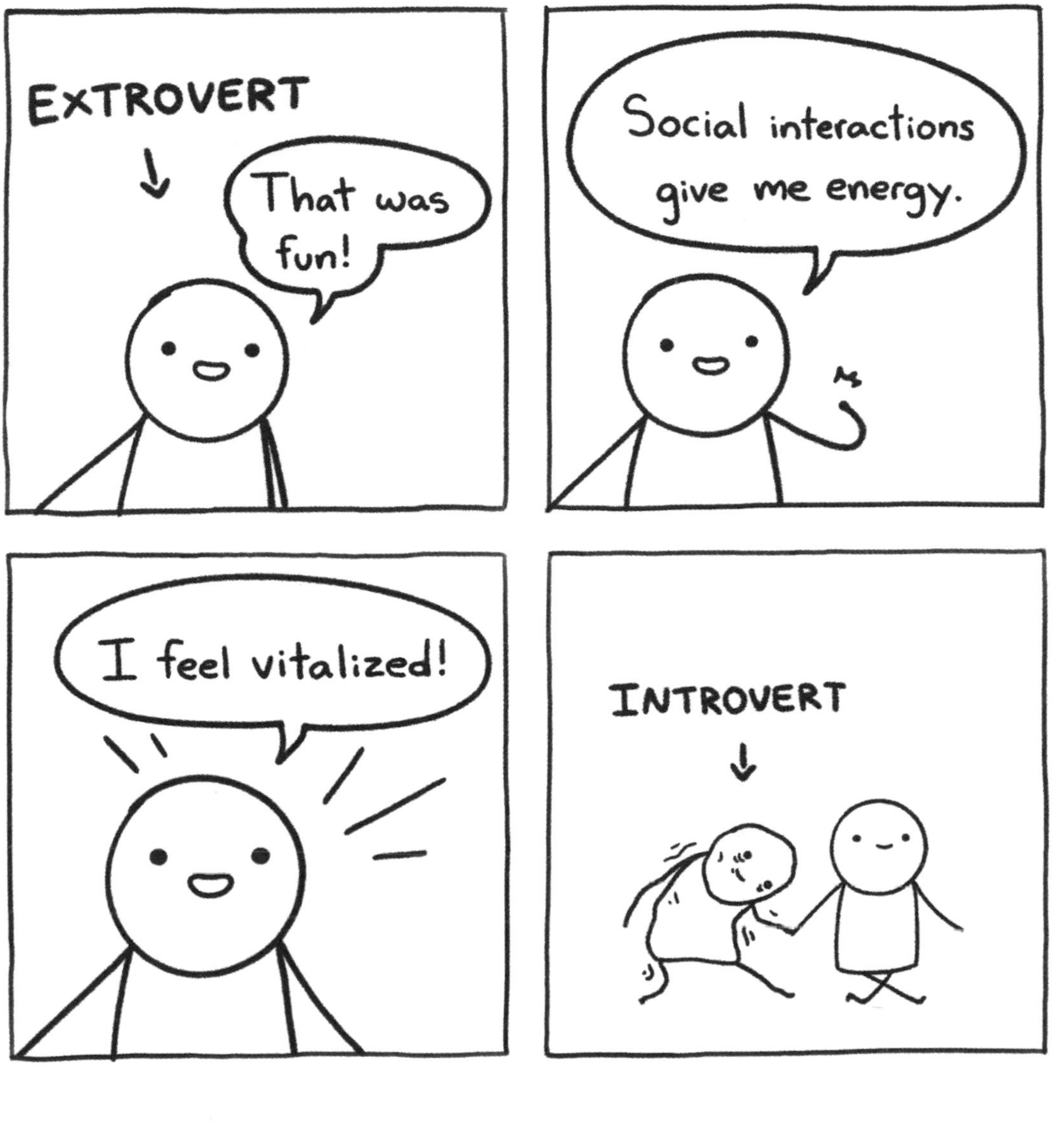
EXTROVERT
That was fun!
Social interactions give me energy.
I feel vitalized!
INTROVERT

CUTE AGGRESSION

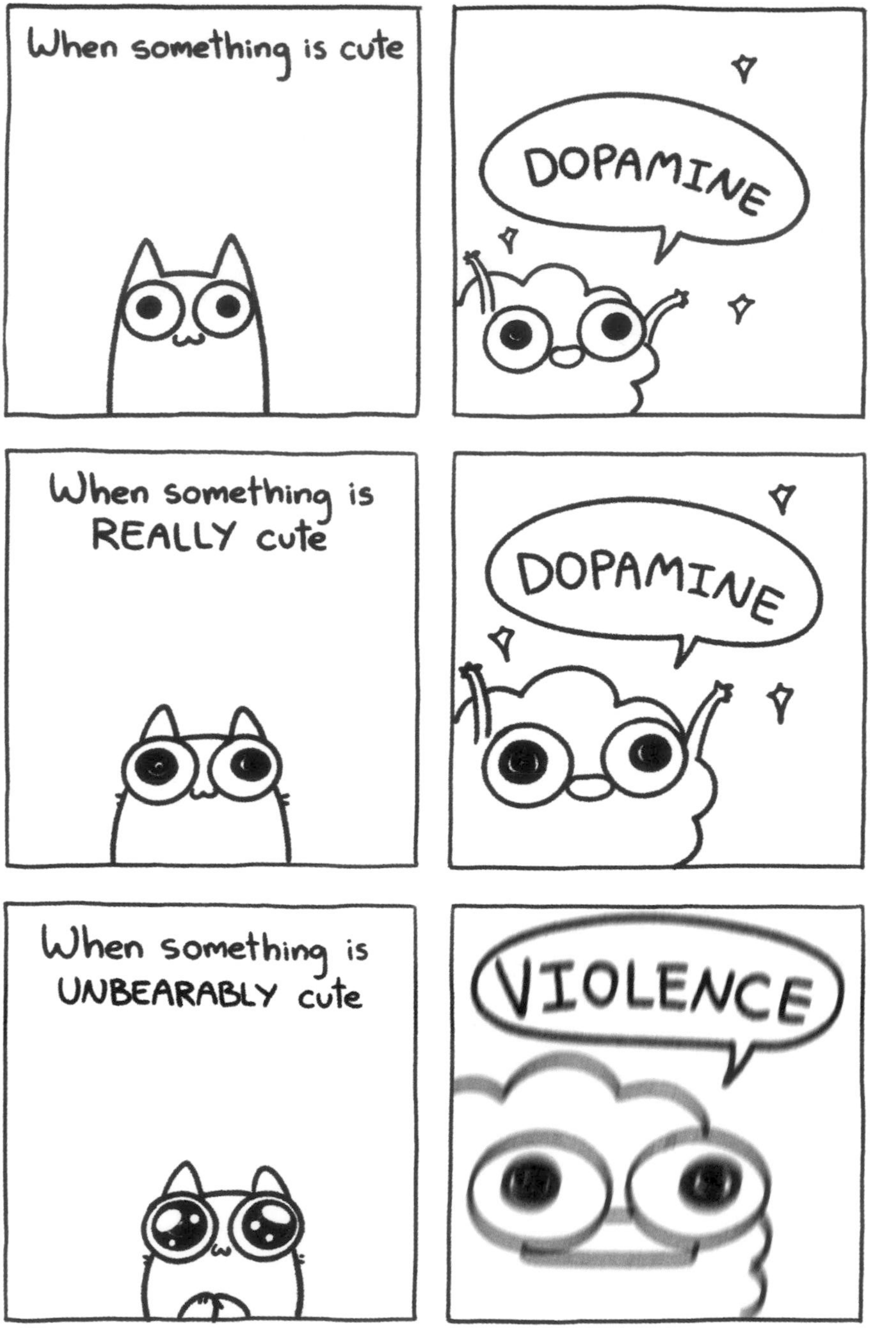
When something is cute
DOPAMINE
When something is REALLY cute
DOPAMINE
When something is UNBEARABLY cute
VIOLENCE

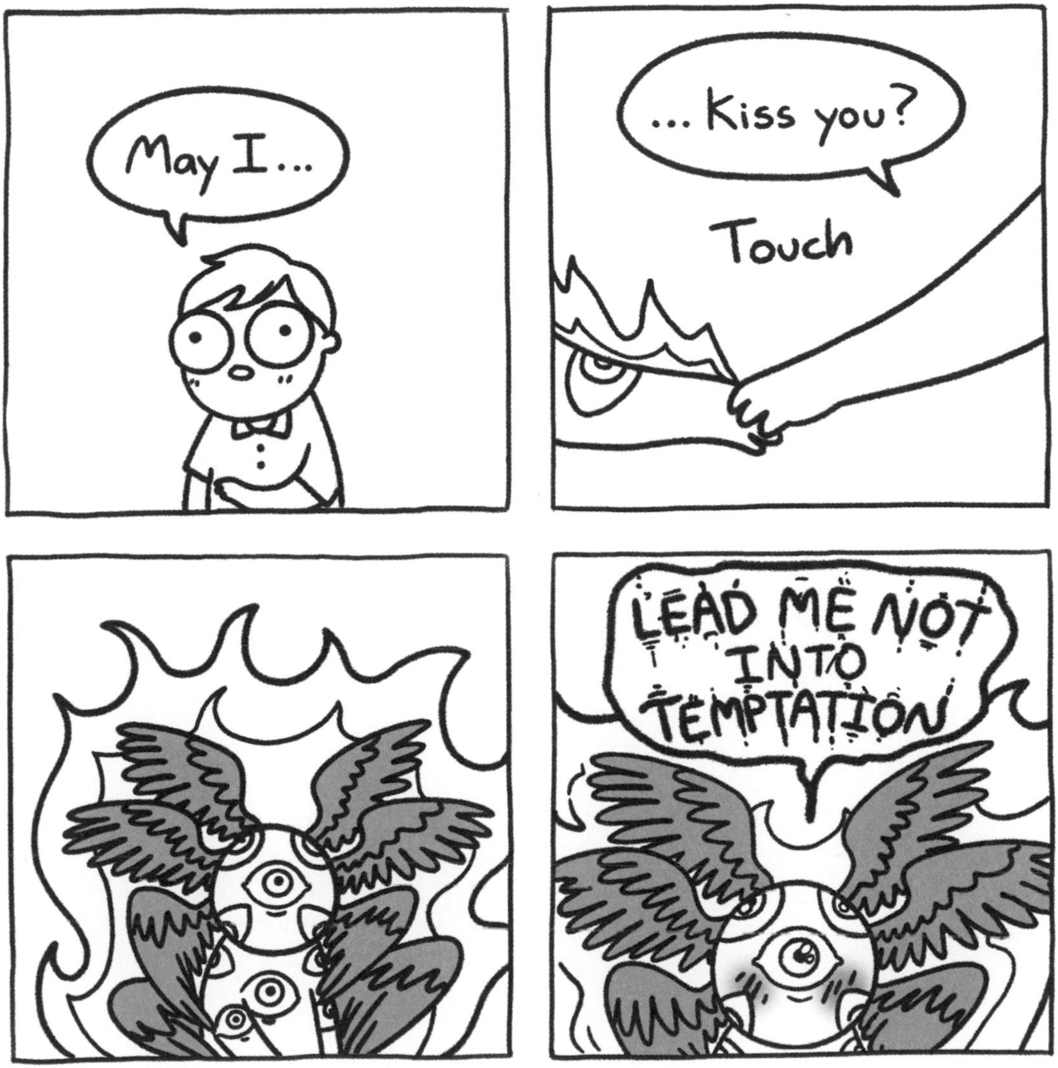
May I...
...Kiss you?
Touch
LEAD ME NOT INTO TEMPTATION

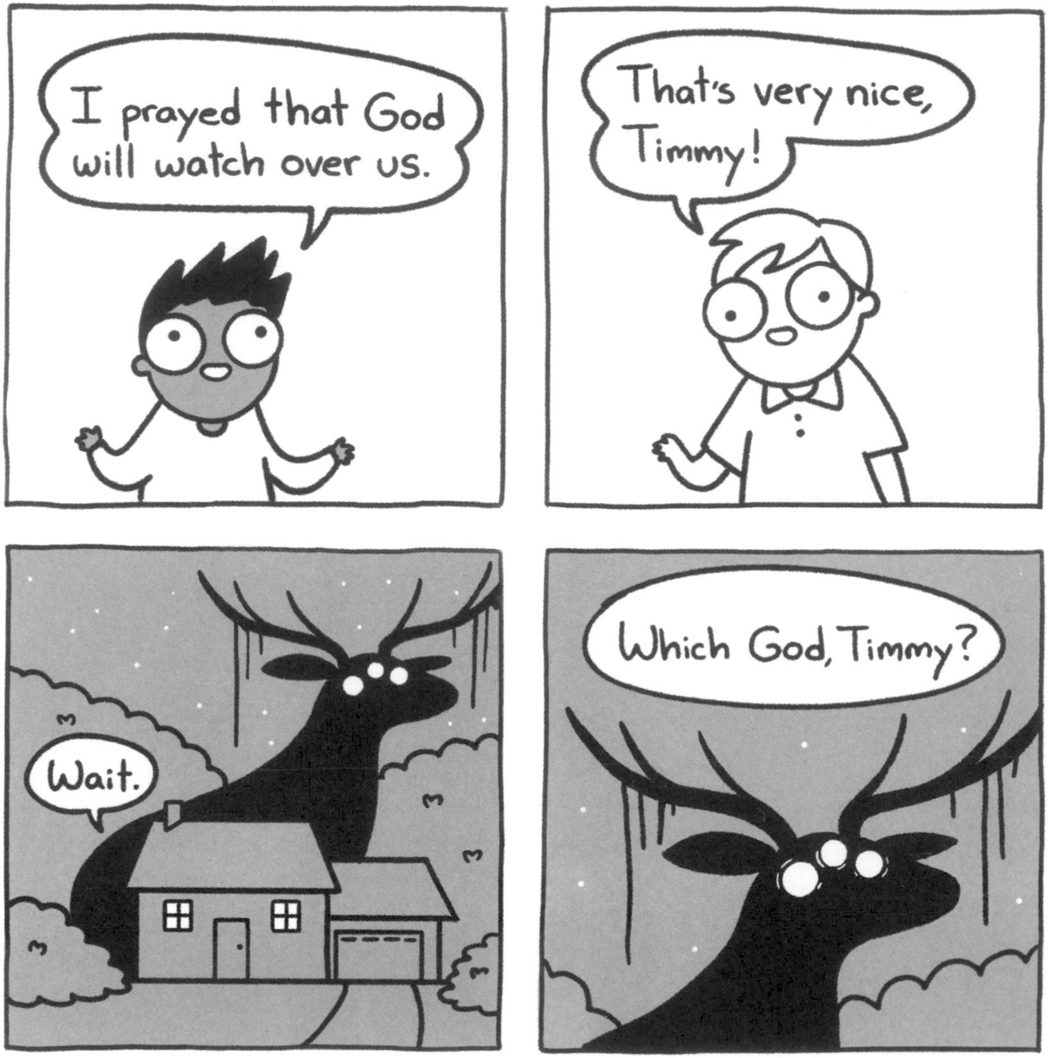
I prayed that God will watch over us.
That's very nice, Timmy!
Wait.
Which God, Timmy?

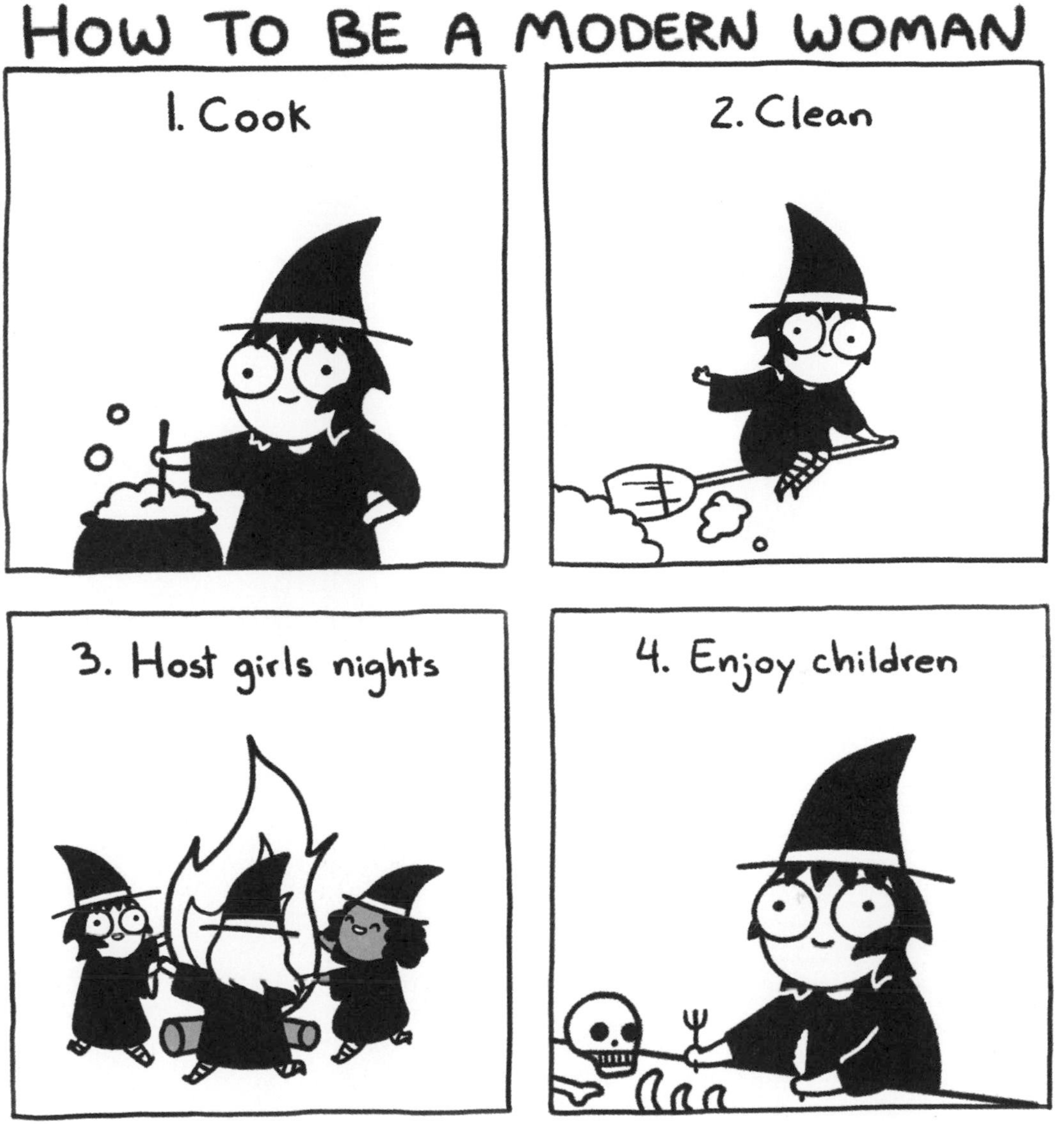
HOW TO BE A MODERN WOMAN
1. Cook
2. Clean
3. Host girls nights
4. Enjoy children

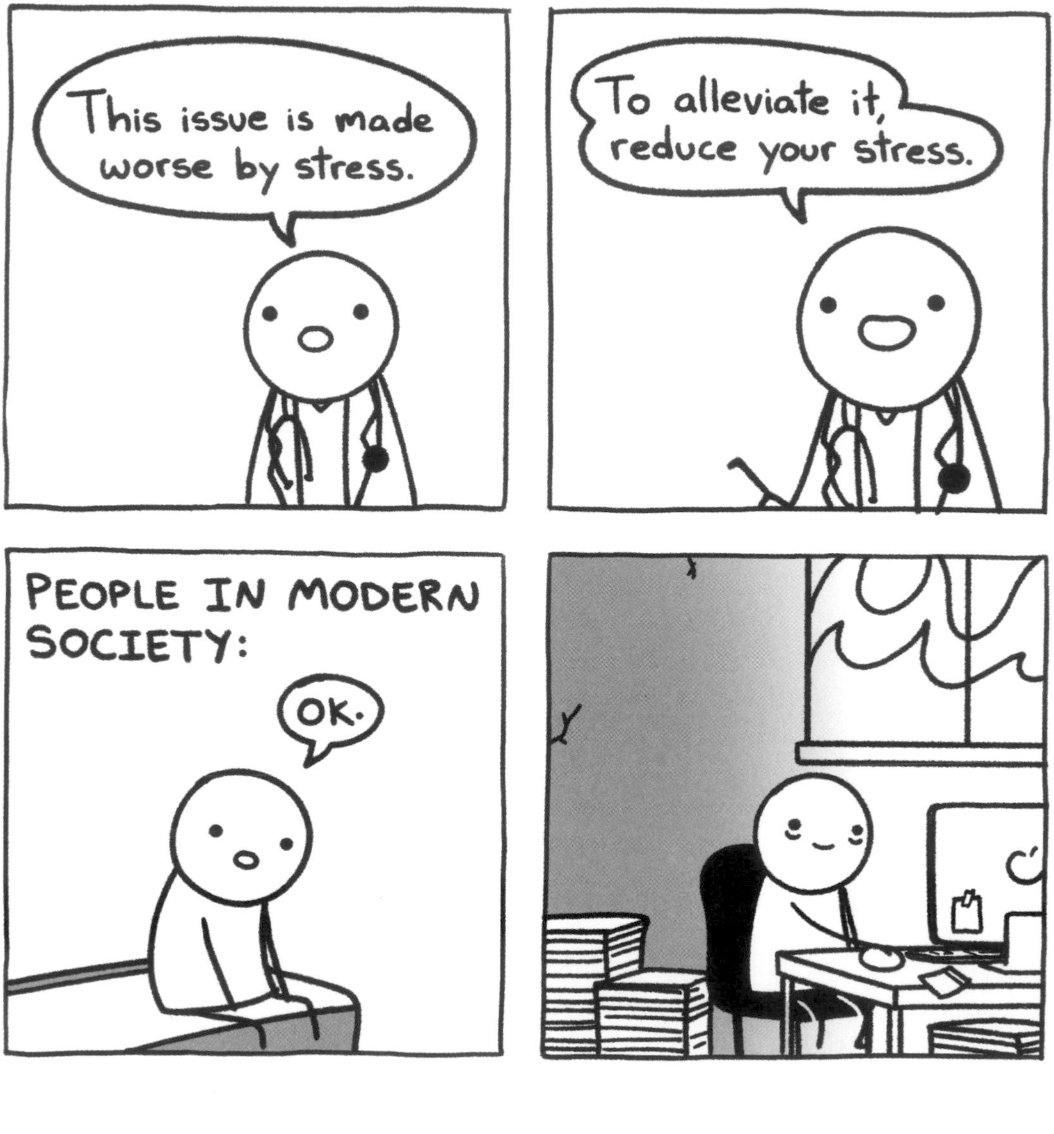
This issue is made worse by stress.
To alleviate it, reduce your stress.
PEOPLE IN MODERN SOCIETY:
OK.

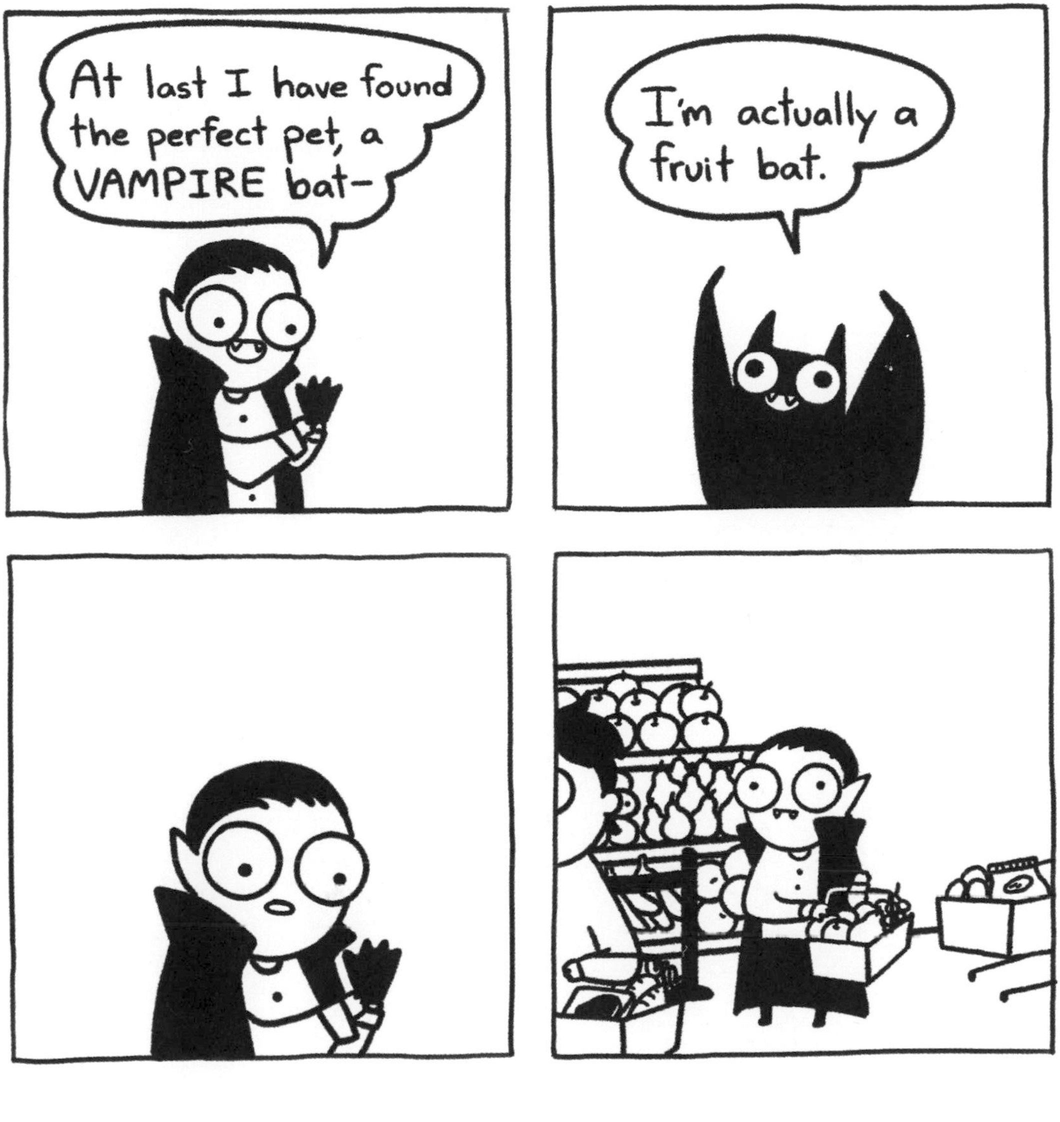
At last I have found the perfect pet, a VAMPIRE bat-
I'm actually a fruit bat.

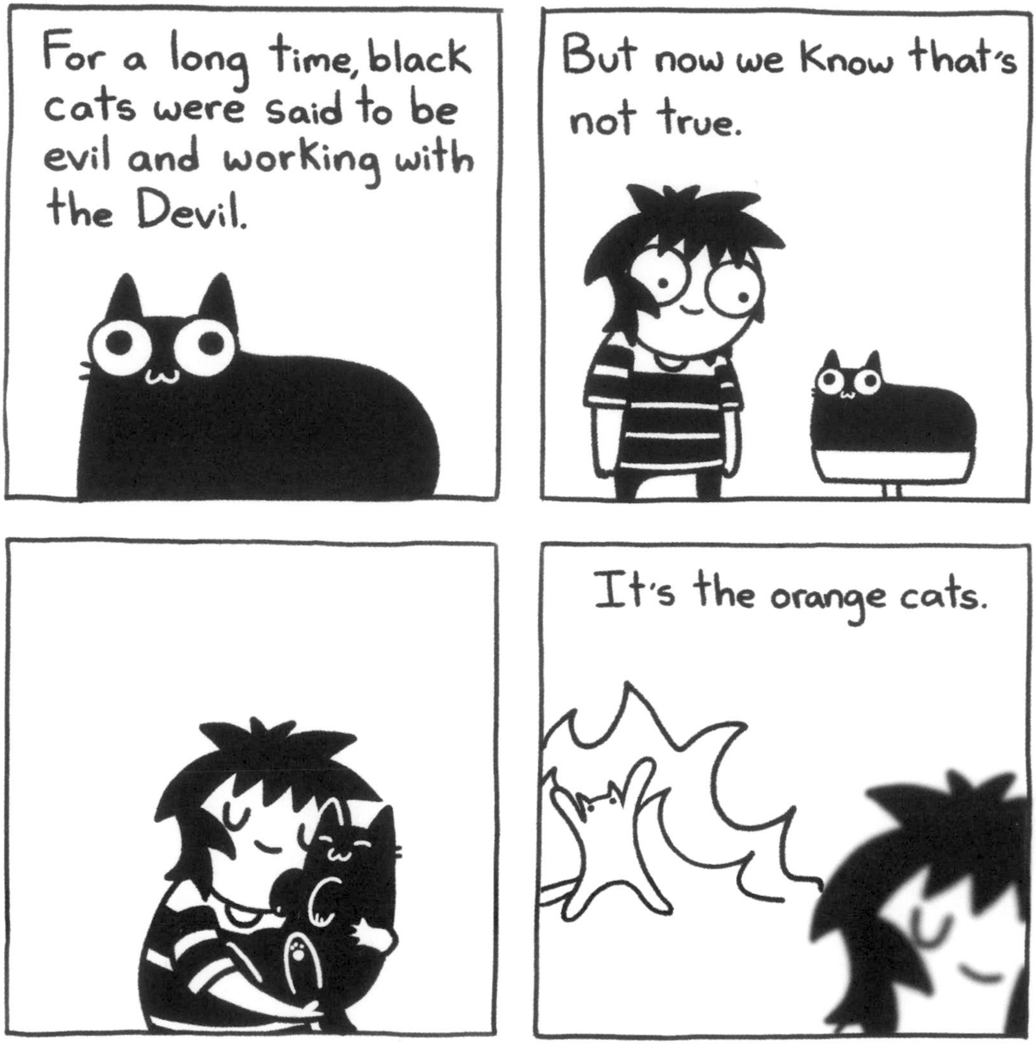
For a long time, black cats were said to be evil and working with the Devil.
But now we Know that's not true.
It's the orange cats.

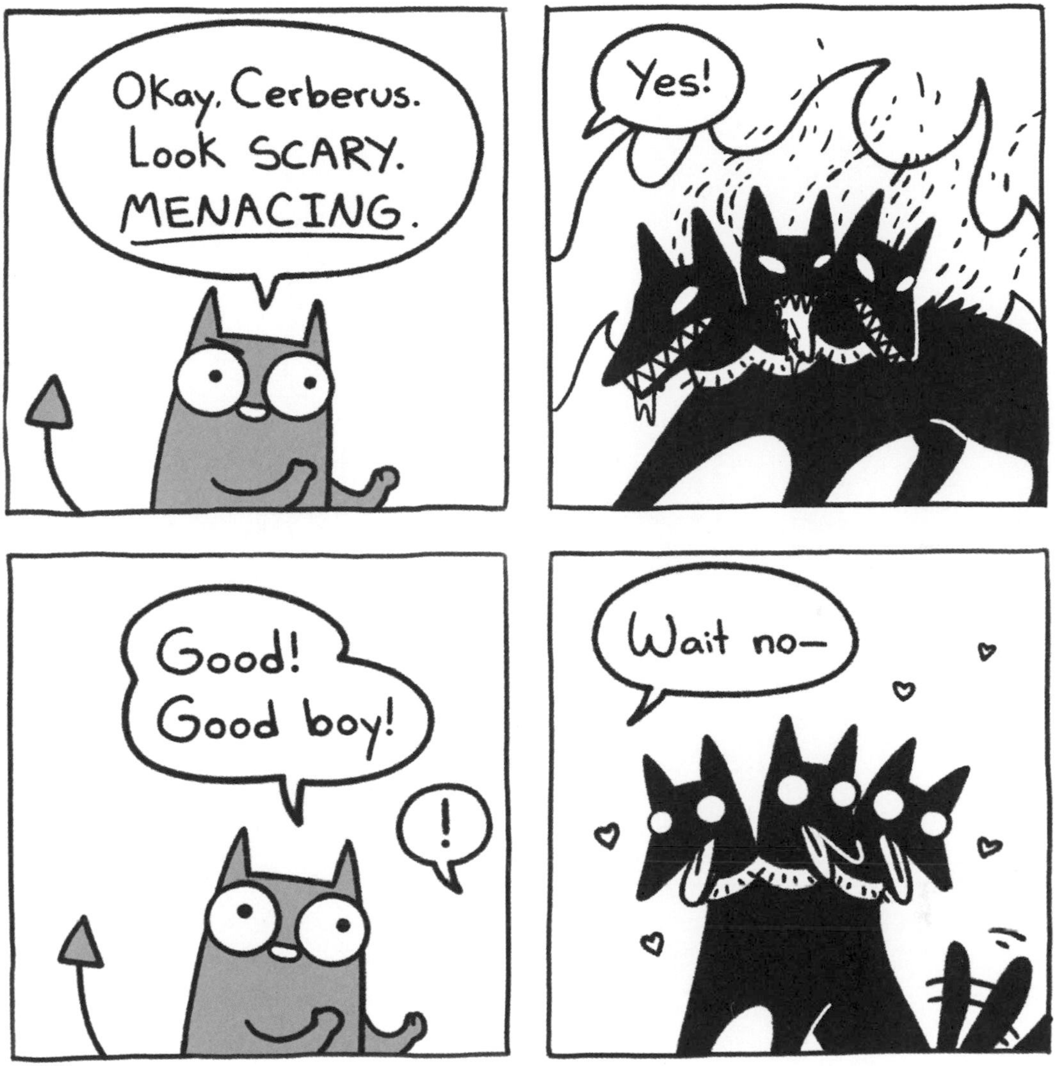
Okay, Cerberus.
Look SCARY.
MENACING.
Yes!
Good!
Good boy!
!
Wait no—

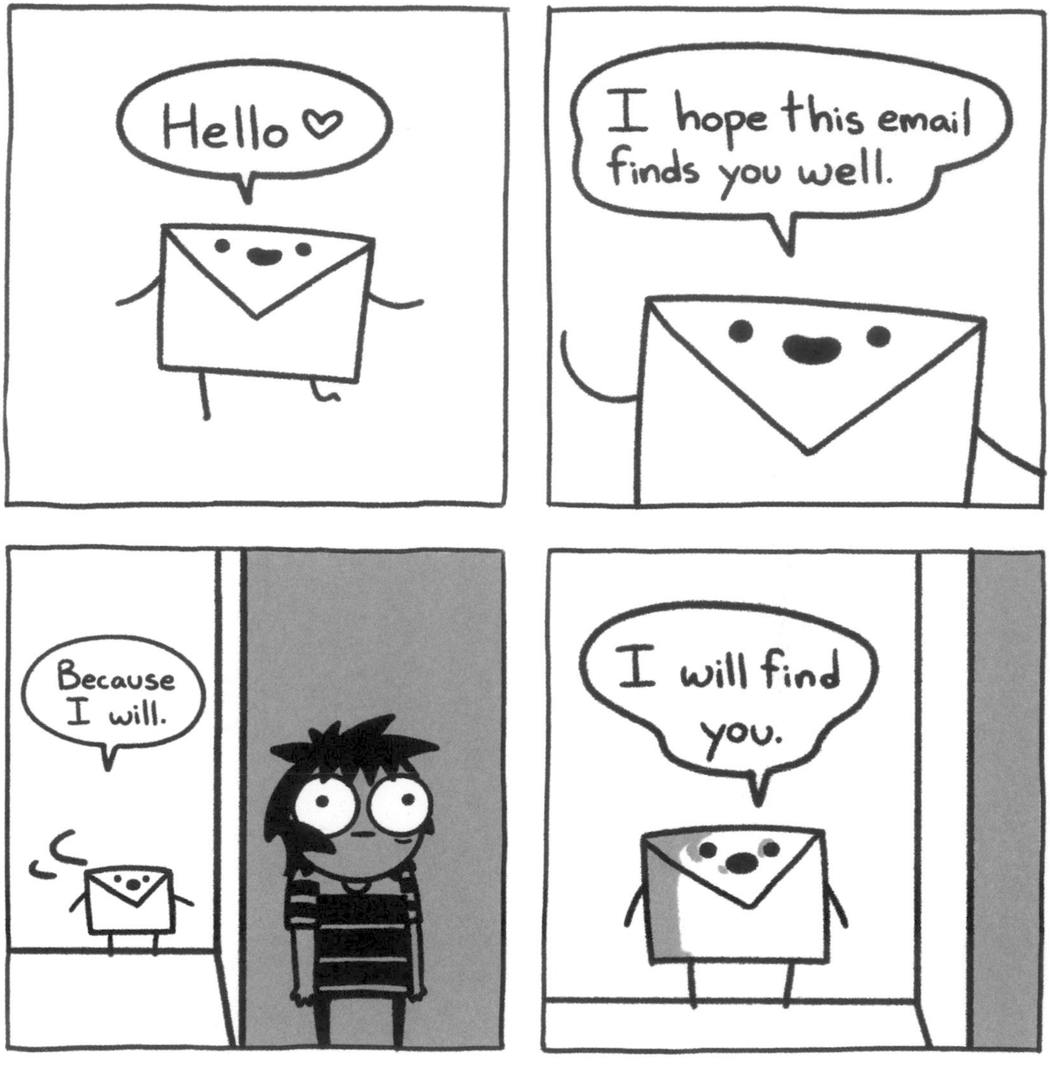

Hello ♡
I hope this email finds you well.
Because I will.
I will find you.

SATANIC RITUAL

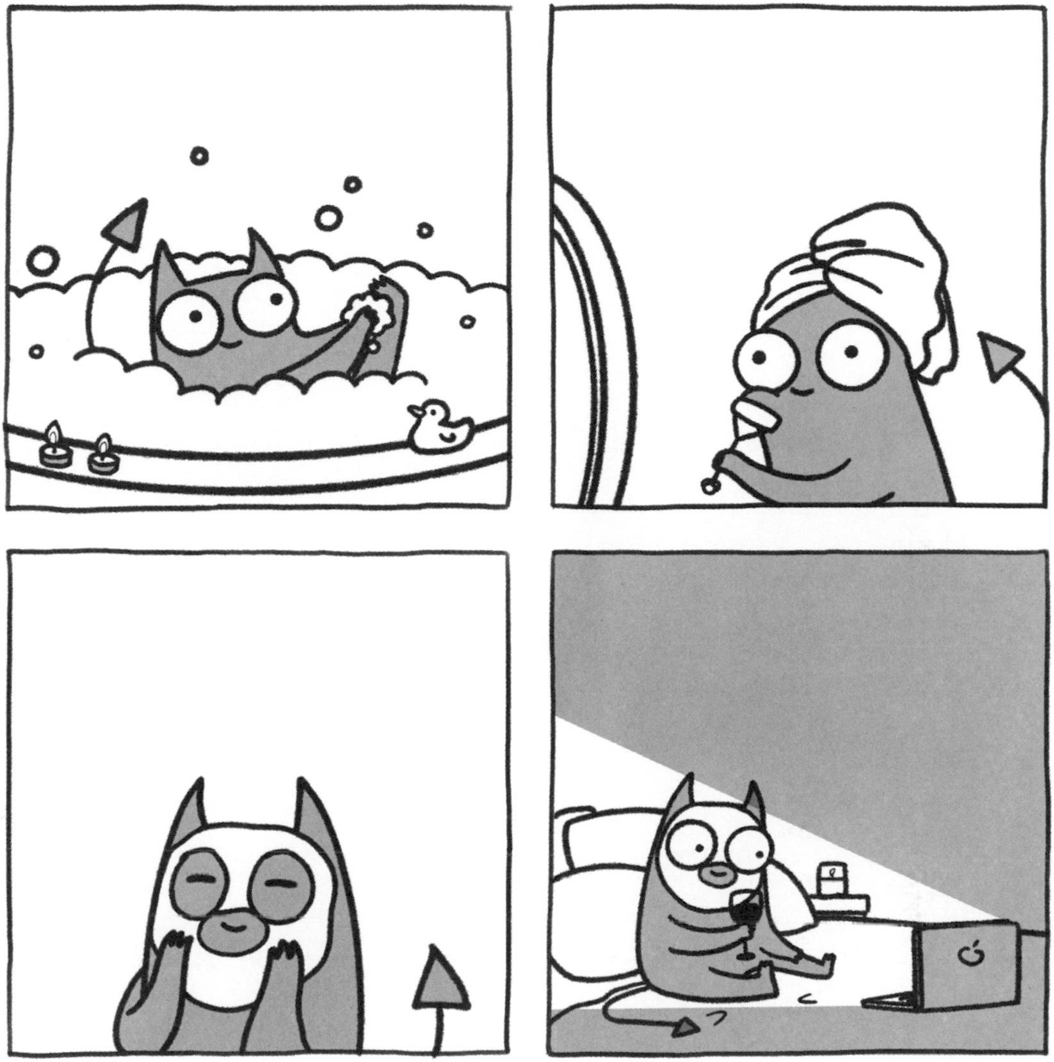

LIFE: THE BARE MINIMUM

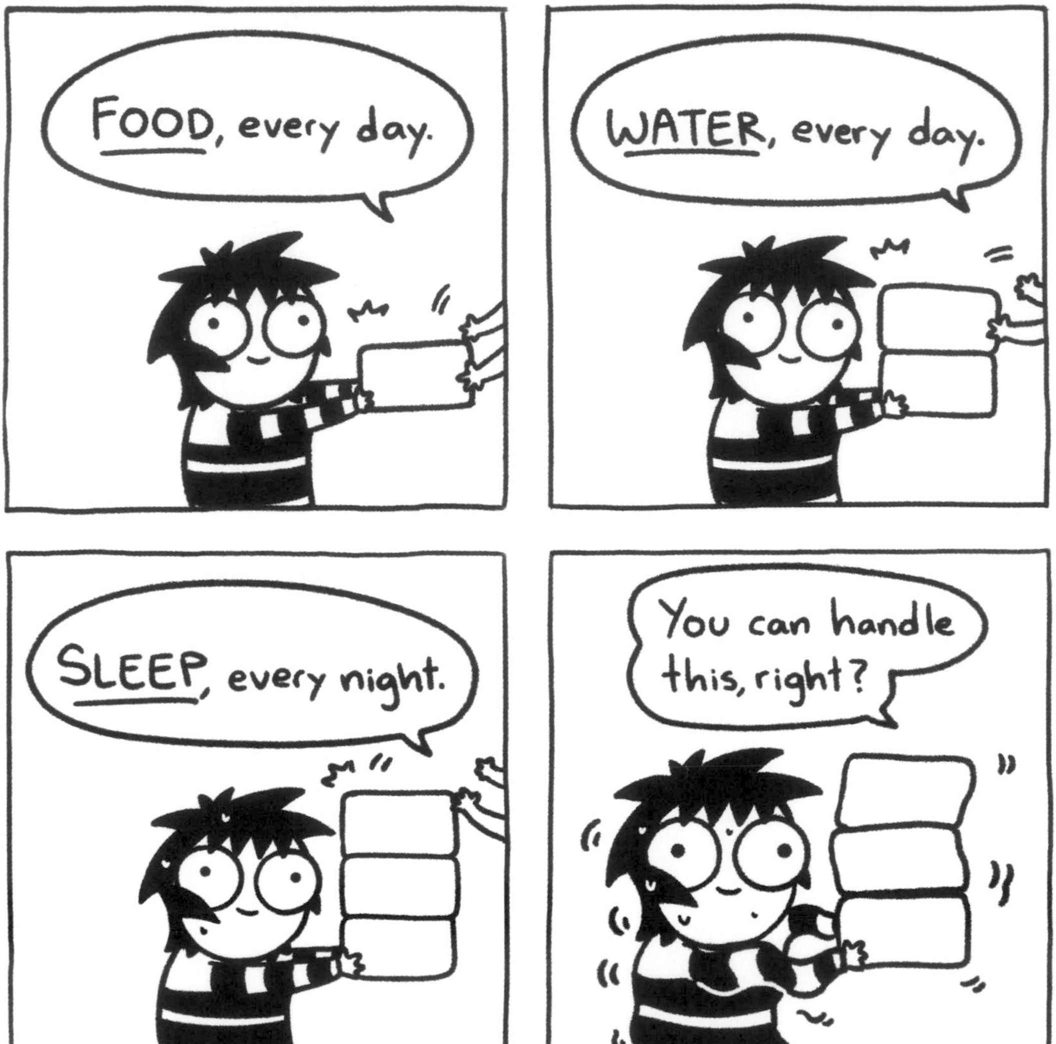
FOOD, every day.
WATER, every day.
SLEEP, every night.
You can handle this, right?

ENGLISH ACCENTS

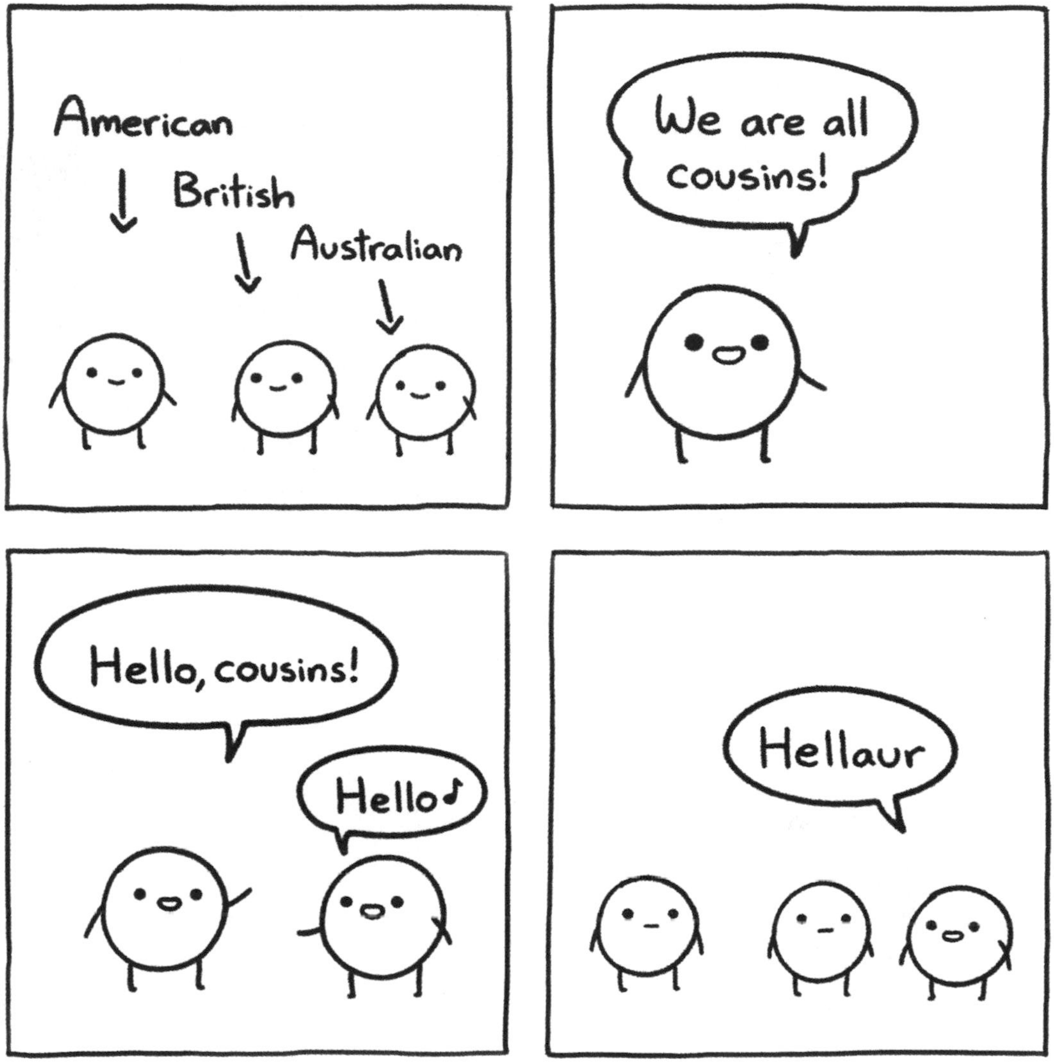
American
British
Australian
We are all cousins!
Hello, cousins!
Hello♪
Hellaur

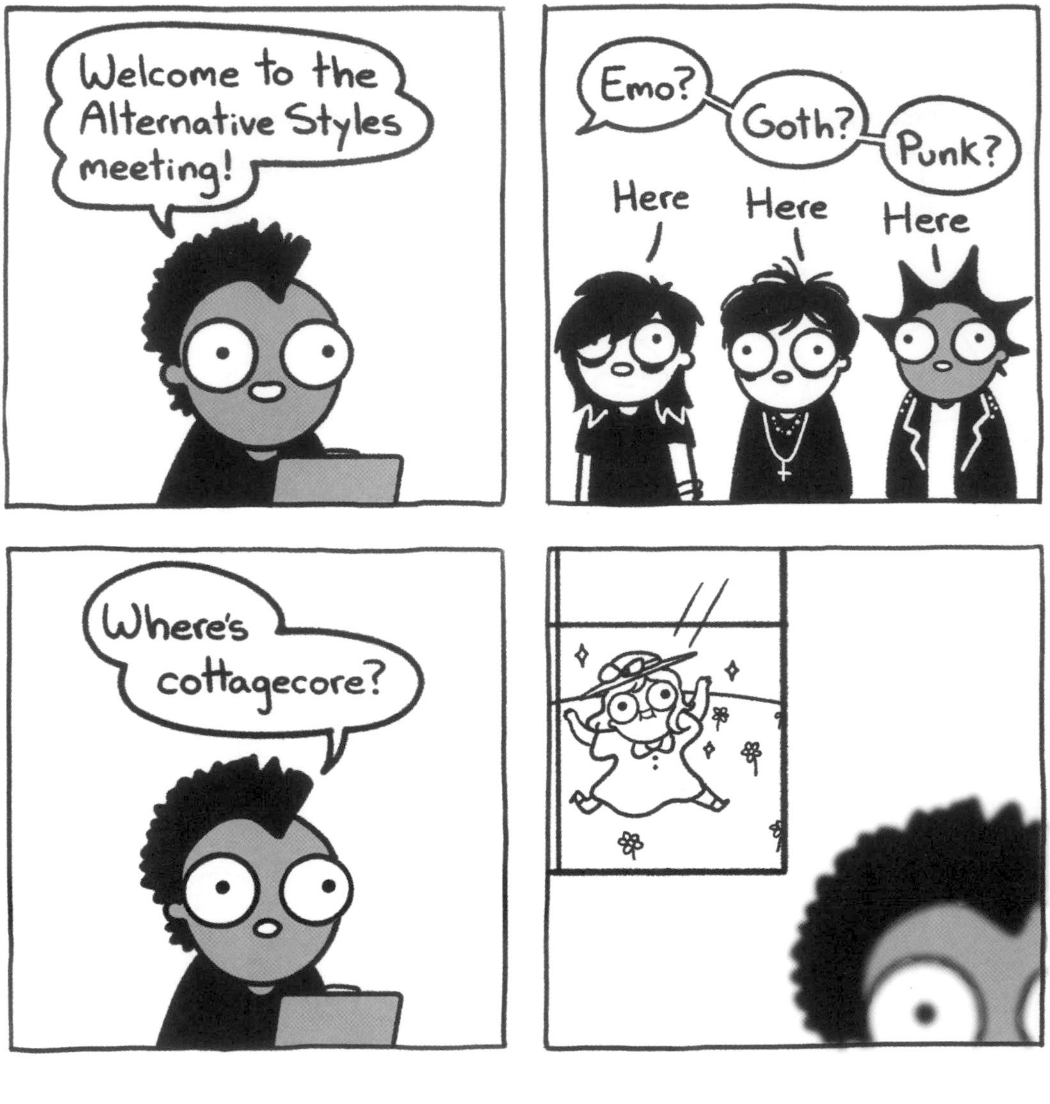
Welcome to the Alternative Styles meeting!
Emo?
Goth?
Punk?
Here
Here
Here
Where's cottagecore?

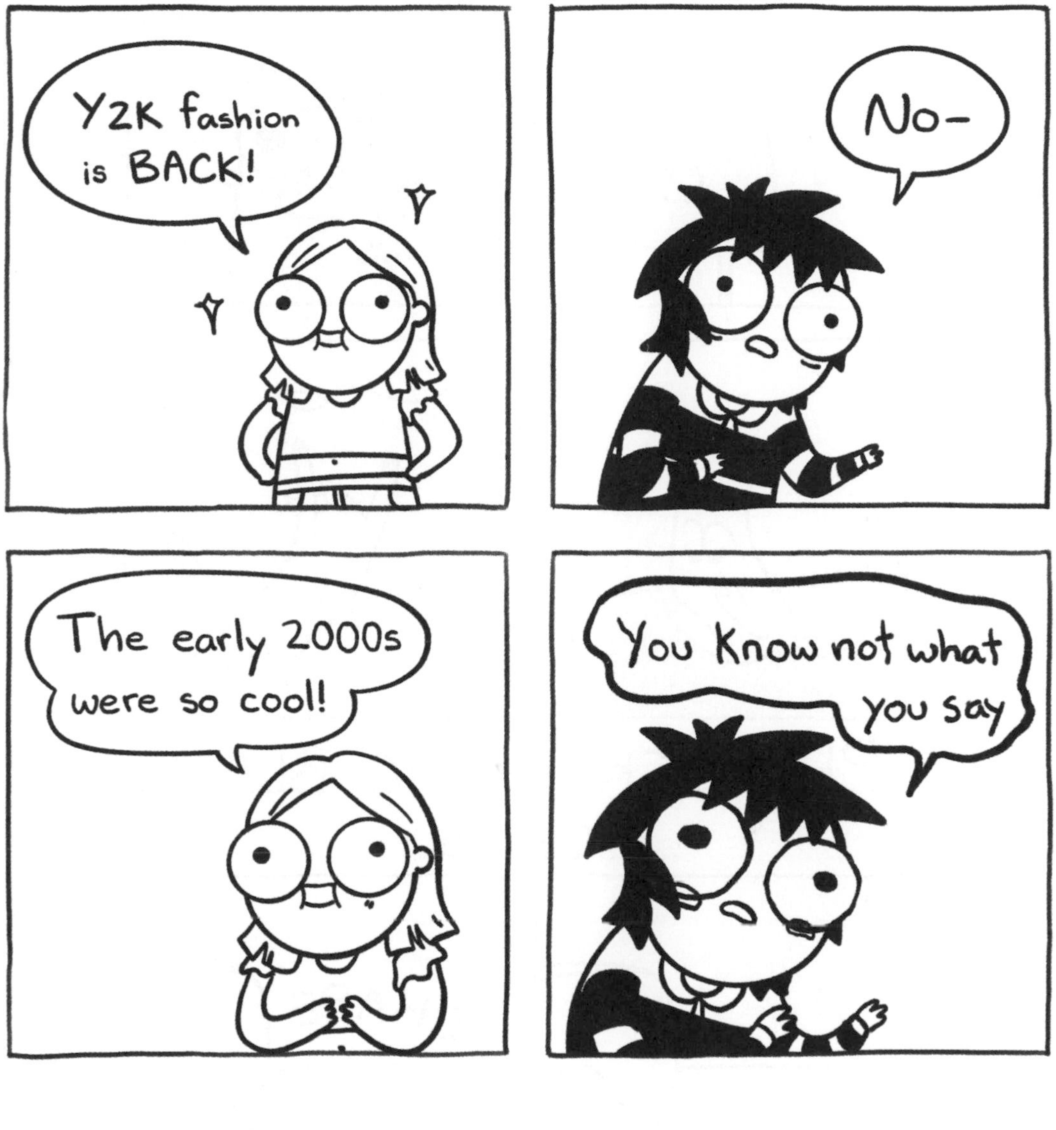
Y2K fashion is BACK!
No-
The early 2000s were so cool!
You know not what you say

PHOTOGRAPHING CATS

PHOTOGRAPHING BLACK CATS

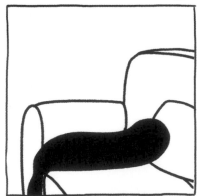
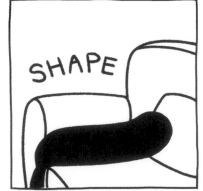

SHAPE

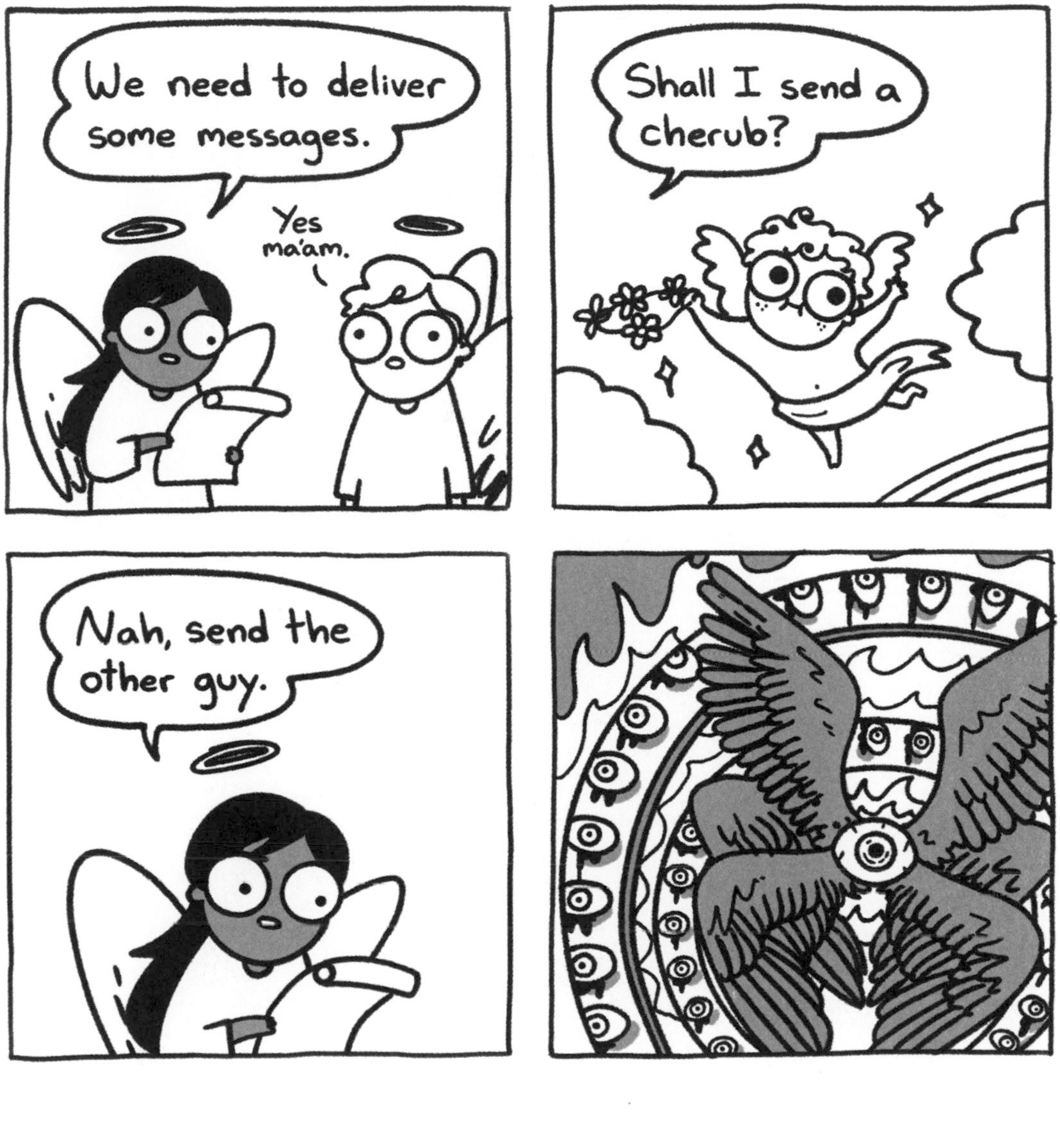
We need to deliver some messages.
Yes ma'am.
Shall I send a cherub?
Nah, send the other guy.

POLTERGEIST

Stuff keeps moving around my house.

I'm terrified. I can't sleep.

Home decor is my passion.

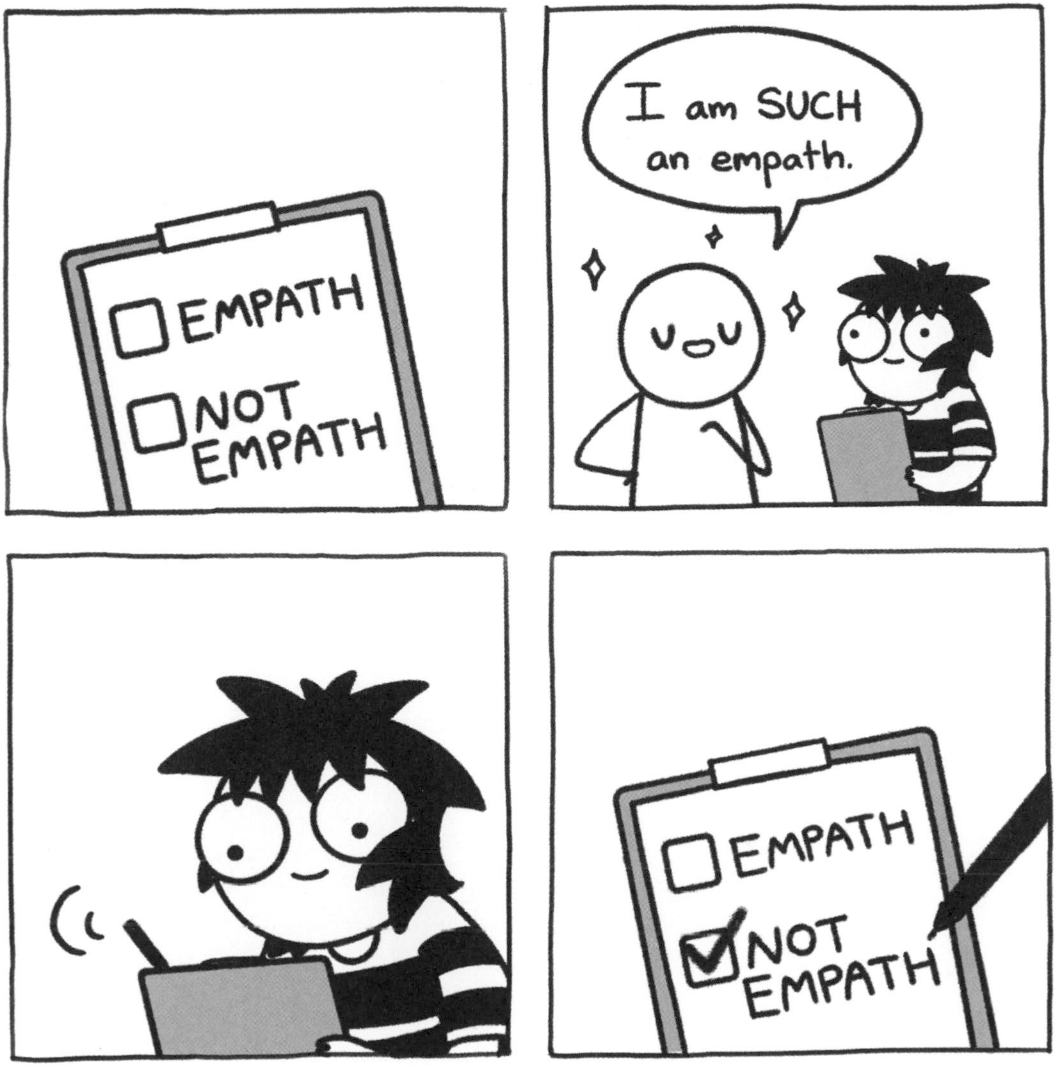
EMPATH
NOT EMPATH
I am SUCH an empath.
EMPATH
NOT EMPATH

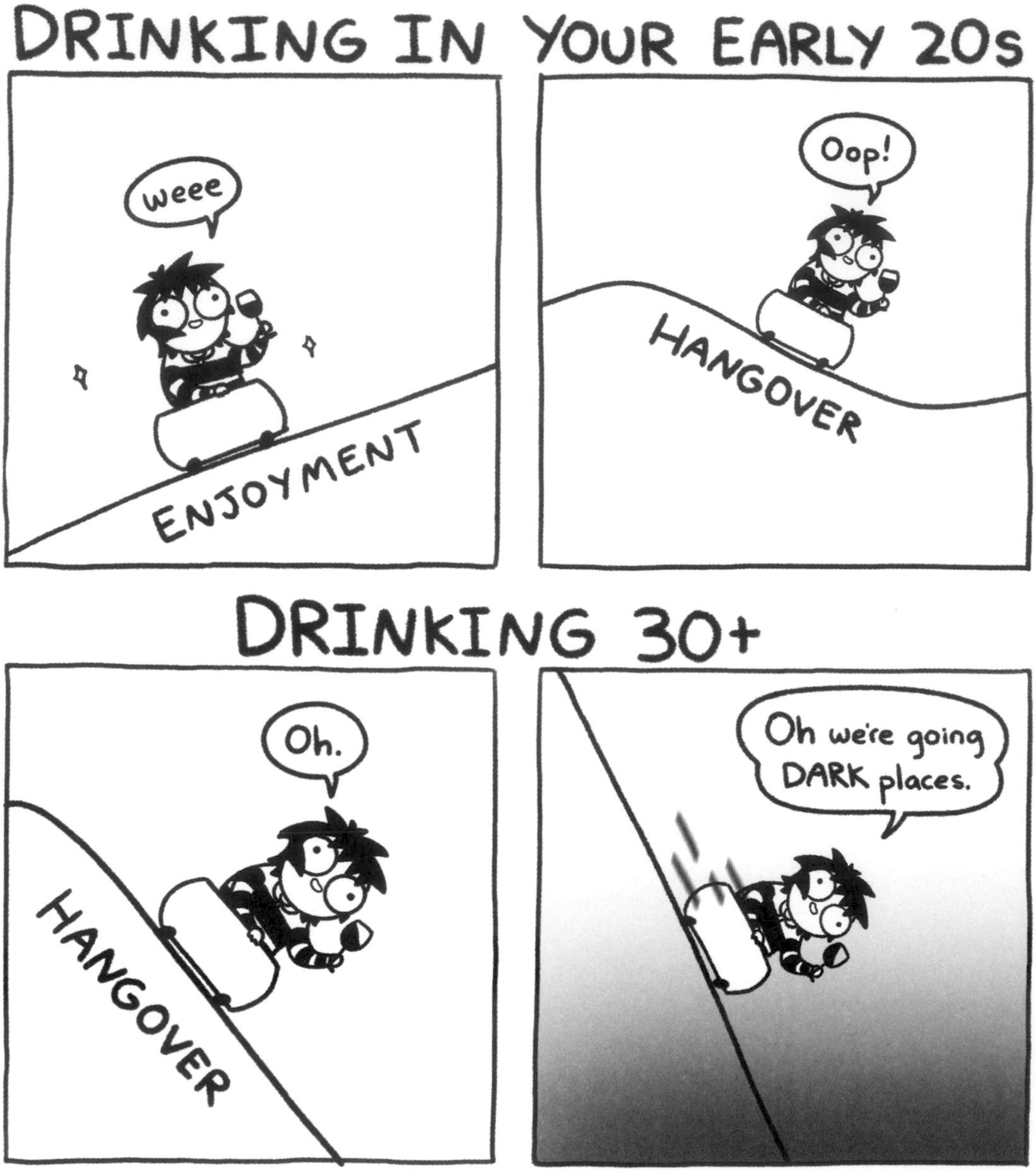
DRINKING IN YOUR EARLY 20s
weee
ENJOYMENT
Oop!
HANGOVER
DRINKING 30+
Oh.
HANGOVER
Oh we're going DARK places.

HOW IT FEELS TO BE ALIVE LATELY

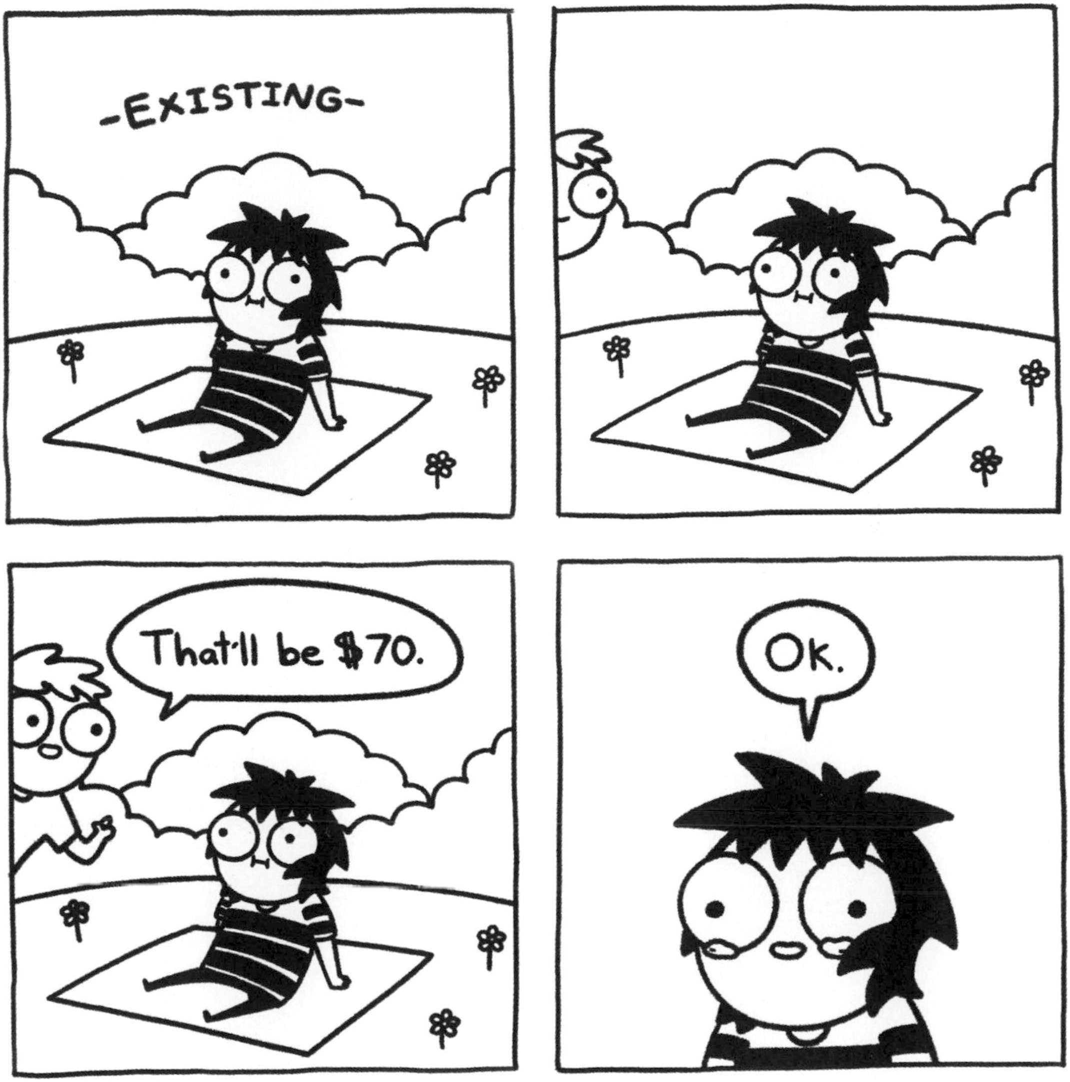
-EXISTING-
That'll be $70.
Ok.

My immune system fighting invaders

My liver fighting toxins

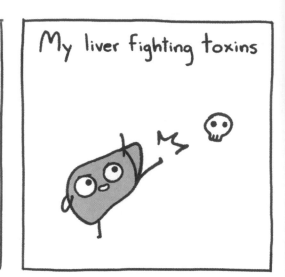

My brain fighting made-up scenarios

SHOWING AFFECTION: SOME PETS

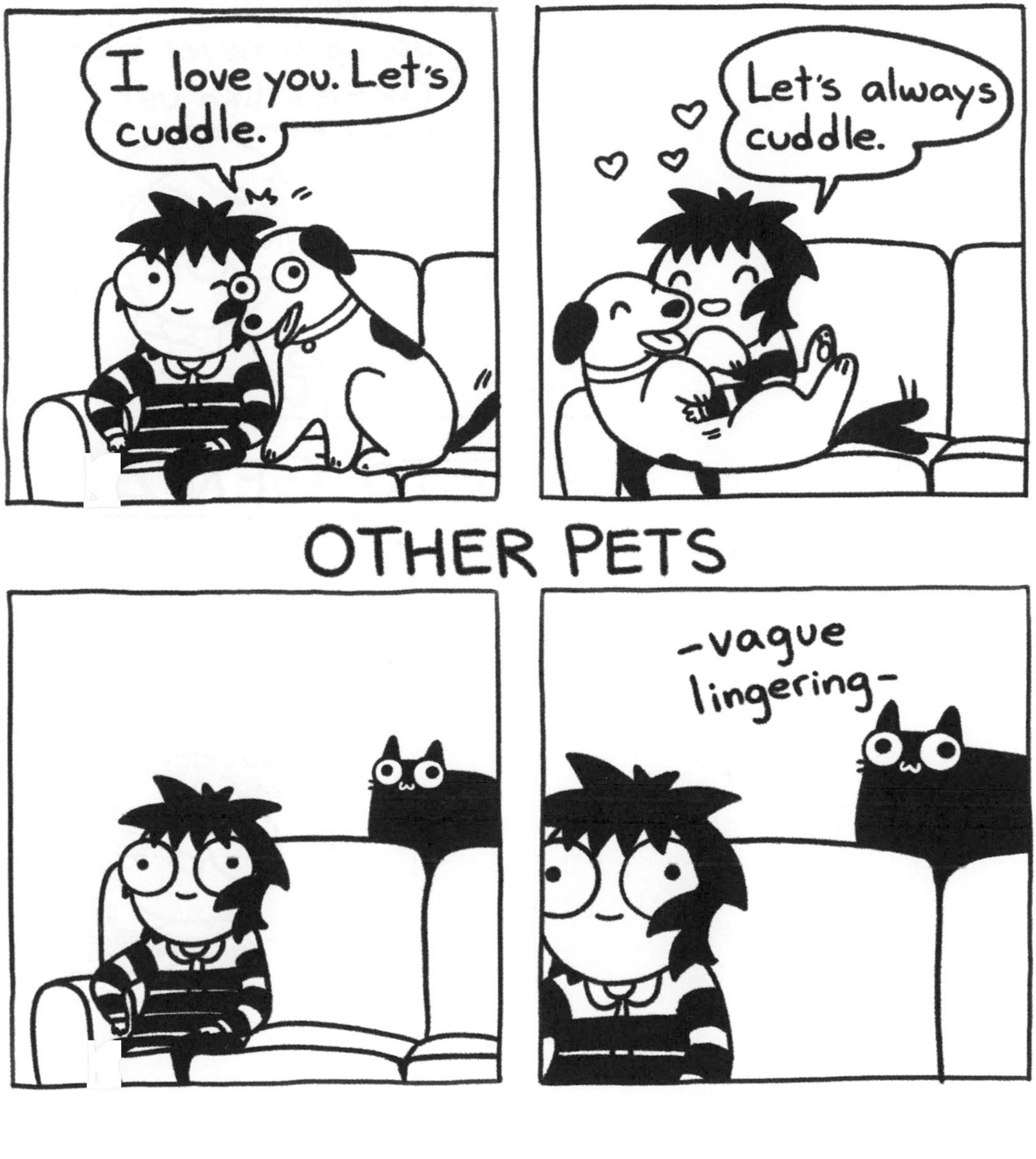
I love you. Let's cuddle.
Let's always cuddle.
OTHER PETS
-vague lingering-

BOOMERS TO MILLENNIALS

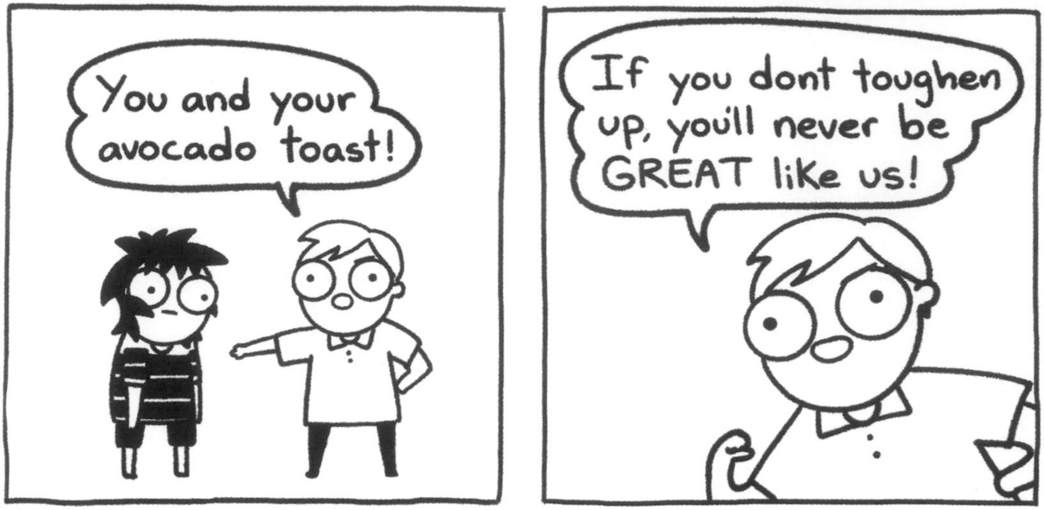
You and your avocado toast!
If you dont toughen up, you'll never be GREAT like us!

MILLENNIALS TO GEN Z

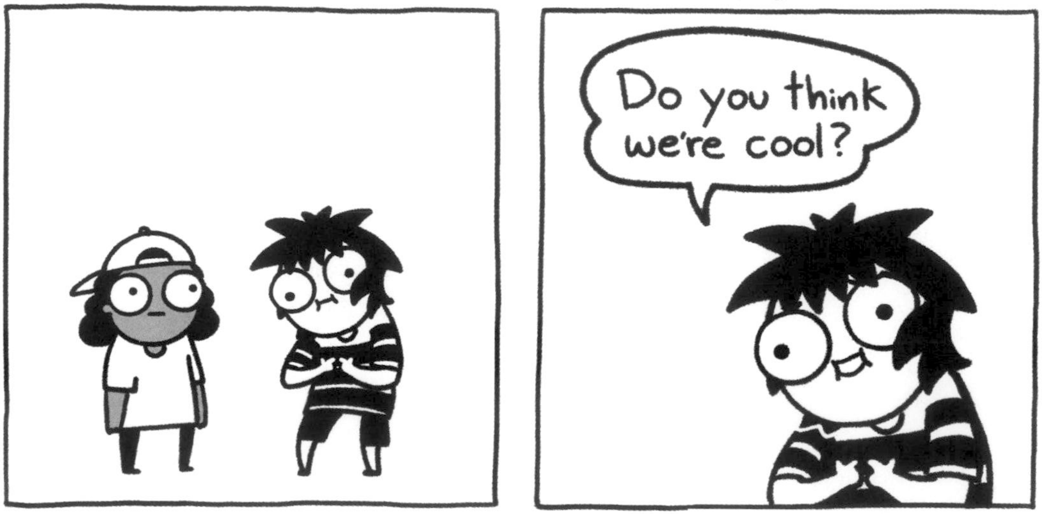
Do you think we're cool?

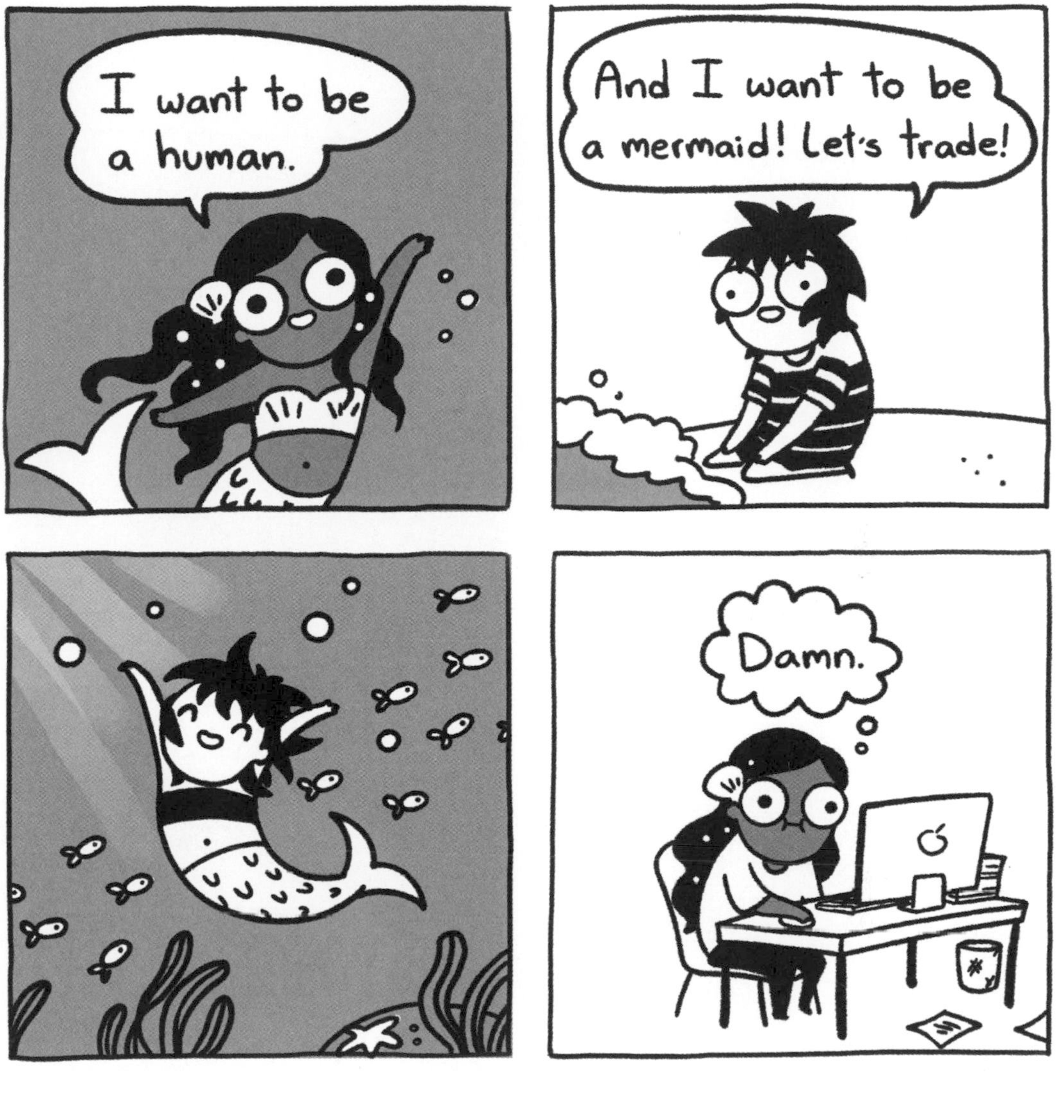
I want to be a human.
And I want to be a mermaid! Let's trade!
Damn.

ME AGE 15

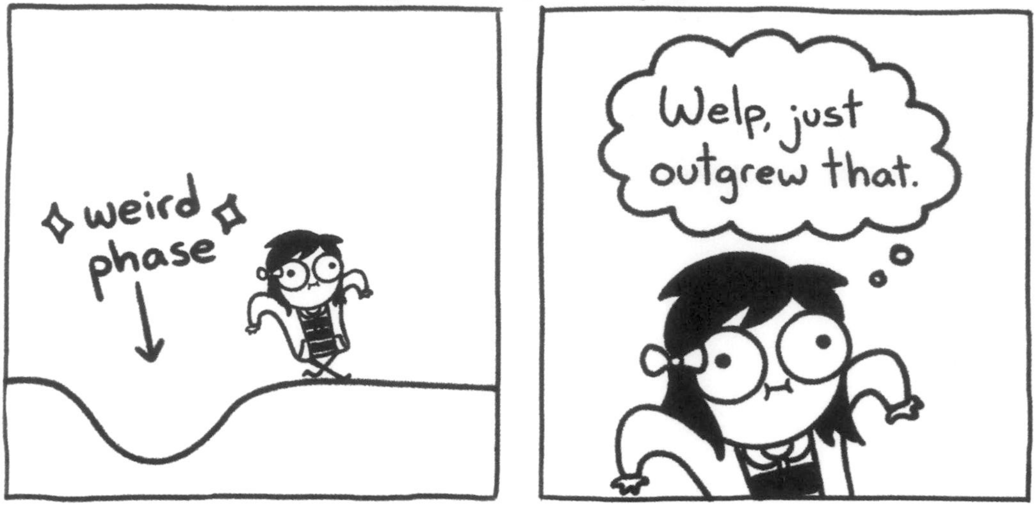
weird phase
Welp, just outgrew that.

ME AGE 30

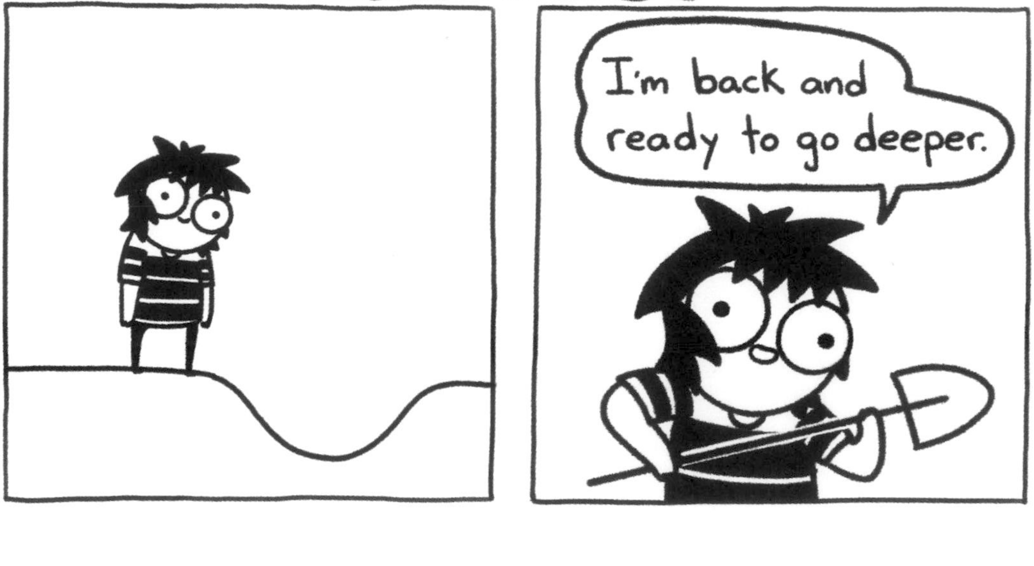
I'm back and ready to go deeper.

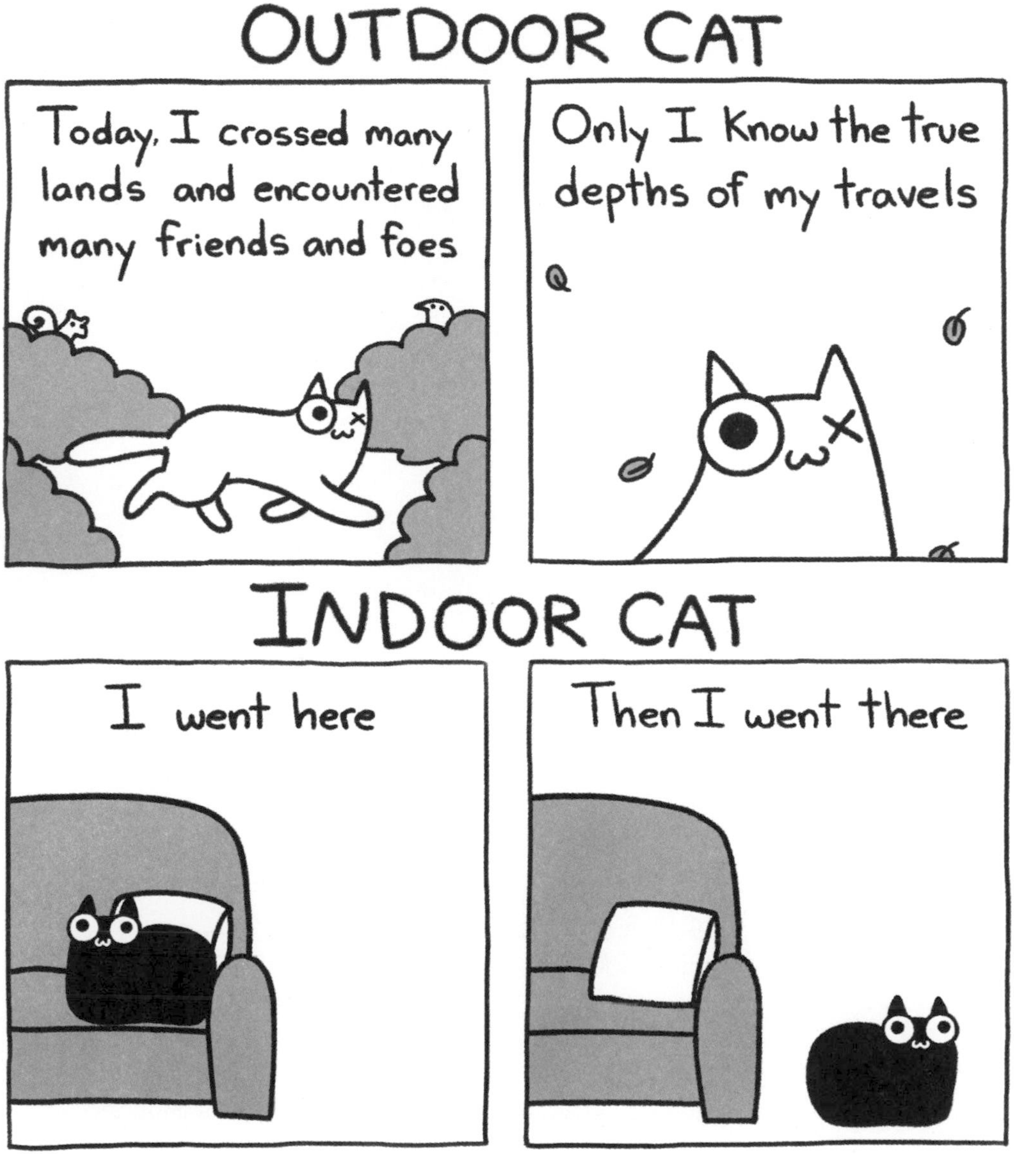
OUTDOOR CAT
Today, I crossed many lands and encountered many friends and foes
Only I Know the true depths of my travels
INDOOR CAT
I went here
Then I went there

CATS LIVING TOGETHER

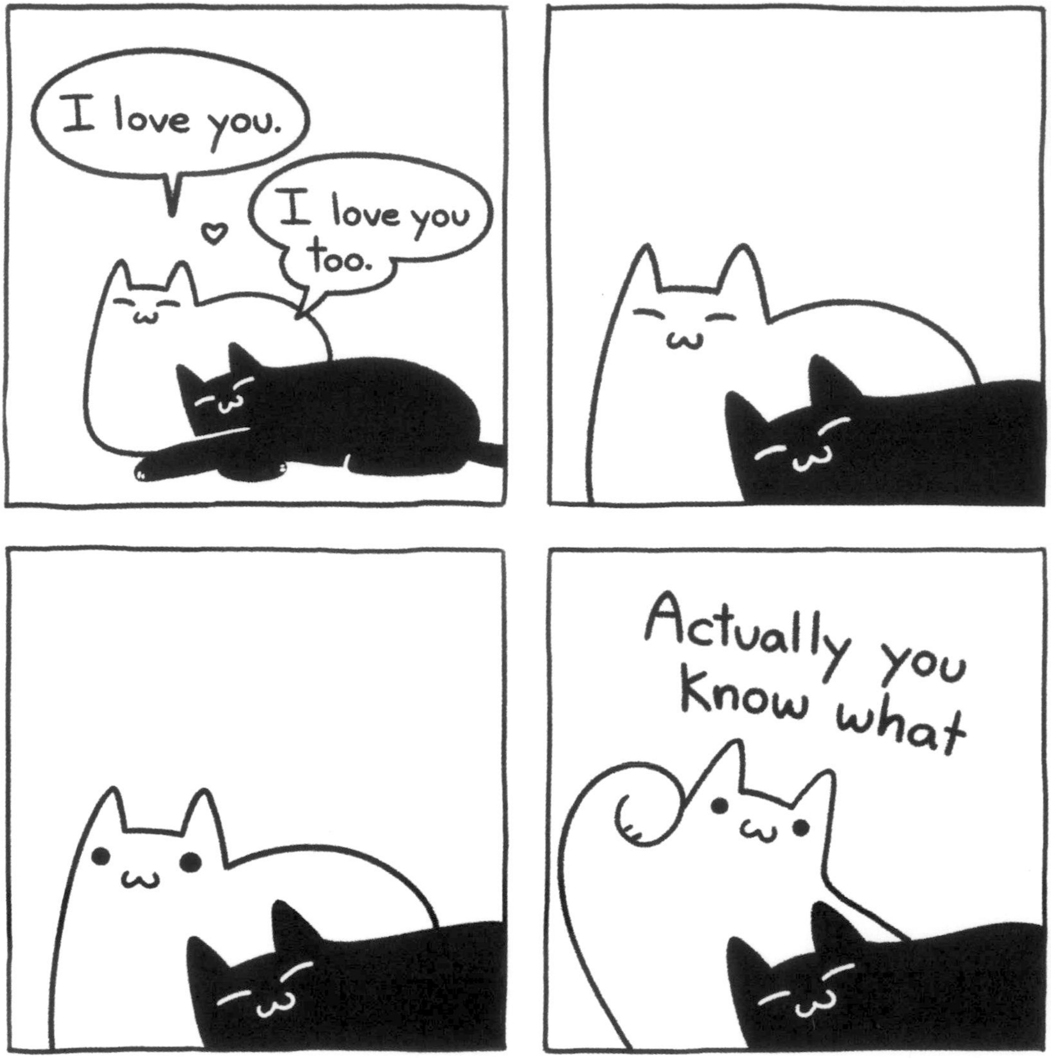

I love you.
I love you too.
Actually you know what

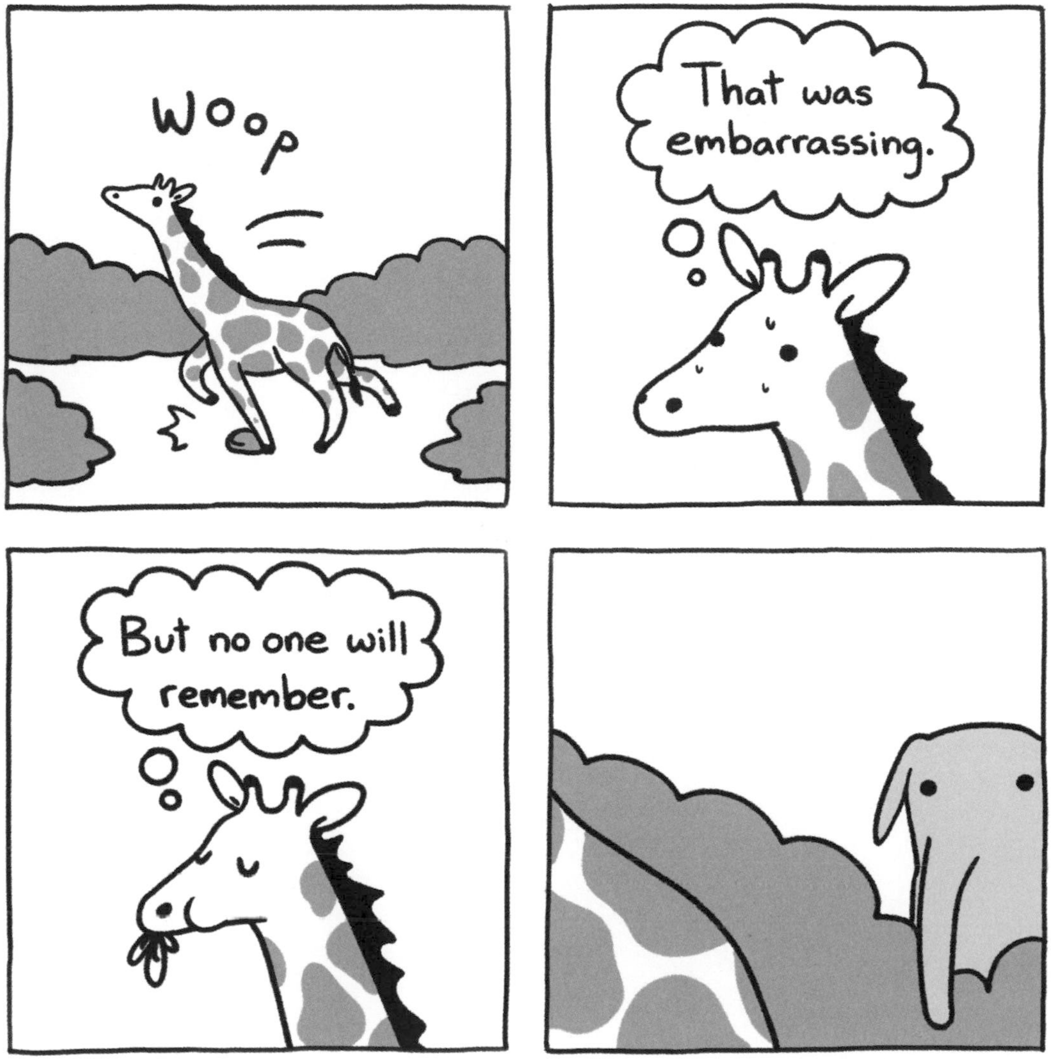
WOOP
That was embarrassing.
But no one will remember.

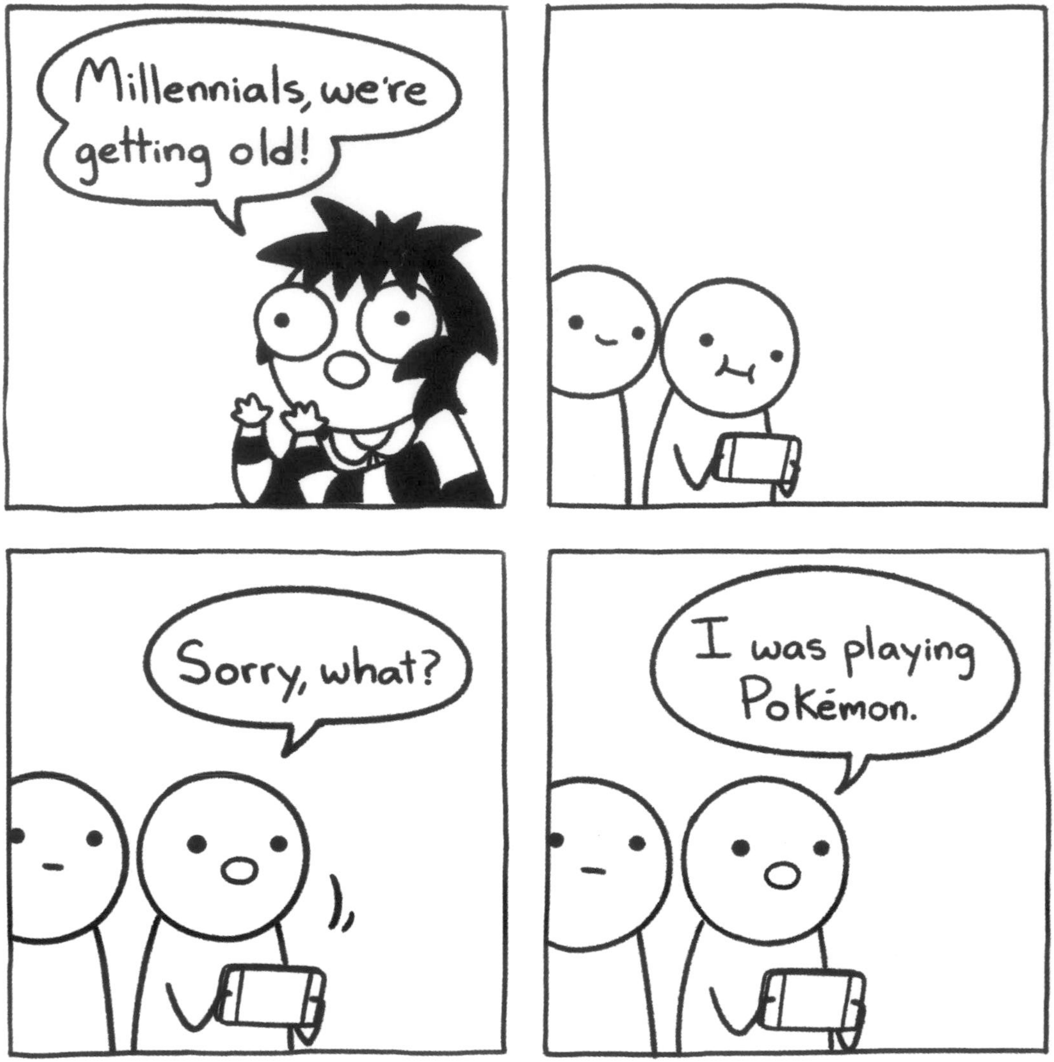
Millennials, we're getting old!
Sorry, what?
I was playing Pokémon.

A DECADE OF SARAH'S SCRIBBLES

Essays and Images by
Sarah Andersen

The Art Critique

How it is:

Good effort. work on shading.

How I perceive it:

You are a bad human being and also you are ugly.

This is the first comic I ever posted to the Internet, all the way back in December 2011. It was drawn on Microsoft Paint and appeared on Tumblr on a blog that I had named *Doodle Time.* I was in my second year at art school.

I had been drawing little comics in my sketchbook since middle school as a way to entertain my friends, but at the time I had no goals of being a cartoonist. I went to art school in the hopes of becoming a children's book illustrator and, at the encouragement of my teachers, created the blog to post my art.

When I began posting my comics as well, I noticed that they were better received by the internet than my illustration works. I'm talking very small scale—the comics would maybe garner something like ten or twenty more "notes" or "likes" than my illustrations, but for me it was enough. This positive encouragement, no matter how small, lit a fire within me and ultimately led to my decision to pursue comics more seriously.

The problem was that I had absolutely no clue how to be a cartoonist or properly draw a comic. You can see in this comic that I wasn't even drawing panels yet. It's drawn on MS Paint, for god's sake! The first year or so of my comics was sporadic. Sometimes, the comics were done digitally; other times, they were scans of my sketchbook. There was a lot of experimenting, failure, and confusion until I finally found a process that worked.

Knowing in retrospect that comics would ultimately become my entire career, the caption I included on this little MS Paint comic really makes me smile.

I wrote:

"I decided to start posting comics I make about my life.

Maybe other art students will relate to this . . ."

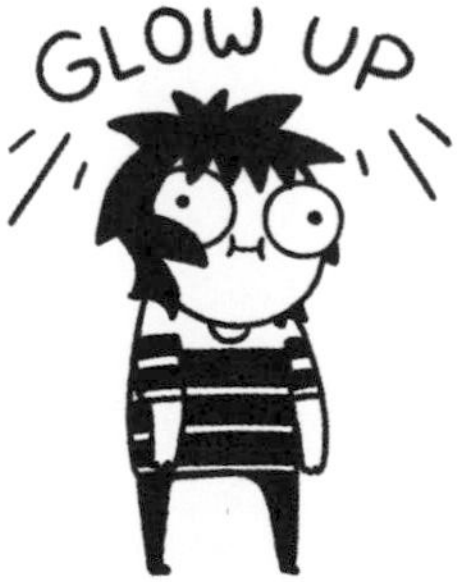
GLOW UP

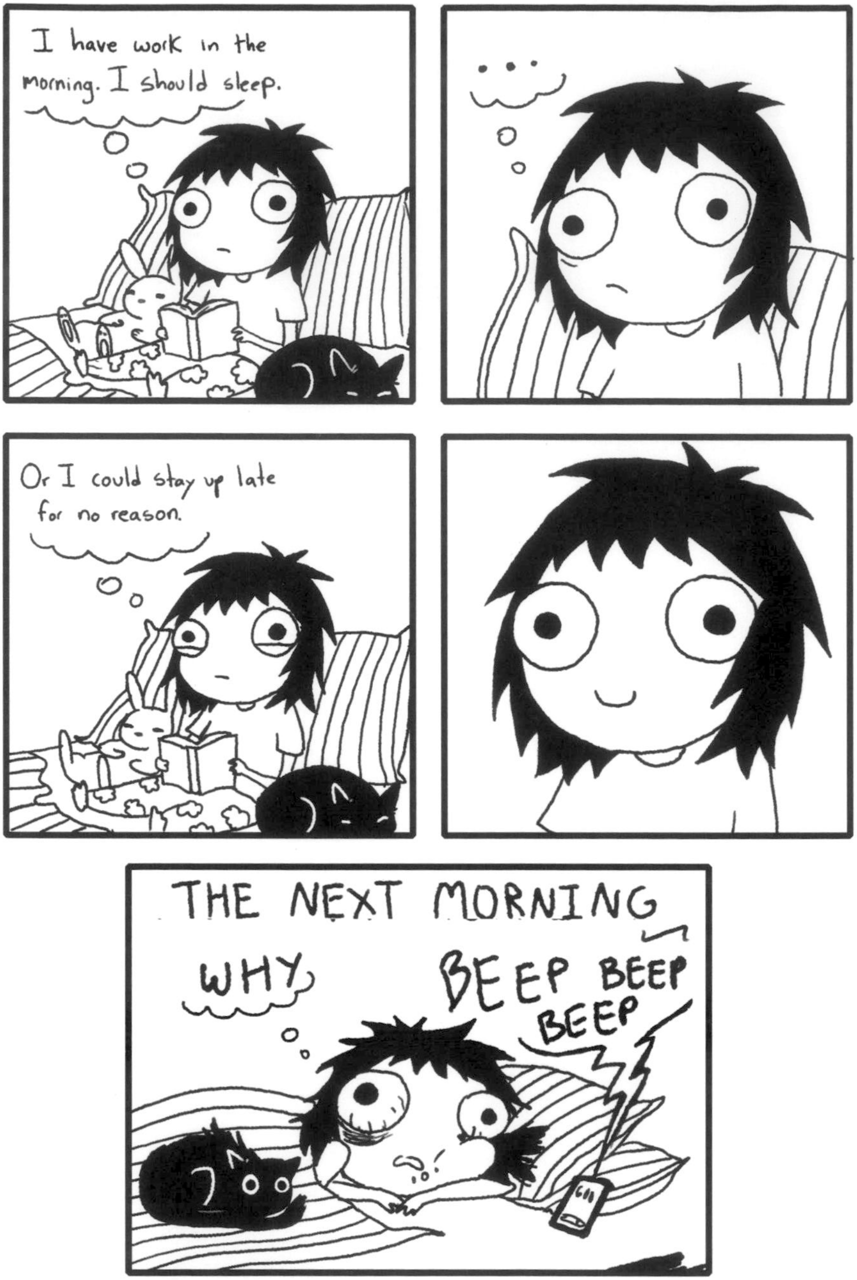
I have work in the morning. I should sleep.
...
Or I could stay up late for no reason.
THE NEXT MORNING
WHY
BEEP BEEP BEEP BEEP
An early comic

The drawing style of my early comics seriously makes me cringe. I can't even read my first book without wincing. To be fair, I wasn't necessarily a *terrible* artist—because I was in art school, I was a decent enough illustrator, but my abilities would fall apart when I tried to draw simple comics. The idea that I couldn't draw at all pervaded my early comics work.

People think simple styles are easier, but without details to cover anything up, simplicity will always reveal your greatest weaknesses. Simplicity requires a steady hand and a lot of confidence, two things I severely lacked at the start of my career. Looking back and seeing the original artwork really makes me think about how much I was still a kid and an amateur. In many ways, simplicity is as sophisticated and challenging an art form as realism and its offshoots.

In my opinion, my comics don't start looking confident and steady until around 2020-ish. That's nearly a decade of drawing. It can take a lot of time and repetition to find your voice. You get to know your style and your characters as you draw them over and over. Practice, practice, practice!

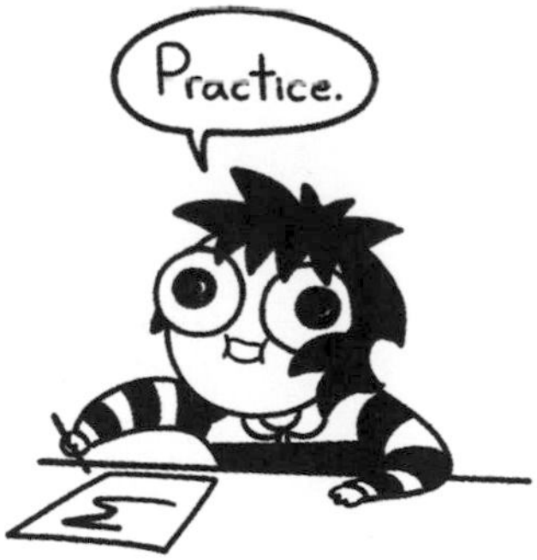
Practice.

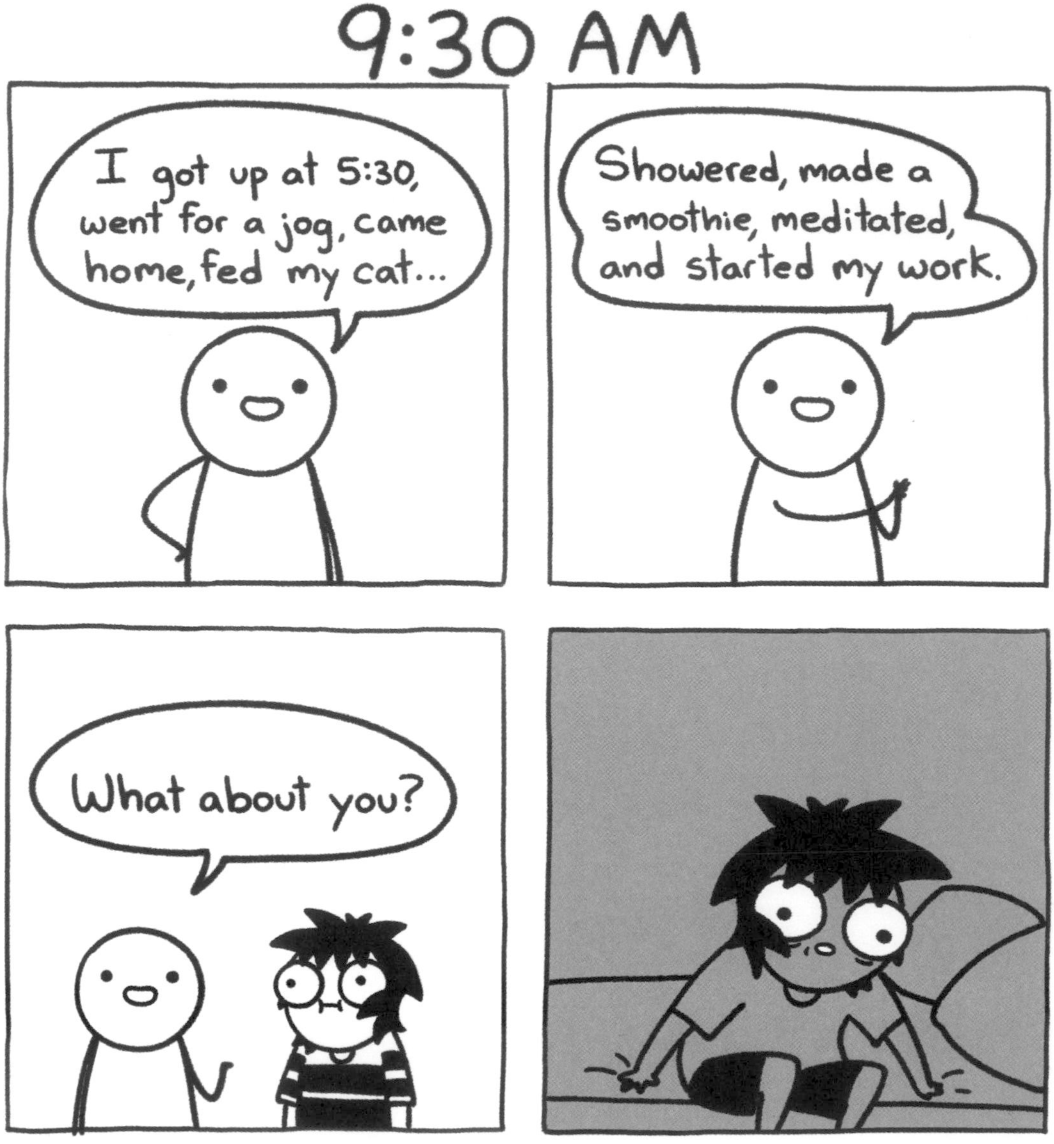
9:30 AM
I got up at 5:30, went for a jog, came home, fed my cat...
Showered, made a smoothie, meditated, and started my work.
What about you?

A recent comic, where my style is cleaner and more confident

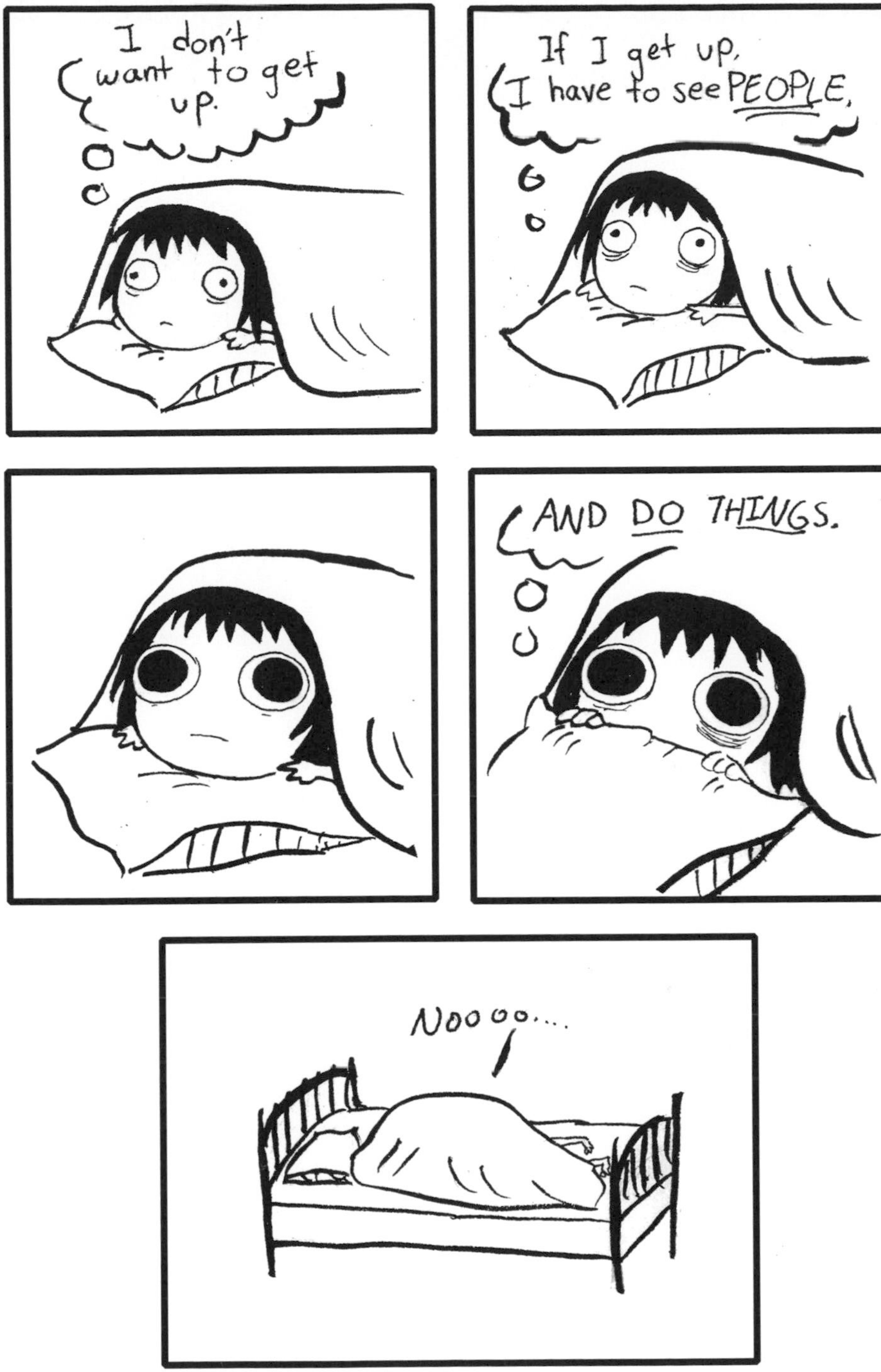
I don't want to get up.
If I get up, I have to see PEOPLE,
AND DO THINGS.
Noooo....

The original drawing and scan

Septemer 2012, you can see I got my act together just a tiny bit here. There are panels! This particular comic was inked by hand and then scanned.

I recall this being my first "hit"—my first real viral moment. It got over one hundred thousand notes on Tumblr. Looking back, I'm struck by how basic the idea is. There's not even really a punch line. Back in 2012, the style of relatable humor that is so ubiquitous today was just getting started, and small, mundane observations could get a lot of traction. Looking back at these comics, sometimes I'm surprised people found them funny at all.

While I find ideas like this sweet, today I feel my comics have to be a lot more clever and punchy to go viral.

've always been a lover of the macabre and, like many people, I joined the true-crime wave of the 2010s. I listened to all kinds of podcasts and had piles of books that told grim and gruesome stories. In recent years, however, I've found myself walking away from the genre. This happened after I read several stomach-churning pieces of writing in which victims' families described the impact such media had on them.

Also around the time of my change of heart, I relistened to an enormously popular true-crime podcast and, instead of trying to "solve the mystery," I put myself in the shoes of the victim's family. How would I feel if all the details of my loved one's murder were being pored over by countless strangers?

I think we need to reassess how and why we tell true-crime stories. Today, it is a genre fundamentally built on someone else's trauma, and it is rampant with people who will harass victims, fawn over serial killers, and wildly speculate, making real-life tragedies into a game of whodunit.

Journalists and writers have a responsibility to report in an ethical manner, to not sensationalize, and to center victims and survivors as opposed to their perpetrators. We need to examine problematic aspects that reveal societal biases, such as why marginalized missing persons don't receive the same media attention as white women. For my part, I regret writing comics about true crime in a casual and jokey manner. I think this contributed to the normalization of a culture that derives entertainment from the pain of others. If I could turn back the clock, I wouldn't write these comics.

I admit, I'm still fascinated with the darker aspects of life, and I understand why people—both writers and readers alike—are drawn to true crime in the first place. But for now, you'll find me in the fiction aisle.

COMMON WOMEN'S INTERESTS

ANIMALS
MAKE UP
FASHION
TRUE CRIME
And that's how they dissolved the body!
CLAP
CLAP
CLAP

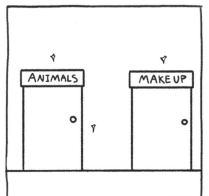

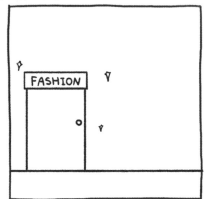

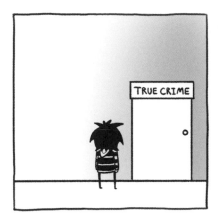

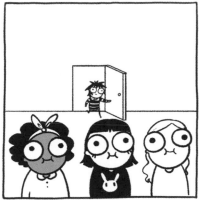

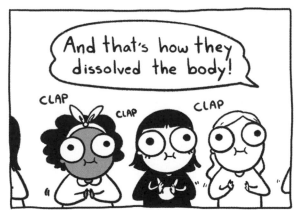

At the beginning of my career, I tried hard to be relatable. A lot of people whose careers depend on social media do this, as it's a reliable way to connect with and maintain audiences. To be clear, I still think relatable humor is great and valuable, especially in the sense that it helps other people feel more normal and "seen." For a long time, this was my mission with *Sarah's Scribbles*.

However, there was also a time when I felt trapped by this format. I think one of my better choices was giving myself the freedom to explore more niche jokes in my mid-twenties. I anticipated less engagement, but to my surprise, I still wound up with positive online reception for a lot of them. This taught me to trust my audience as well. I'm truly grateful for this encouragement because it took me on a creative path that I personally believe led to my strongest work.

The trust in my audience and a newfound confidence to explore led to two other series, *FANGS* and *Cryptid Club*. I felt free to dive into subjects that were a bit more "out there"—vampires, werewolves, and cryptids—and instead of reaching for relatability, during these projects I was able to dive into topics I truly loved. This passion fueled the creative energy in the pages and resulted in a whole new mode of thinking and writing for me.

Not only did this creative freedom lead to new projects but, in my opinion, it strengthened *Sarah's Scribbles* as well. When you compare this book with my first, there are entire paradigm shifts in what I'm writing about. *Sarah's Scribbles* now includes all kinds of wild characters, like biblically accurate angels, Dracula, ghosts, and more.

Overall, I would summarize this shift as going from writing what I know to writing what I love. I'd encourage all artists and writers to lean into this, as your passion for a subject will shine through in your work.

Eat him
Pro
Con
Date him
Pro
Con

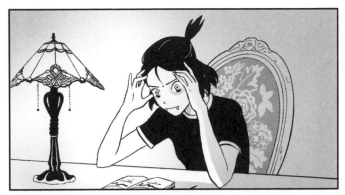

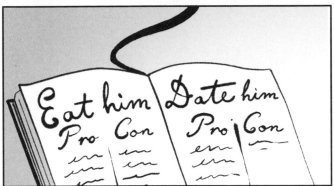

FANGS ***is a love story between a vampire and a werewolf. I still think Elsie, the vampire, is my finest creation.***

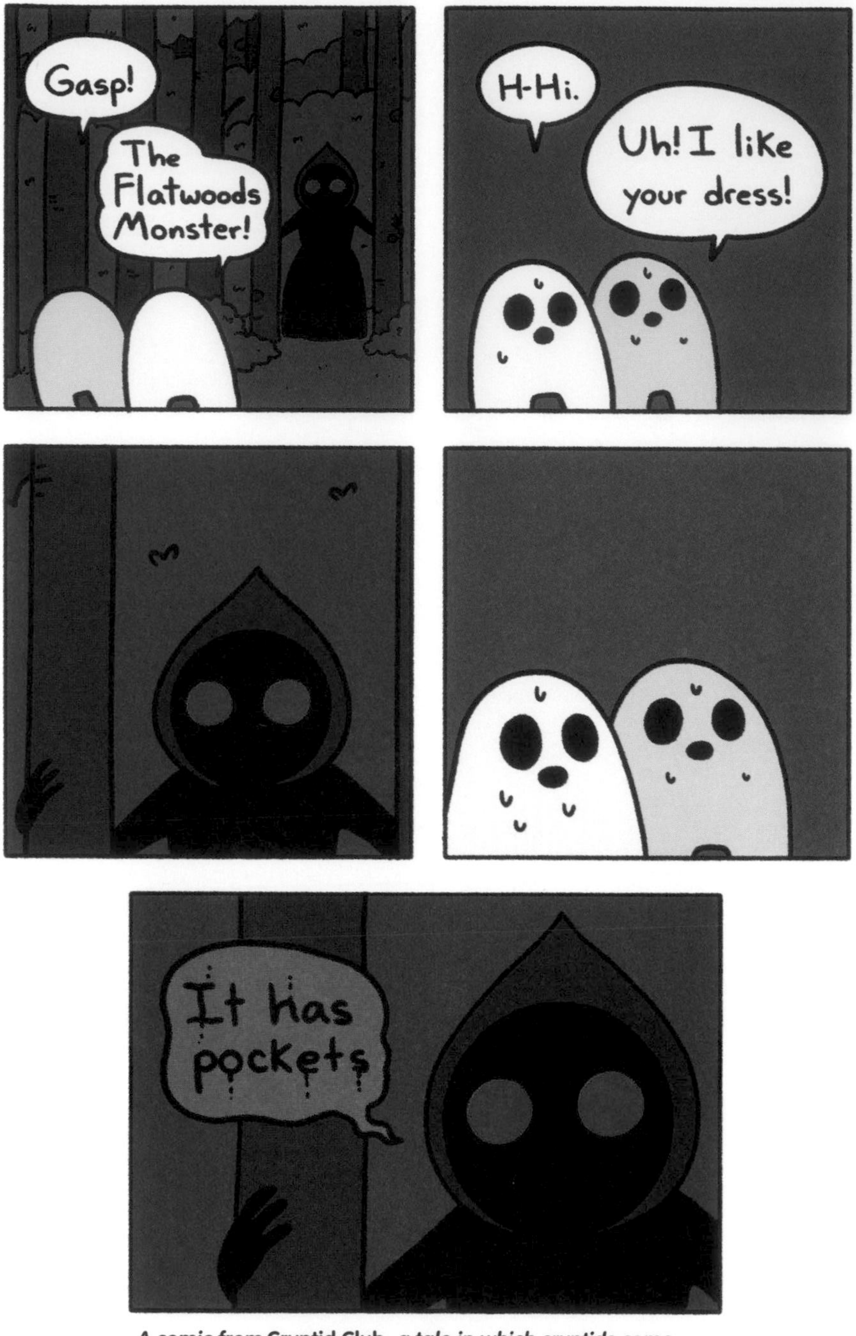

Gasp!
The Flatwoods Monster!
H-Hi.
Uh! I like your dress!
It has pockets

A comic from Cryptid Club*, a tale in which cryptids come together to understand each other.*

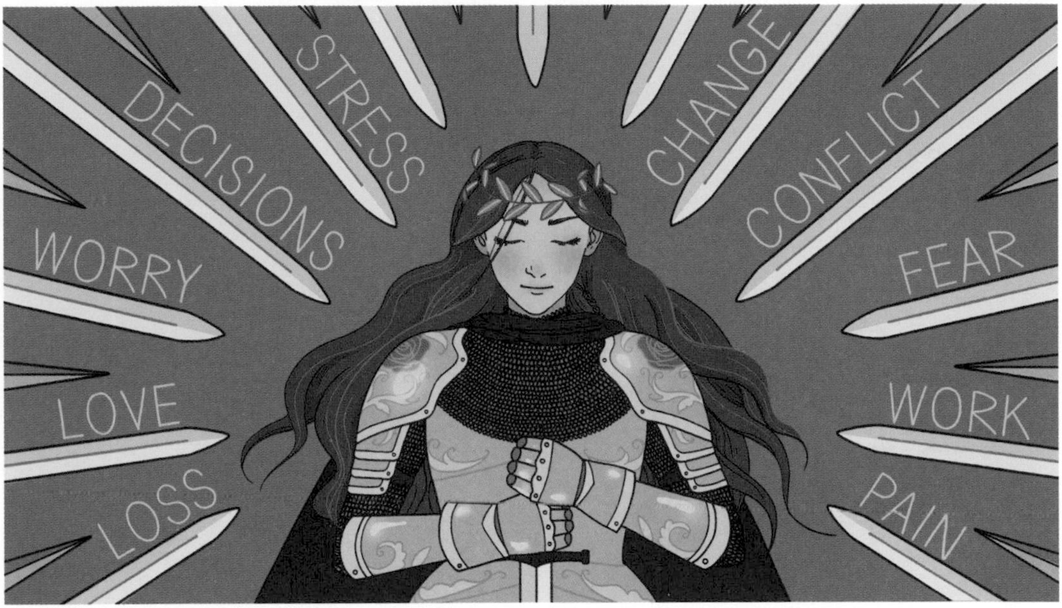
STRESS
DECISIONS
WORRY
LOVE
LOSS
CHANGE
CONFLICT
FEAR
WORK
PAIN

An example of my editorial cartooning work.

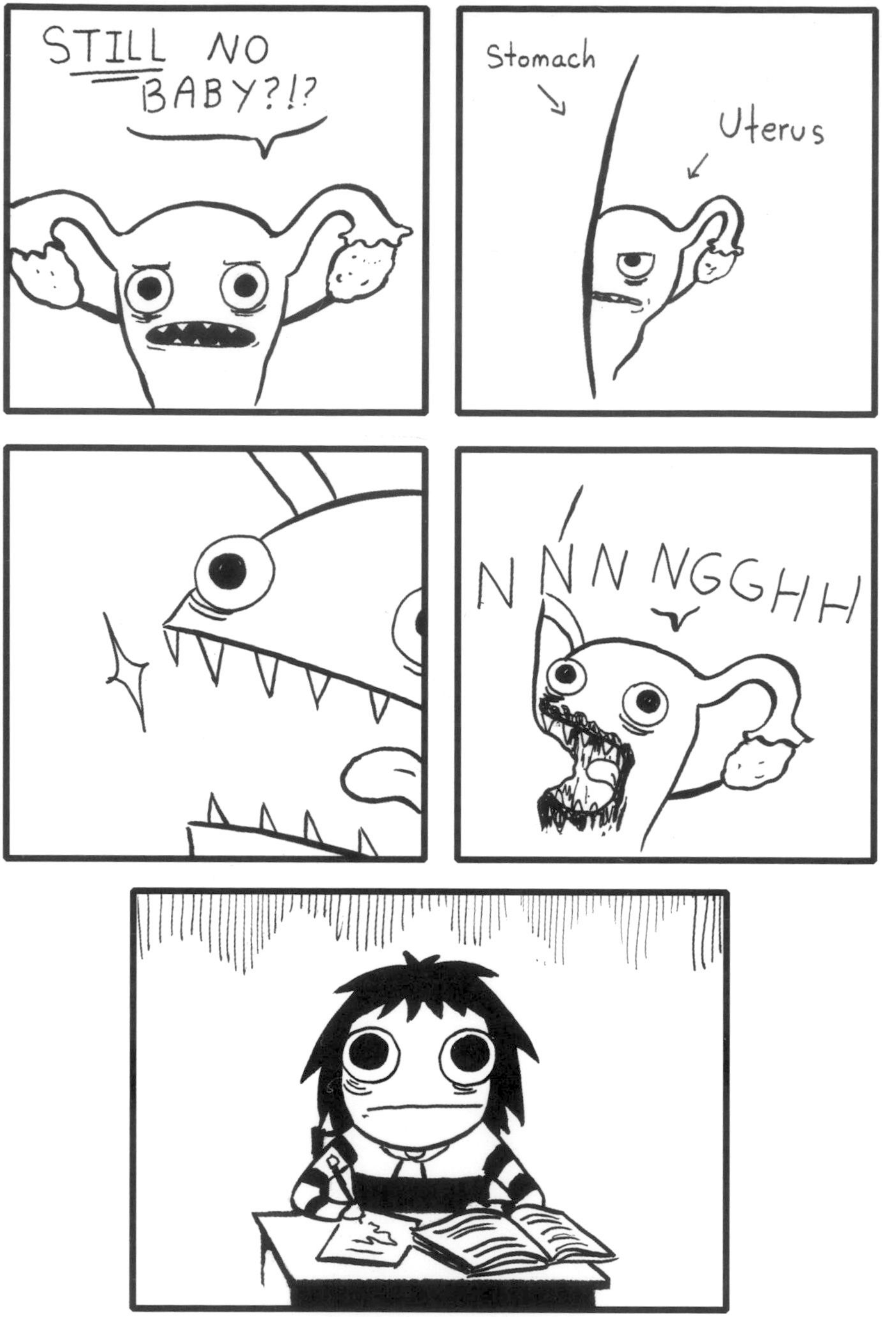
STILL NO BABY?!?
Stomach
Uterus
N N N NGGHH

The uterus character, like all* Sarah's Scribbles *characters, has evolved significantly in design.

Ah, the uterus, the primary antagonist of *Sarah's Scribbles* (other than alarm clocks). This was its first appearance in one of my comics. I wrote this comic in a far more conservative time, and I recall my classmates being shocked that I would upload it. I remember this comic receiving a strong reaction, much like the way people feel about their actual uteruses. Over time, the uterus became one of the most recognizable characters in the entire series, and I'm glad for it. After all the grief this organ has caused, I'm happy to have been part of collective venting.

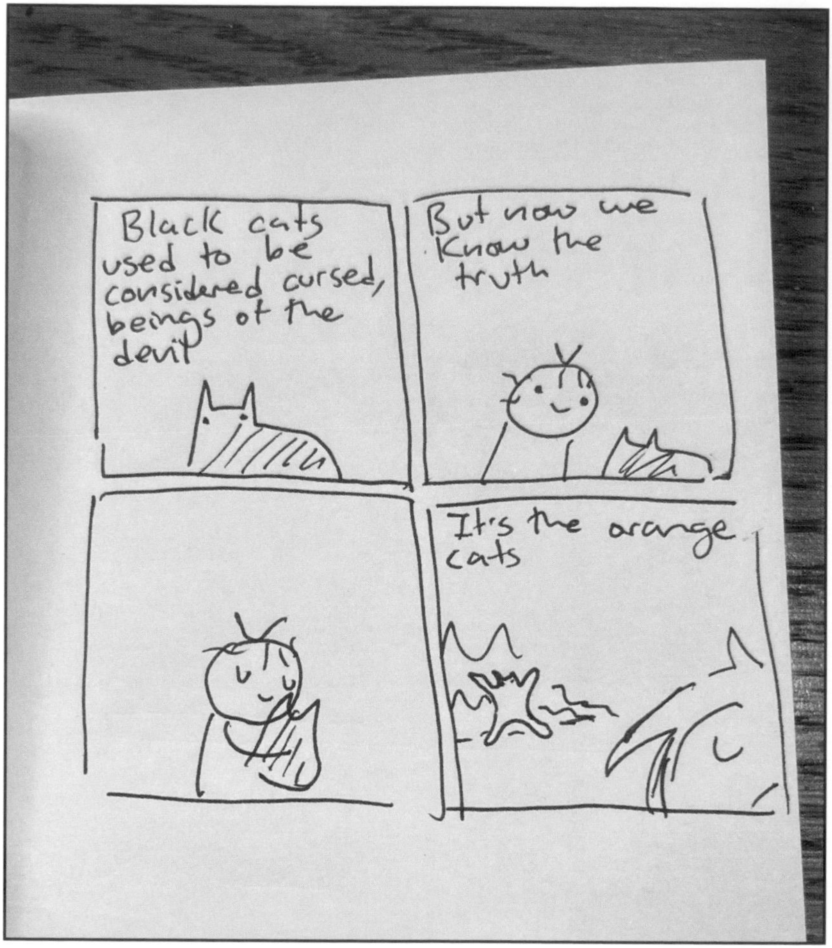
Black cats used to be considered cursed, beings of the devil
But now we know the truth
It's the orange cats

The idea sketch. You can see it's quite simple.

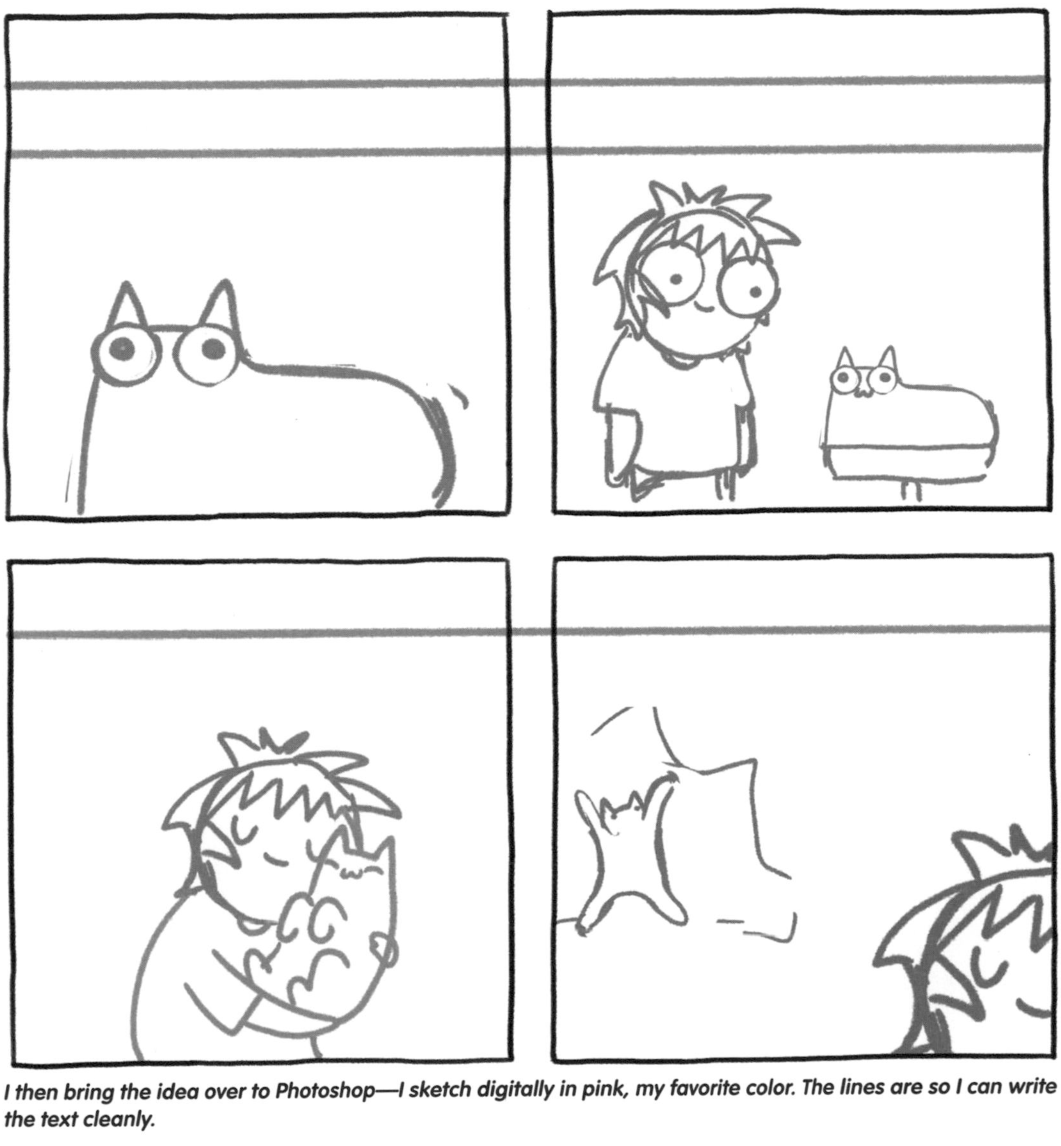

I then bring the idea over to Photoshop—I sketch digitally in pink, my favorite color. The lines are so I can write the text cleanly.

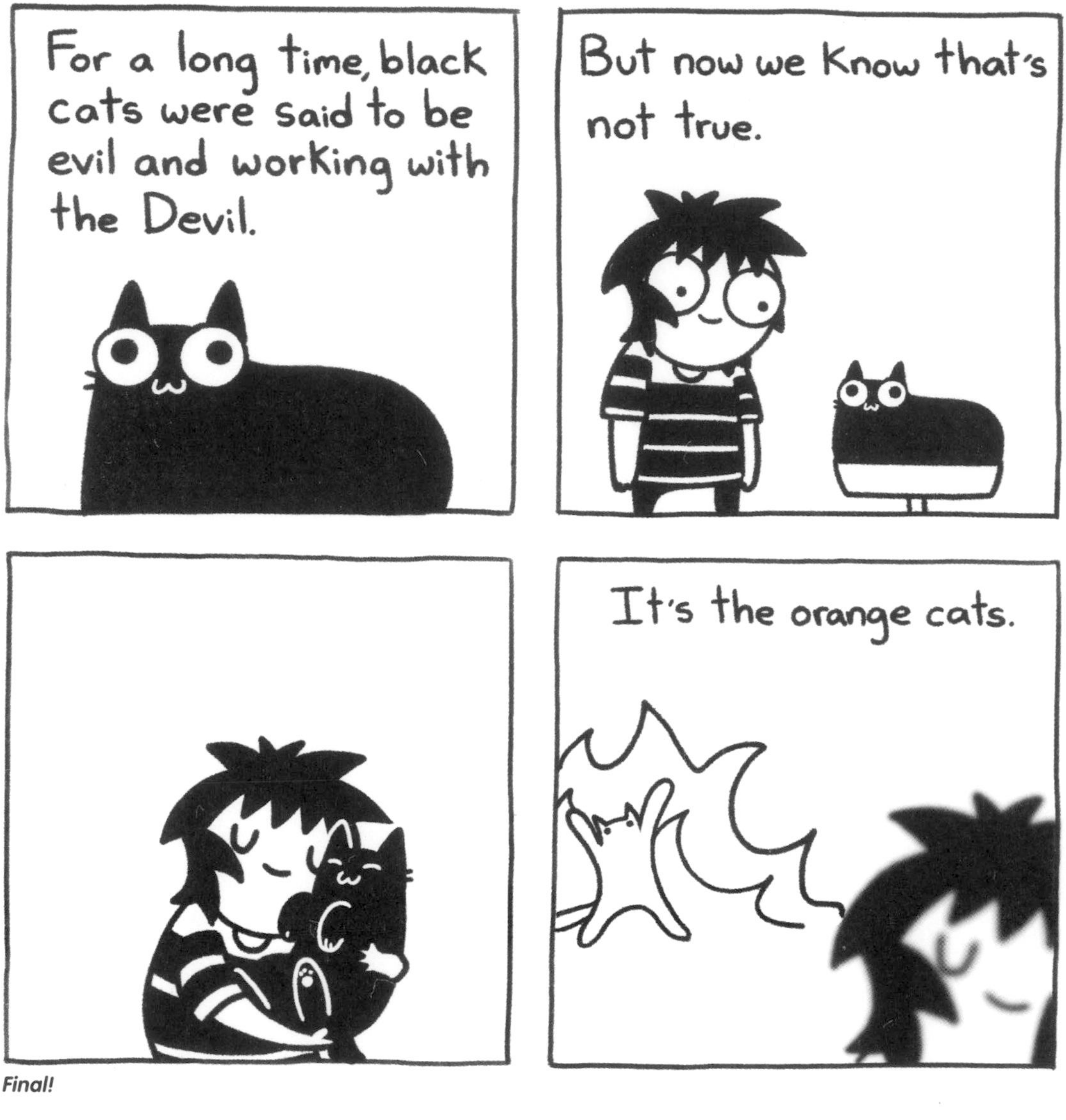
For a long time, black cats were said to be evil and working with the Devil.
But now we know that's not true.
It's the orange cats.

Final!

My process can be broken down into two simple parts: idea generation and final drawing. The first part, coming up with an idea, is infinitely more challenging than creating the final drawing.

For me, three things are necessary for coming up with an idea: a pen, a sketchbook, and a cup of coffee. (This part is not a joke. No coffee, no comics.) I keep my sketchbooks unsophisticated and sloppy. While I'm jealous of artists who have beautiful and organized sketchbooks, if I get hung up on the details of making my sketchbook look "nice," I will simply never come up with an idea. I try to leave every trace of perfectionism at the door and just let my mind flow.

As for finding the ideas, there's not much rhyme or reason to it. I try to ask myself a lot of questions—*What do I feel excited about at the moment? What's going on in the news? Has my cat done something odd or funny?* I haven't got this down to any kind of science, and the process can feel random. Sometimes, an idea will appear the moment I sit down to draw; sometimes, I'll struggle with my sketchbooks for days before I have something I like.

In comparison, drawing is a walk in the park. I'll redo the sketch in Photoshop and finalize the linework through my Wacom Cintiq tablet. While Photoshop is my go-to for *Sarah's Scribbles,* it's certainly not the only program I'd recommend. I did all of *FANGS* in Procreate.

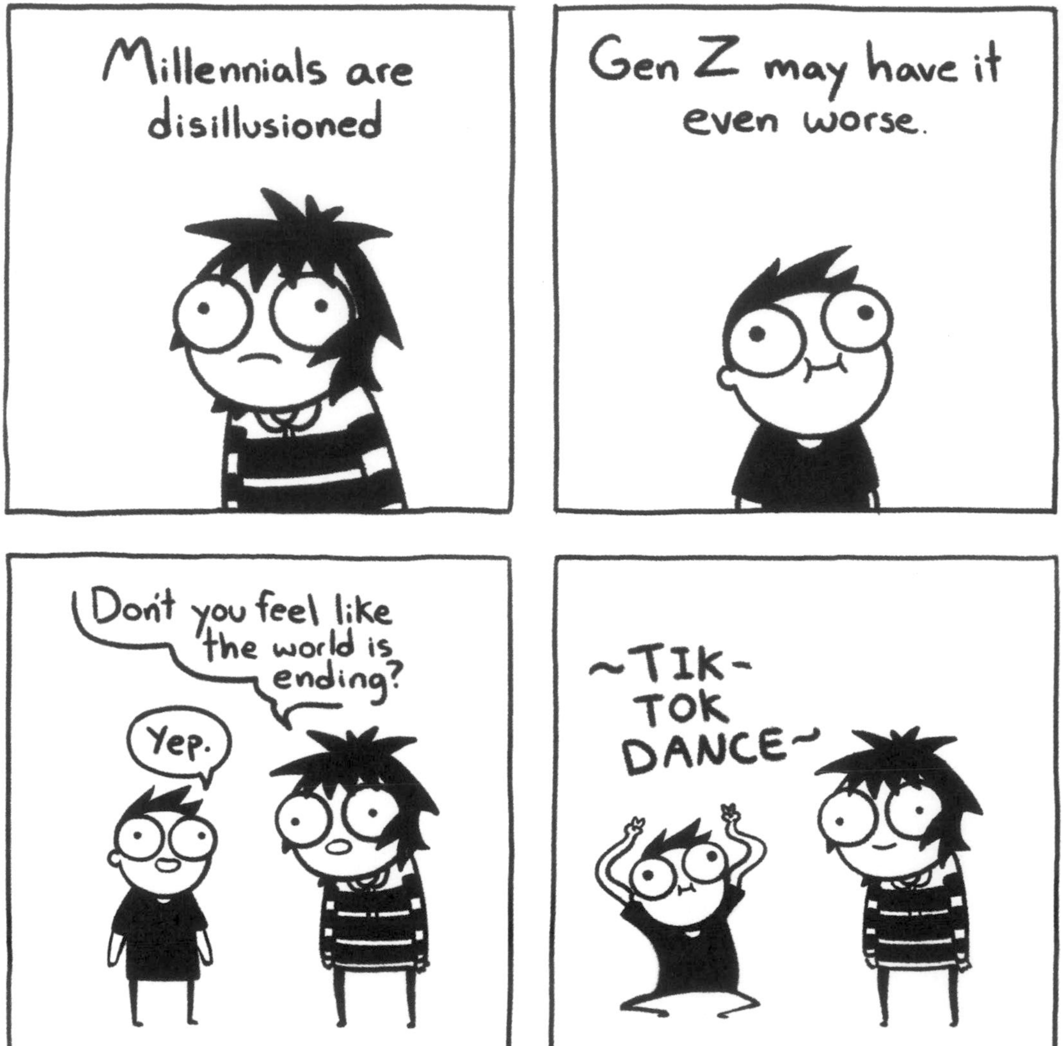
Millennials are disillusioned
Gen Z may have it even worse.
Don't you feel like the world is ending?
Yep.
~TIK-TOK DANCE~

When I started writing comics, I was writing about my own youth. Now, I'm starting to write comics about my age.

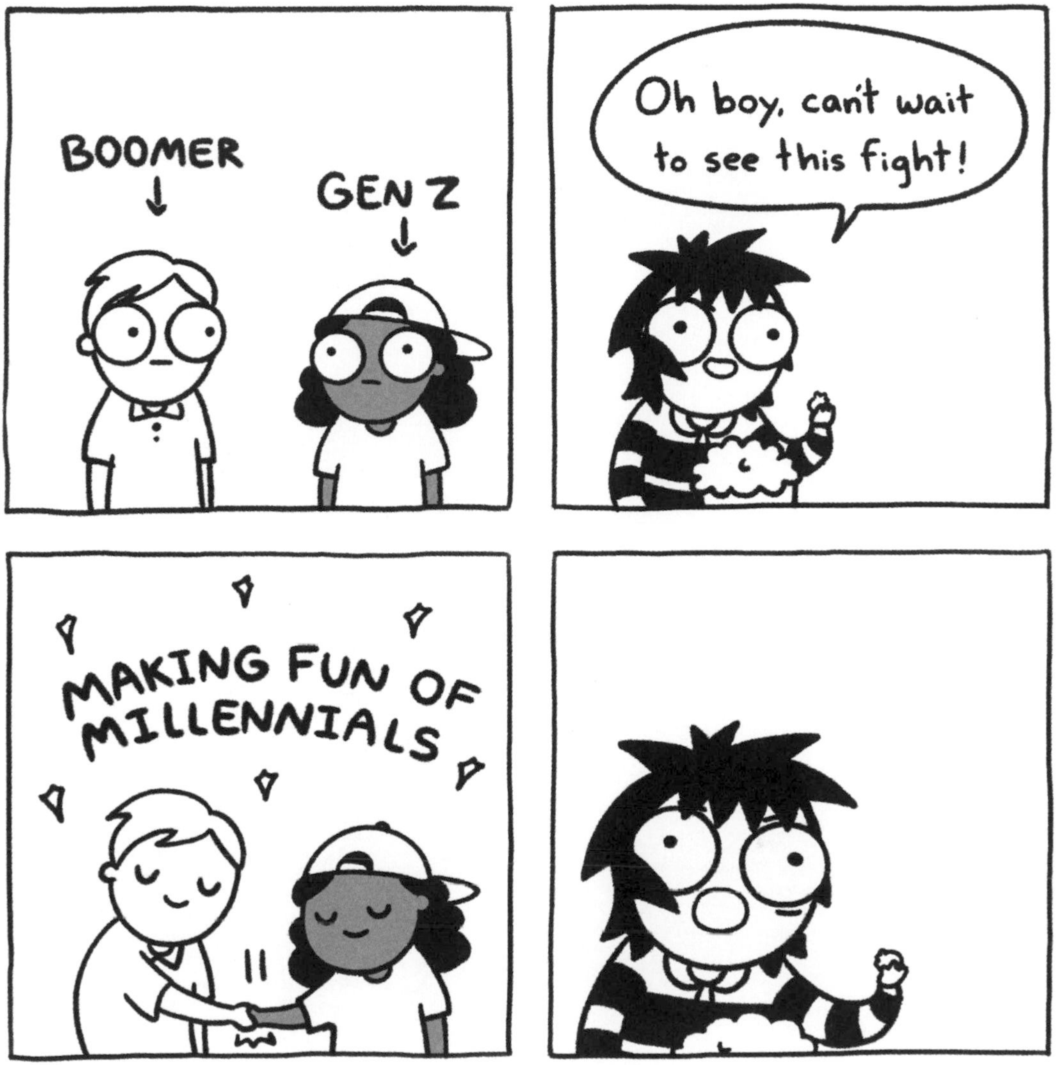
BOOMER
GEN Z
Oh boy, can't wait to see this fight!
MAKING FUN OF MILLENNIALS

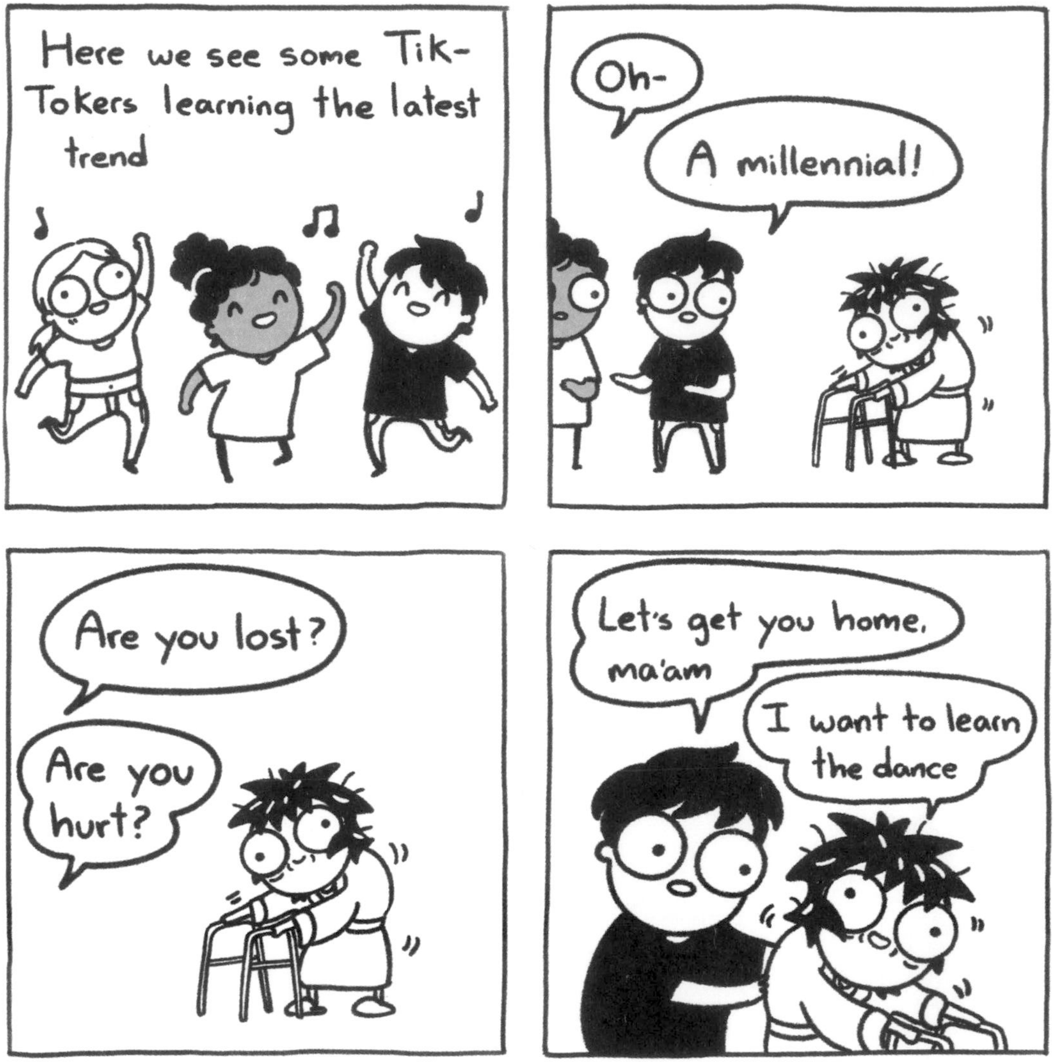

Here we see some Tik-Tokers learning the latest trend
Oh-
A millennial!
Are you lost?
Are you hurt?
Let's get you home, ma'am
I want to learn the dance

I will always be defined as a "millennial" cartoonist, for better or for worse. At the time I started writing comics, millennials were heavily scrutinized by older generations as the selfie-taking, Starbucks-sipping, avocado toast–munching generation. Millennials were subversive (and annoying) to their elders in many ways. Typical markers of adulthood were and continue to be nearly impossible to reach at the same age as boomers reached them, if they were ever reachable at all: buying a house, having kids, finding a steady and well-paying career. I also believe that the Internet allowed millennials to be more transparent about simple day-to-day struggles, and we made troves of memes and jokes that broke through the idea of maintaining a perfectly respectable veneer. This combination of factors, perhaps, gave older generations the impression that we were lazy and stuck in a state of permanent adolescence.

A lot of millennials reached adulthood and found that our happily-ever-afters weren't going to happen in the way we envisioned. And while that's unfair, I also believe this upset gave rise to a generation of thinkers who are now able to take unique and different paths in life. A lot of millennials I know challenge the status quo, resulting in new approaches to relationships, politics, careers, and purpose. I got lucky in my career, but I have also found myself pursuing a completely different life path than I expected. I find myself surrounded by peers who may not be married and living in a house but who have found meaning in life by maintaining strong friendships, pursuing their passions, and trying to change the world around them for the better. After mucking through our own disappointment, I believe that millennials may have laid the groundwork for Gen Z to be a truly revolutionary generation.

I have no interest in putting down Gen Z or nitpicking them. When I write comics about intergenerational differences, of which there are myriad, I try not to make the punch line at the expense of Gen Z. Every Gen Z person I've met is sharper, funnier, and more socially aware than I ever was in my teenage-hood or early twenties. There is sometimes a pessimism about them that makes me sad, because I wish we had succeeded in handing them a better world, one that isn't ravaged by climate change, late-stage capitalism, and unending culture wars. There's an instinct online to pit Gen Z and millennials against each other in the same way boomers and millennials waged war, but my hope is that we can have the grace to reach out to Gen Z in a way that is positive and productive. Despite currently being branded as "cringey"—and we are sometimes, I admit it!—millennials did so much pondering and transforming in their youth that I hope we can pass some of our wisdom down. In the end, we are two generations that were given the short end of the stick, and we should try to band together to forge a new path.

Much has been said about the fact that I don't write a lot about Gen X. A lot of this comes down to the simple fact that I don't know Gen Xers well enough to be insightful about them. I was raised by boomers and surrounded by millennials. I'm sorry, Gen X. I love you; I just don't know how to represent you accurately. Your music rocks, though!

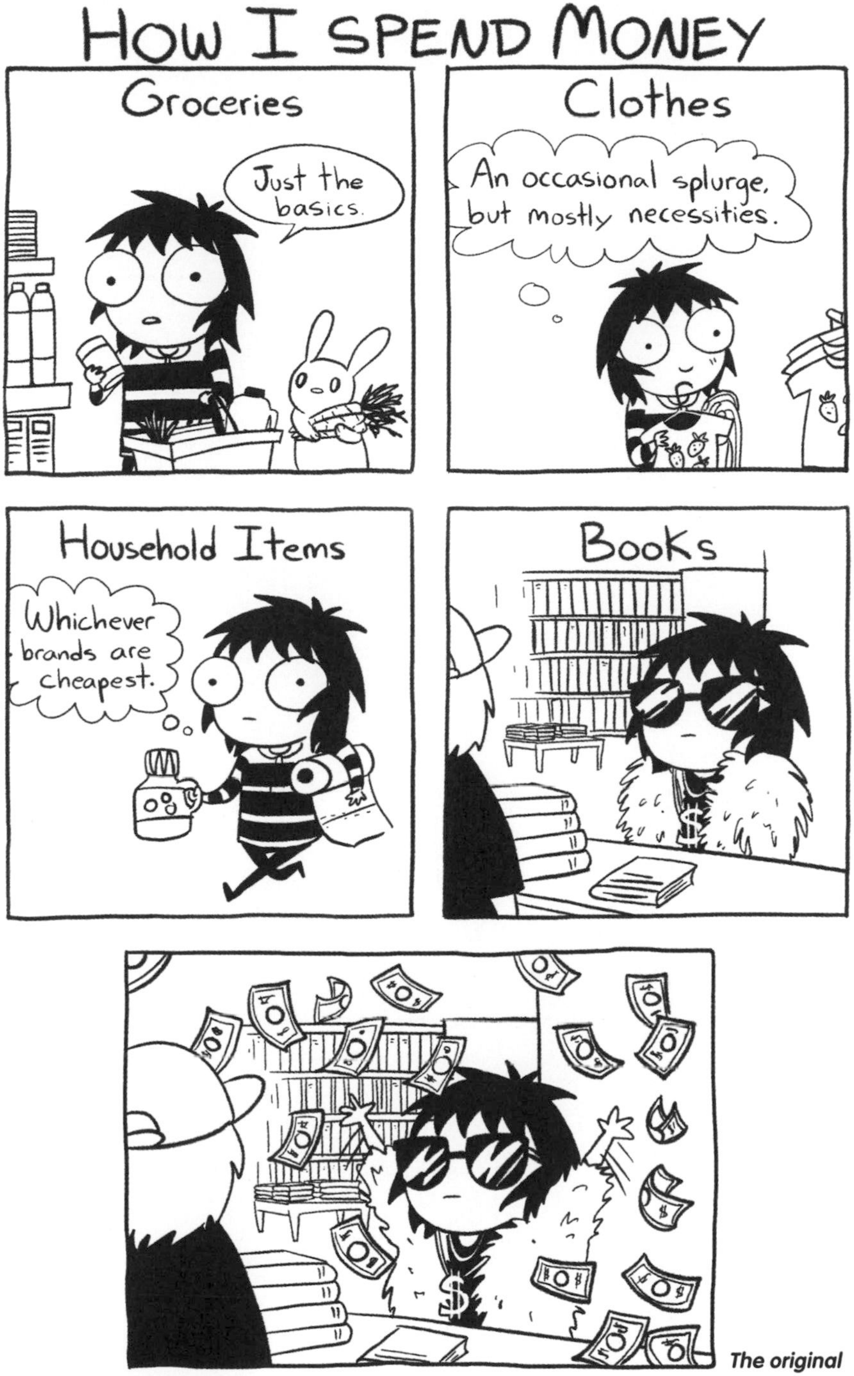
HOW I SPEND MONEY
Groceries
Just the basics.
Clothes
An occasional splurge, but mostly necessities.
Household Items
Whichever brands are cheapest.
Books

The original

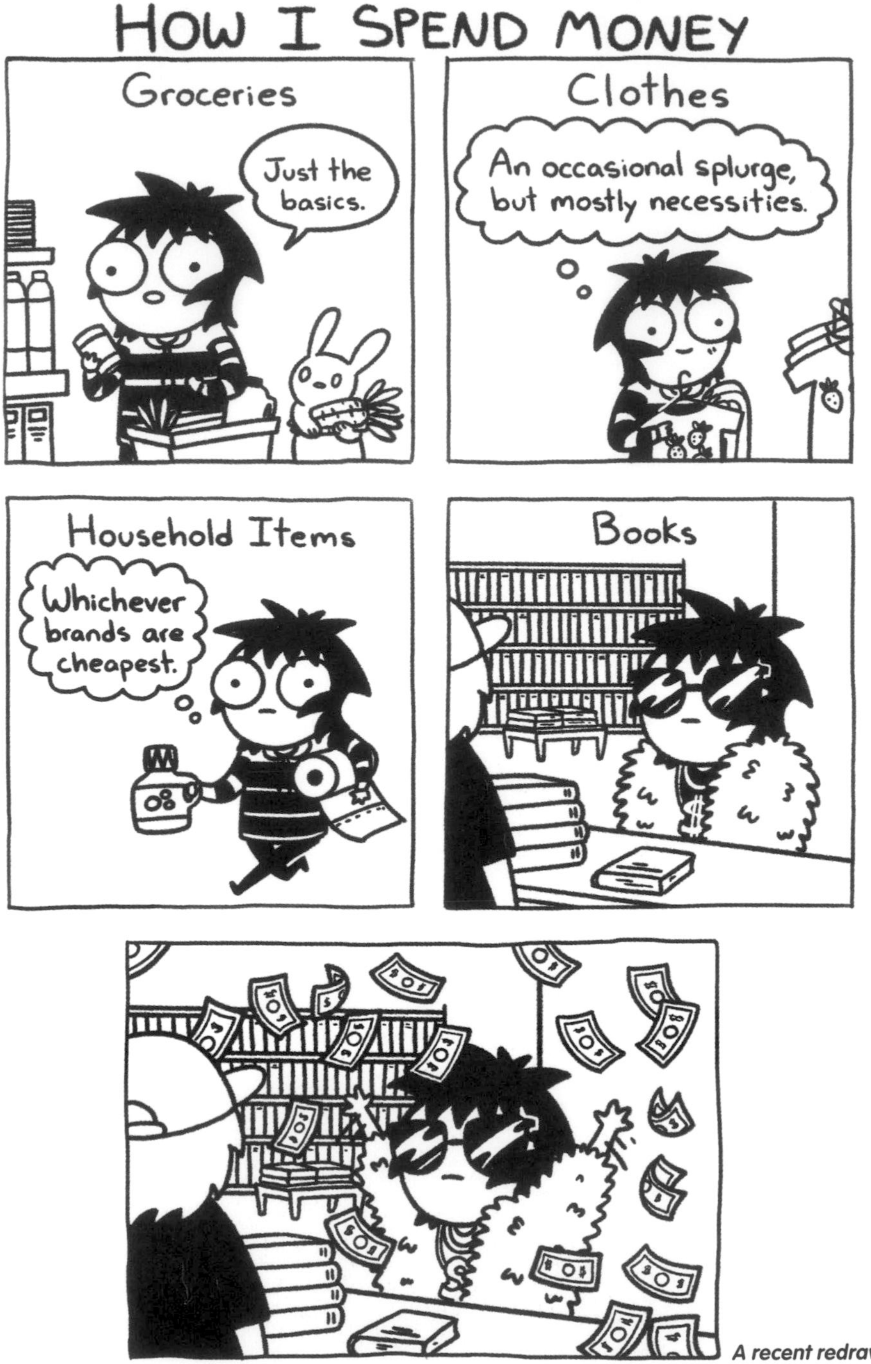
HOW I SPEND MONEY
Groceries
Just the basics.
Clothes
An occasional splurge, but mostly necessities.
Household Items
Whichever brands are cheapest.
Books

A recent redraw

I think this is the most meme-ified comic of my entire career. People edit the final panels to reflect all sorts of interests, from records to mushroom foraging. The viral nature of this comic surprised me a lot. I only uploaded it because I was so wrapped up in meeting a separate deadline that I picked a comic from my scrap pile. I expected it to underperform. As a cartoonist, sometimes you get strong feelings about what will be received well versus what won't, but in the end the reception is unpredictable.

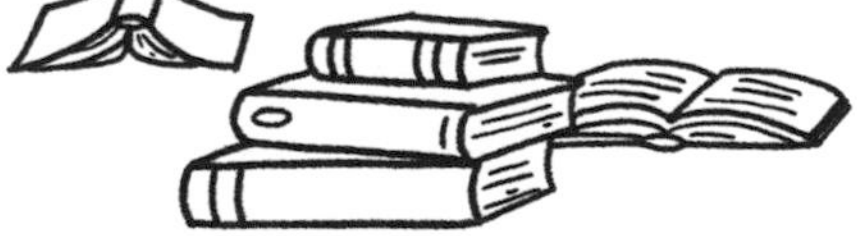

Another comic I regret. If I'm honest, there are quite a few of these, and it was hard to pick out which to reflect on. It's amazing how much your views can change over a decade. Some of my older comics have antiquated views on gender roles; others are overly self-critical of my appearance to the point of being toxic. However, this comic really stood out to me as something I have done a full 180 on.

While it's true that stress and anxiety cause or worsen some conditions, the past few years have been a major realization for me in terms of health care. The system can be complex and inaccessible to the point of madness, bogging down doctors and nurses who entered the field out of a genuine desire to do good. In our clinics, pain is often dismissed or minimized, with serious conditions frequently being chocked up to anxiety. And while anxiety is in and of itself serious, there's an entire world of other causes for physical pain or discomfort that often go unexamined.

When I turned thirty, I was diagnosed with a rare GI condition that was repaired through surgery. I only went to a new doctor because I randomly stumbled upon a TikTok of someone talking about their experience with the same condition. I spent thirty years of my life with constant stomachaches and nausea, and after doctors' visits were unproductive in my teenage years, I had gaslit myself into believing that my pain was a physical manifestation of stress.

This experience fundamentally changed how I view pain. Though the mind is powerful, not everything is mental. Some conditions have a complex road to diagnosis, and so often people, especially women, are not given the care that they deserve. My heart goes out to all of those who, like I once did, know deep down that something is wrong but haven't been able to find answers yet.

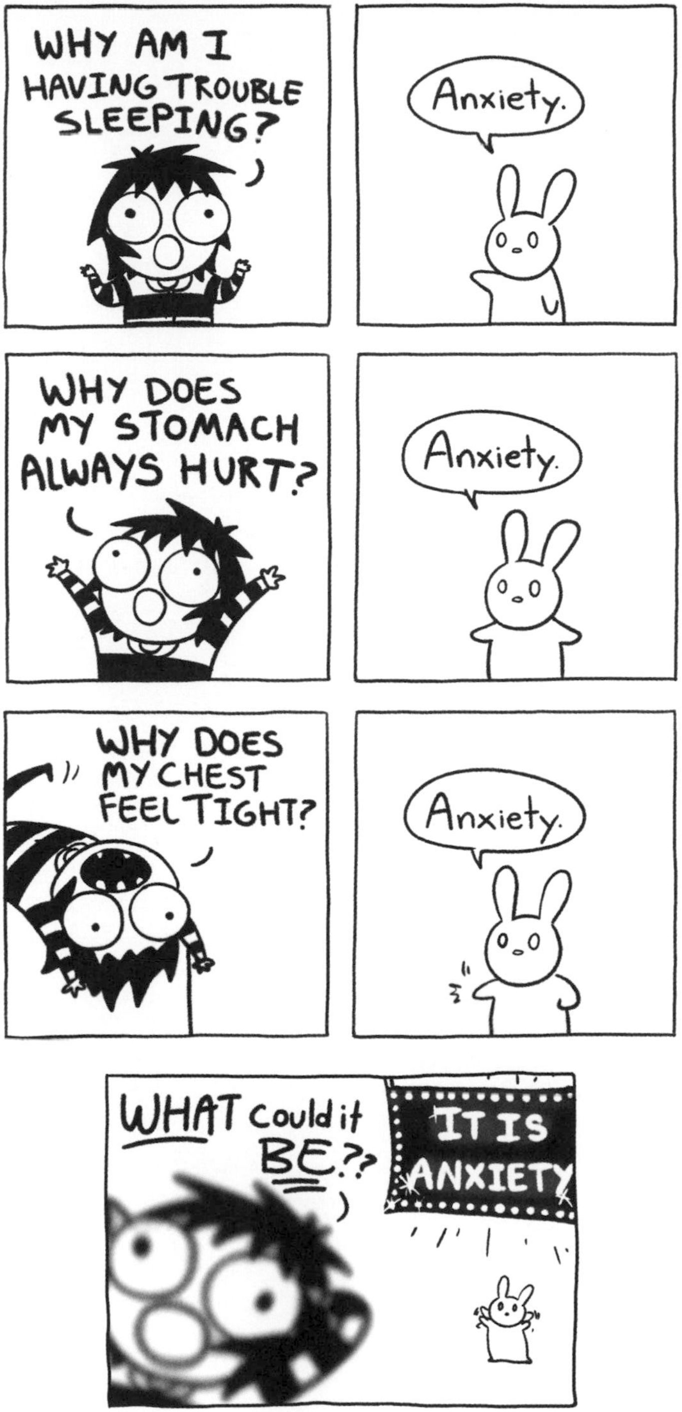
WHY AM I HAVING TROUBLE SLEEPING?
Anxiety.
WHY DOES MY STOMACH ALWAYS HURT?
Anxiety.
WHY DOES MY CHEST FEEL TIGHT?
Anxiety.
WHAT could it BE??
IT IS ANXIETY

In 2017, I underwent a harassment campaign from a particularly vile section of the Internet. At complete random, a white supremacist forum started editing my work and spreading it to reflect their repulsive Nazi ideas. I've written about this experience before, but I still find that a lot of people don't know it happened and how monumentally it affected my life and work.

This is the comic that I personally saw them editing the most, so I want to give it a moment to stand on its own without any sinister message. In the months that followed, I had a difficult time writing because I was so afraid of how my message might get twisted and corrupted. I forced myself to continue because I was desperate for the legacy of *Sarah's Scribbles* not to succumb to racism, and in the end the harassment did eventually die out, months after it began.

In hindsight, it was a massive learning experience for me. In an attempt to understand what was happening, I started educating myself more seriously about politics and social issues. In my own privilege, I had felt relatively optimistic under the then-recent Obama presidency, but the harassment led me to confront how much I had missed. To this day, white supremacy and systemic racism is still an active and malignant presence in the United States. Before the harassment campaign, if someone had told me that there were Nazis operating in the U.S. in any sort of significant way, I might have been doubtful. I watched a similar shock echo through the U.S. after the Charlottesville rally.

While I don't wish this experience on anyone, it allowed me to shed my naivety and truly educate myself. It was through a lot of reading, as well as listening to speakers and educators, that my past ignorance fell away and I became more informed. I have tried to use that knowledge to show up in a productive way in my private and professional life. I am forever grateful to the many activists and writers whose material helped me take a negative experience and contextualize it. Through this second education, I was able to mold myself into someone new: someone with more perspective and someone capable of greater compassion.

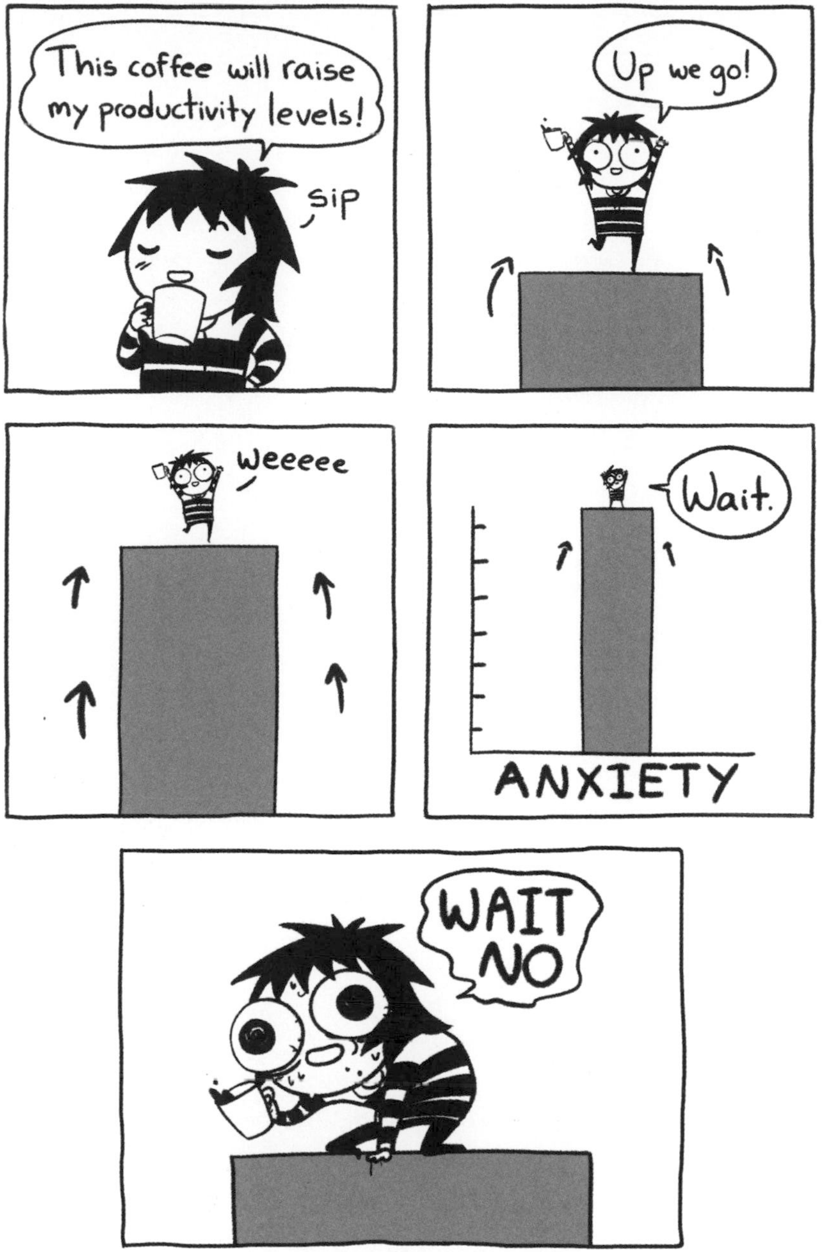
This coffee will raise my productivity levels!
sip
Up we go!
weeeee
Wait.
ANXIETY
WAIT NO

For years, I felt some kind of fight-or-flight reaction when I saw this comic, because it was edited and spread widely by white supremacists to reflect an anti-immigrant message, something I would never condone.

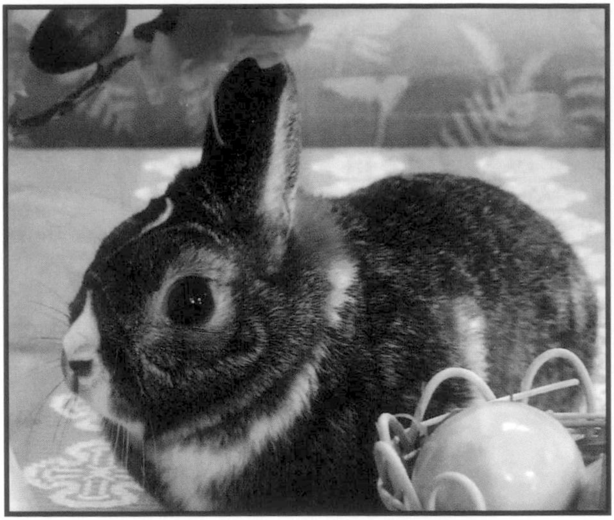

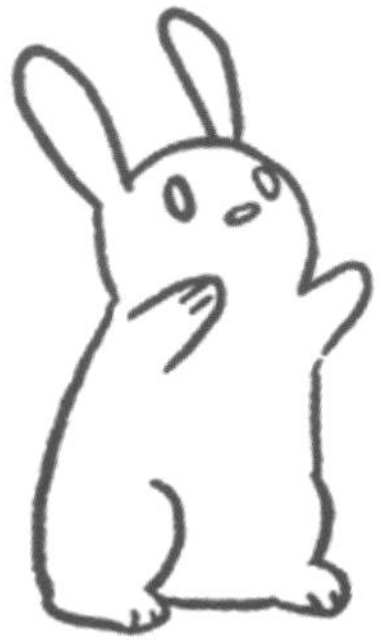

Sunshine, my childhood pet, next to the character he inspired

Harley, the true star of Sarah's Scribbles

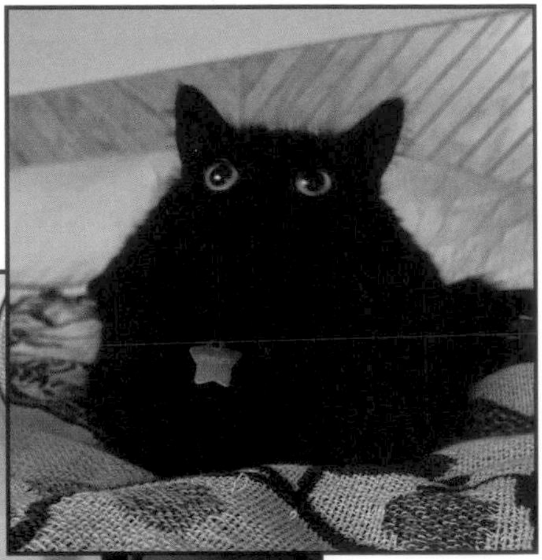

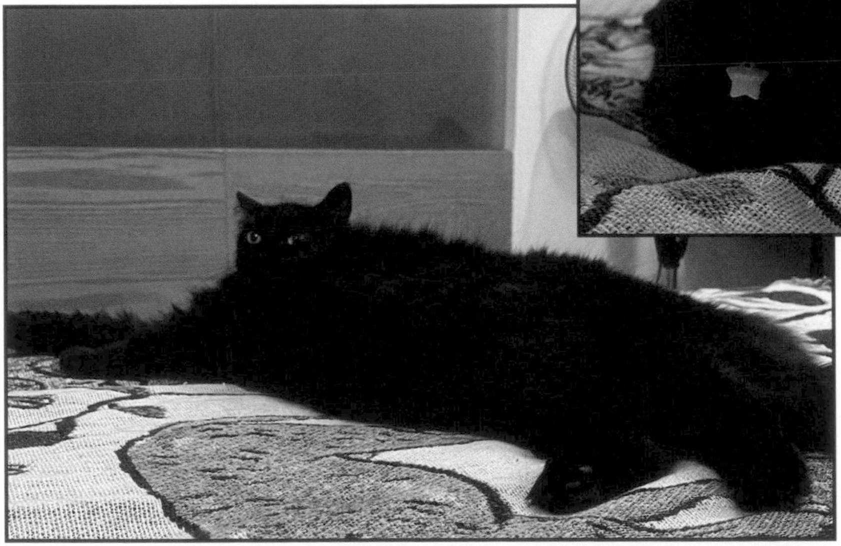

A lot of people want to know if the animals of *Sarah's Scribbles* are real, and they are! Pets are family members, and I'm happy to introduce you to mine.

In the early years of *Sarah's Scribbles,* not knowing how to otherwise externalize the main character's thoughts, I often drew "Sarah" in conversation with a rabbit. I was drawing from the animal-human dynamic in *Calvin and Hobbes,* my favorite newspaper comic, as well as my childhood pet, a rabbit named Sunshine.

Some pets are just special. He was just as calm, sweet, and wise as the comic rabbit was portrayed, and we spent many hours of my childhood and teenage-hood cuddling together on the couch while I drew, read, or watched TV. Now that he's passed, from time to time, he comes to visit me in my dreams.

The cat is, of course, also real and is based on the cat I have today, Harley. I've often heard people express how surprised they are at how identical she is to the comic version of herself, down to the large, expressive eyes. She's amazing—funny, sweet, stubborn, and often unintentionally hilarious. She frequently interrupts my writing by coming to yell at me for food, and in turn I interrupt her napping and daydreaming by coming to give her pets.

As for the dog, it's an amalgamation of my friends' pets and a character I designed to write about dogs and my love for them. One of my big goals in the future is to own a dog; I just need approval from Miss Harley.

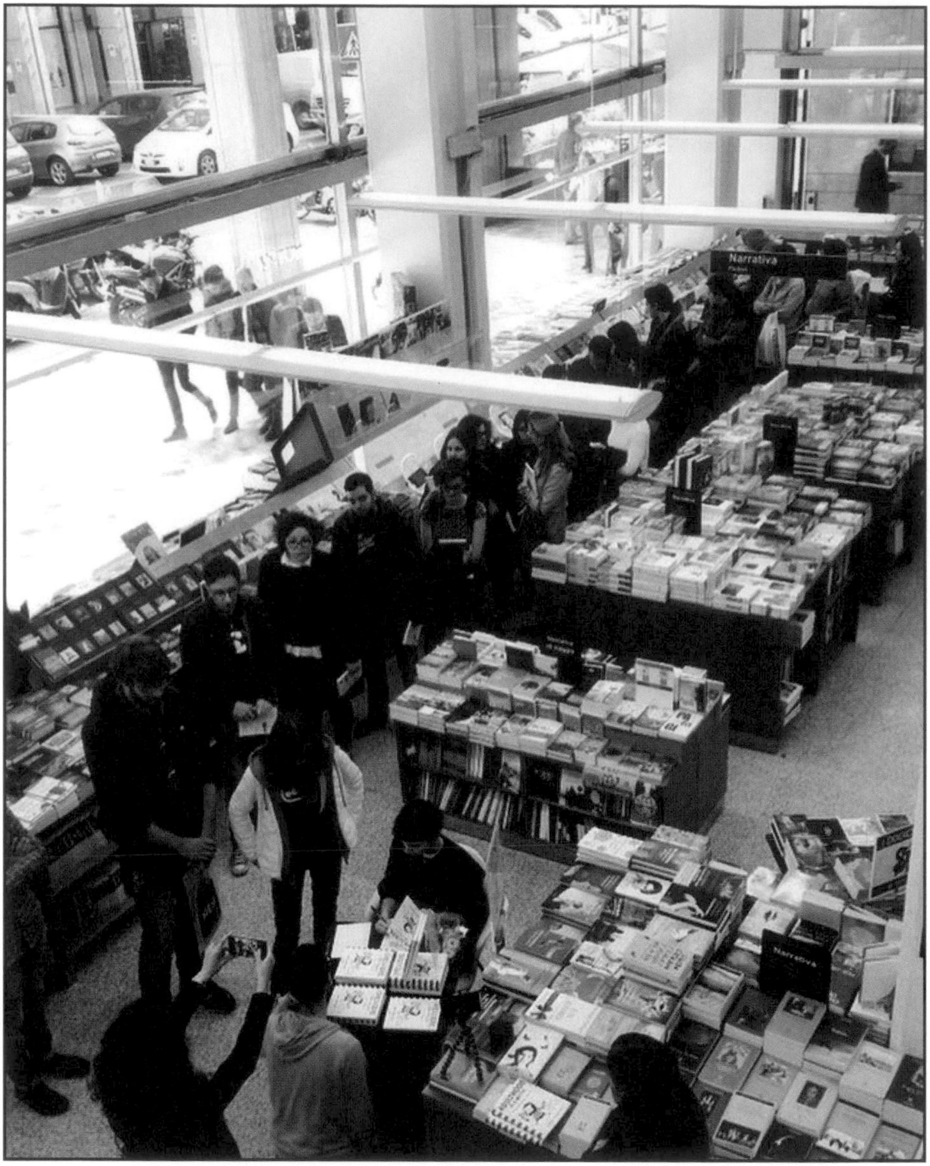
Narrativa
Narrativa

This photo was taken at my first ever book tour. I couldn't believe that so many people had shown up. I was so nervous that my hands were shaking when I signed books. I had believed I was an adult, but I was so young and really had no clue what lay ahead of me.

I mentioned in an earlier essay that I used to be naive. Severely so. When I started drawing comics, I was coming off the heels of the explosive careers of women like Allie Brosh and Kate Beaton. At the time, I truly believed that my gender wouldn't impact my career significantly, and I dove in totally unprepared.

I noticed misogyny first online, when people found photos of me and obsessed over my pixie cut. There was a consensus at the time that I'd be much prettier if I had long hair, to the point that someone photoshopped long hair onto me to "prove" this point. I noticed it when people started making explicit images of my characters or of myself. I noticed it when I got obsessive, repetitive messages that kept up for months from men declaring their love for me in graphic detail. I noticed it just recently, a few months ago, when someone made sexualized deepfakes not of one of my characters but of me.

Perhaps my most disappointing experiences were in person. When I attended comic cons or art events, I started dreading the appearance of what I called in my mind "that guy." A man, usually one in the industry and with power, who would cross my boundaries, make odd or sexual remarks, or keep his hands lingering around me in ways that would make my skin crawl. At times, before a convention or a signing, I'd try to tell myself that it wouldn't happen again, that the past times had just been unfortunate but random occurrences. But "that guy" is always there. I felt most deflated when men who I admired, sometimes since childhood, turned out to be "that guy." I saw them as heroes, and in turn, they saw me as an object.

I thought a combination of power and age might mitigate some of these interactions—I'm now in my thirties and have spent a decade in the industry. It hasn't helped.

When I decided to write this particular entry, I asked myself why I would write it. Does it come off as complaining when I point out the misogyny and harassment I experience when I have otherwise been so fortunate and have had such a kind and loyal readership?

In response to this self-doubt, I wish to counter these negative experiences with something that often happened alongside them. A woman pulling me aside, having noticed an odd interaction and asking if I was all right. Someone sharing that she had the same experience. Emails and messages of support when I would occasionally speak up. Once, even a hashtag in support of me! A man believing me and taking steps to protect me. All of this added up to a quiet but powerful consensus, a consensus I wish to share with all of you reading.

I'm no longer one of a handful of female webcomic artists. Young artists are in a clash with the old art world, one that sadly often enabled predatory behavior and exhibited a dismissive attitude toward artists who didn't fall into a very specific category. But, now, art and webcomics are exploding with talent from women and people across the gender spectrum, and so I would like to tell them that if they have these negative experiences, they are real. We see it, too, and it's not okay. At times, navigating these types of waters feels exhausting to the point of being impossible, but it's not, and we are here to offer you a life raft. This world, this industry, will change. Do reach out.

Turning thirty is a little like hitting puberty again. Your body changes in weird ways (I got my first gray hair!), people view you differently ("you look good" changes to "you look young"), and it's a time when people find themselves questioning a lot about their identity and their lives. Just recently, for the first time, I was asked in an interview what my secret to looking youthful is!

In the beginning of my career, in my early twenties, I wrote about how much I struggled to be an adult, to the extent that my first book was called *Adulthood Is a Myth*. By the time I hit thirty, I had gotten a grip on some of the day-to-day things like cooking, hitting my deadlines, and baseline self-care, but I was surprised to find how much I still didn't know.

I dreaded turning thirty and wrote doomsday-style comics about it. However, I had hoped that by the time I actually *turned* thirty, I would have fully unlearned some of the antiquated thinking that declares women "old" at that age. Or that being "old" is even a bad thing! It is a privilege to age, and while I knew that intellectually, alas, it is difficult to emotionally shed concepts that have been ingrained in us since childhood. I turned thirty and panicked.

But with the panic came a lot of self-reflection. We tell ourselves over and over again that there will be a point in our lives where we have it "all figured out." At thirty, I certainly didn't. And at thirty-one, I still don't. And somehow life keeps going. I'm deeply confused about what I want next in life, how to proceed in my career, and what sorts of things I want to focus on. Do I want to write more? Illustrate more? Do I want to abandon it all and go raise some chickens in the woods? Who knows?!

But what I do know firmly is this: While I may not know what will come next, I do know myself much more deeply than I did at twenty. I know my boundaries, I know what I like, I know how I need others to treat me and how I need to treat others. I have a very strong sense of "me." I often look back at teenage and early twenties me, who was so lost in her sense of self that she just followed others or accepted conditional love in a hope of finding something meaningful. Sometimes, I wish I could take her place or give her a hug. The paradox, of course, being that I had to go through those years and those feelings in order to become a better and more defined version of myself.

Being thirty is weird, an age full of contradictions. I feel simultaneously much more at peace but still lost and confused. I feel young, but goddamn, my back hurts. Perhaps this confusion is a gift. If I "had it all figured out," maybe that would be limiting. Being lost also means that there are things to be found, new opportunities to grow and explore.

BIRTHDAYS

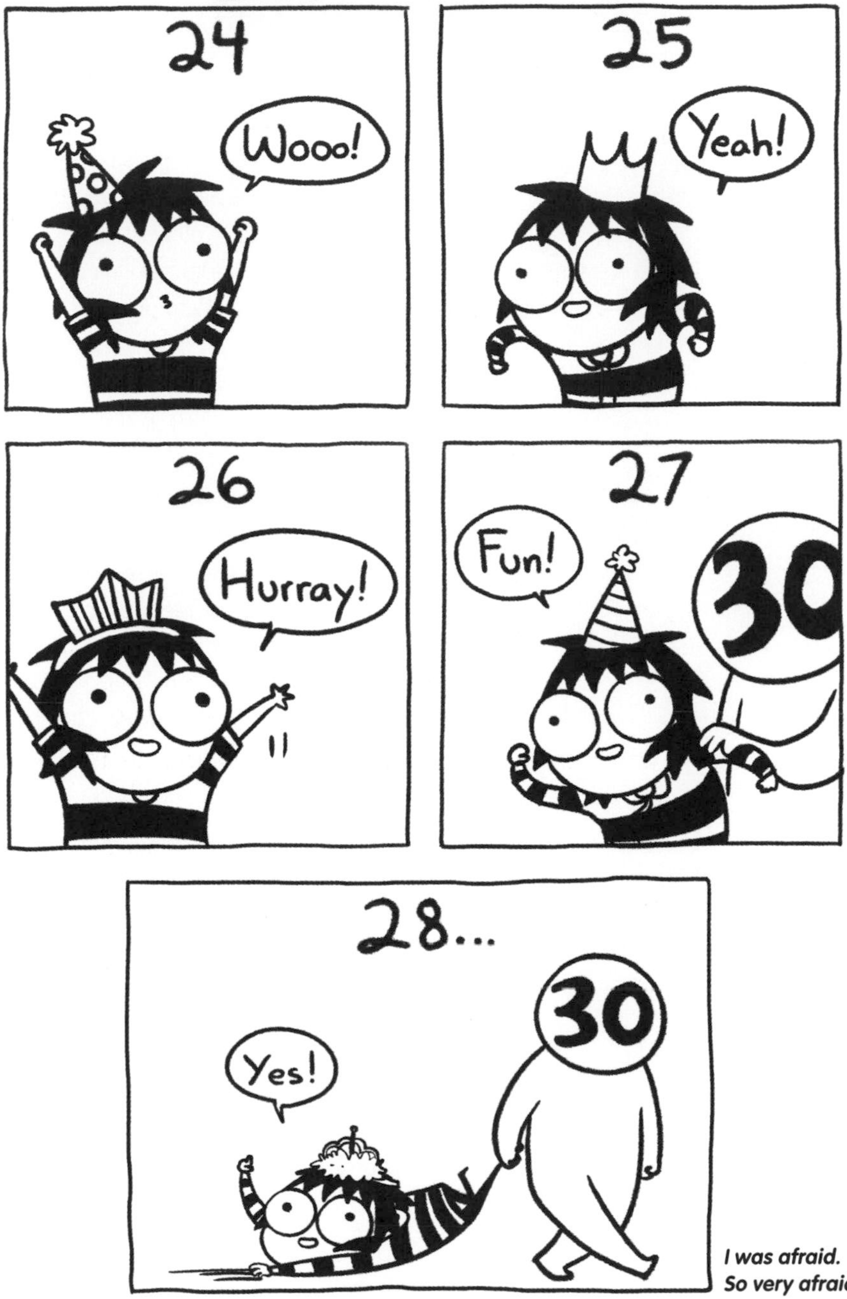
24
Wooo!
25
Yeah!
26
Hurray!
27
Fun!
30
28...
Yes!
30

I was afraid.
So very afraid.

Sarah's Scribbles started, oddly enough, during a time in my life that was pretty miserable. As a college student who struggled to make friends and keep up with the new challenges of adulthood, I was at my most lost and confused when I drew those first panels. I was plagued with feelings that I was fundamentally different from others. Everyone around me seemed to possess some kind of veneer of perfection that I couldn't understand or attain. "This is supposed to be the time of my life," I frequently thought, "so why isn't it?"

That is all to say, *Sarah's Scribbles* was a way for me to vent my own frustration. And the response I got was unexpected and powerful. Suddenly, thousands of people online were saying that they could relate to my feelings. That, yes, being a young adult is hard. That being a human is really hard! Slowly, over time, I felt the veil that divided myself from the world start to lift. We are all different, but sometimes in the details and in the small things, we are actually exactly alike.

This is a profound lesson that you, my reader, gave to me. Over a decade later, I'm no longer a college student stuck in a rut, but I am still continuing to search for the small things that connect us. To be able to do this work is the privilege of my life, and it is all thanks to you.

Thank you to everyone who picked up this book or who read, shared, and perhaps chuckled at my comics over the years—I am so grateful.

About the Author

Sarah Andersen is a cartoonist and illustrator from
New England. She likes coffee, cats, and covens.

Adulthood Is a Gift!

Andrews McMeel Publishing
a division of Andrews McMeel Universal
1130 Walnut Street, Kansas City, Missouri 64106

www.andrewsmcmeel.com

24 25 26 27 28 SDB 10 9 8 7 6 5 4 3 2 1
ISBN: 978-1-5248-9040-7
Library of Congress Control Number: 2024931642

Editor: Lucas Wetzel
Art Director: Diane Marsh
Production Editor: Elizabeth A. Garcia
Production Manager: Tamara Haus

ATTENTION: SCHOOLS AND BUSINESSES
Andrews McMeel books are available at quantity discounts with
bulk purchase for educational, business, or sales promotional
use. For information, please e-mail the Andrews McMeel
Publishing Special Sales Department: sales@amuniversal.com.

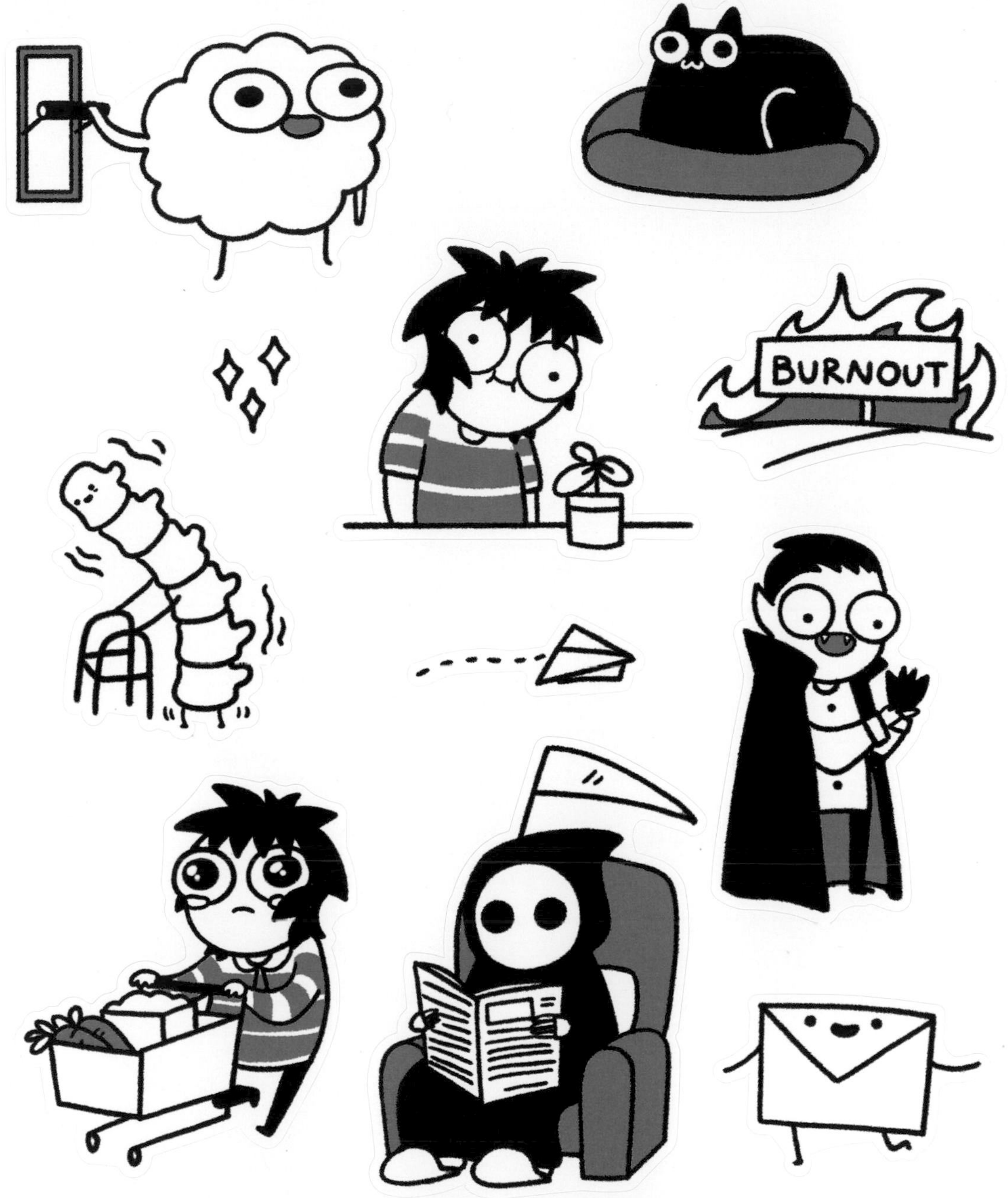
BURNOUT